I0138122

THE CHURCH OF THE REVOLUTIONARY AGE: FACING NEW DESTINIES

VOLUME 1

THE CHURCH OF THE REVOLUTIONARY AGE:
FACING NEW DESTINIES

VOLUME I

Henri Daniel-Rops

Translated from the French
L'Église des Temps Classiques:
L'Ère des Grands Craquements
by John Warrington

CLUNY
Providence, Rhode Island

HENRI DANIEL-ROPS

THE HISTORY OF THE CHURCH OF CHRIST

VOLUME I
The Church of Apostles and Martyrs (2 VOLS.)

VOLUME II
The Church in the Dark Ages (2 VOLS.)

VOLUME III
The Church of Cathedral and Crusade (2 VOLS.)

VOLUME IV
A Religious Revolution: The Protestant Reformation (2 VOLS.)

VOLUME V
An Age of Renewal: The Catholic Reformation (2 VOLS.)

VOLUME VI
The Church of the Classical Age: The Great Century of Souls (2 VOLS.)

VOLUME VII
The Church of the Classical Age: The Era of Great Splintering (2 VOLS.)

VOLUME VIII
The Church of the Revolutionary Age: Facing New Destinies (2 VOLS.)

VOLUME IX
The Church of the Revolutionary Age: A Fight for God (2 VOLS.)

VOLUME X
The Church of the Revolutionary Age: Christian Brotherhood (2 VOLS.)

CLUNY MEDIA EDITION, 2024

This Cluny edition is a republication of Chapters I–IV of the 1965 edition of *The Church in an Age of Revolution*, a translation of *L'Église des Révolutions: En face des nouveaux destins*, published by E. P. Dutton & Co., Inc.

....

With the approval of the author, this English version of *L'Église des Révolutions* has been slightly condensed.

For this Cluny edition, citation and reference styles have been updated and developed, as needed, for the purposes of clarity and accessibility.

For more information regarding this title or any other Cluny Media publication, please write to info@clunymedia.com, or to Cluny Media, P.O. Box 1664, Providence, RI 02901

VISIT US ONLINE AT WWW.CLUNYMEDIA.COM

ISBN (paperback) | 978-1685952990
ISBN (hardcover) | 978-1685953010

NIHIL OBSTAT: Joannes M. T. Barton, S.T.D., *Censor deputatus*
IMPRIMATUR: Patritius Carey, *Vic. Gen.*
WESTMONASTERII, DIE 16 FEBUUARII, 1965

The *Nihil obstat* and *Imprimatur* are a declaration that a book or pamphlet is considered to be free from doctrinal or moral error. It is not implied that those who have granted the *Nihil obstat* and *Imprimatur* agree with the contents, opinions or statements expressed.

Cover design by Clarke & Clarke
Cover image: Eugène Delacroix, *Christ on the Sea of Galilee* (detail), c. 1854, oil on canvas
Courtesy of Wikimedia Commons

CONTENTS

NOTE TO THE TEXT

This is a translation of *En face des nouveaux destins*, dealing with the period 1789–1870—the first part of *L'Eglise des Révolutions*, which latter forms the sixth volume of M. Daniel-Rops's *Histoire de l'Eglise du Christ*. (THE TRANSLATOR)

CHAPTER I

An Epoch of History

I. REVOLUTION WITH THE CHURCH?

VERSAILLES, May 4, 1789. As the doors of Notre-Dame swing open the voice of an organ reaches expectant crowds. Led by a cross-bearer the procession comes into view, its order predetermined by strict etiquette. First to appear are hundreds of men dressed in sober black and small tricorn hats. Next, far more elegant, members of the nobility in black and white satin embroidered with gold, their plumed headgear stirring in the breeze. Behind them walk a small group of bishops and cardinals resplendent in violet and purple, followed by two long files of cassocked priests. Each carries a candle in his right hand. Then, beneath a cloth-of-gold canopy, the Archbishop of Paris bears the Blessed Sacrament in a monstrance flashing like the sun. Immediately after him steps the king, wearing his great coronation mantle of blue adorned with golden fleurs-de-lis; he is attended by the queen, the princes and princesses of the blood and senior officers of the orders of chivalry. That slow *cortège* takes more than an hour to reach its destination, the church of Saint-Louis. Every building along the route has hung out some piece of gorgeous tapestry, and the pavements are crowded with a throng of people held back by an unbroken line of troops. The three Estates of the Most Christian Realm are on their way to attend a Mass of the Holy Ghost, begging God to enlighten the deliberations of the States-General which are to open on the following day.

Thus, with full Catholic ceremonial, began the revolutionary crisis which was destined to rock the Church in France for ten long years, until she appeared to be on the brink of irremediable ruin. But who in that hour of glory foresaw so dark a future? Who thought that this meeting of the States-General, convoked to save France from bankruptcy, would mark the opening of a tragic drama and inaugurate what Joseph de Maistre called "an epoch of history"? Here and there a note of anxiety was heard, as when M. Emery, superior of Saint-Sulpice, wrote to a friend: "What may be the consequences of an assembly so restive as the States-General at a time when the links of subordination and obedience are already so weak?" For the most part, however, there was an air of optimism, strengthened by the lists of grievances brought by the deputies on behalf of their constituents.

France proclaimed almost unanimously that Catholicism was the religion of the realm and should remain so. There was no objection to the Church, to her keeping of the civil registers, to her control of education, or to her strict teaching on the indissolubility of marriage. True, there was a demand for reforms, in which the clergy themselves were not slow to join. Many voters considered that there must be an end of fiscal privilege, of exemption from taxes, of seignorial rights and of tithes; ecclesiastical revenues must be more equitably distributed, the wealth of bishops must be restricted and parish priests assured of a decent salary; there must also be more centres for the education of youth. Nor were the regular clergy overlooked: *commendam* must cease; "useless and depopulated" abbeys must be closed; abbots and monks must be compelled to live according to the spirit of their rule.

Now all those aims were perfectly reasonable; Frenchmen desired indeed to reorganize their Church, but they had no wish to destroy it or to bring about a radical transformation. If there had to be a revolution—and who in that springtide dreamed of such a thing?—it must be effected in harmony with the Church, not in her despite. Many minds were possessed by a truly religious fervour; the new France, emerging from the expected reforms, would be more just, more brotherly than the old.

How then are we to explain the fact that within less than a year the situation was completely altered? In the assembly which opened on May 5, there were certainly determined adversaries of Catholicism; but far more numerous than these were the faithless friends or false brethren of Holy Church. A great many deputies, Catholic in name and even in practice, had been won over in varying degrees to the ideas of the *philosophes* and freethinkers; many sincere believers, too, were attached to Jansenism, Richerism and Gallicanism. All those factors helped to create an atmosphere of sullen hostility towards Rome and towards the Pope, favourable to the control of religion by the State as well as to "democratization" of the hierarchic structure.

Some historians maintain that the forces inimical to the Church were directed by Freemasonry. The question remains undecided.[1] In 1789 the anti-Catholic forces were sufficiently powerful to dispense with secret leadership. They could have been resisted only by a Church united, coherent and governed by far-sighted men of unquestioned authority; but the Church in France had no such qualities, nor had those responsible for her guidance.

The clergy was represented in the States-General by two hundred and eight parish priests and forty-seven bishops, a disproportion which revealed a latent cleavage between the aristocratic episcopate and its plebeian subordinates. The "presbyterian" tendencies[2] that found expression in some clerical quarters were not predominant; but when it came to making known their views, the parochial clergy undoubtedly had more confidence in their fellow-priests than in their bishops. They felt that they belonged to the Third Estate. Even the prelates were far from single-minded: though sceptics like Mgr. Talleyrand of Autun were few and far between, there was a group of liberal-minded bishops in favour of drastic reforms. They were opposed by others more conservative, who, though clinging to the old order if not to their own privileges, suffered from disquiet of conscience and hesitated as to choice of means.

The first revolutionary gesture in the formal sense, marking a resolve to defy the king's authority, came from the lower clergy. It was precipitated by

1. *The Church of the Classical Age: The Era of Great Splintering* (Providence, RI: Cluny, 2024), Volume 1, Chapter I, section 17.
2. Ibid., Volume 2, Chapter V, section 9.

the problem of how the assembly should vote. By Estates, each with a single voice? In that case the Third would derive no benefit from containing twice as many deputies as each of the others. By heads then? That would give the Third alone one-half of the suffrages. Vicomte Mirabeau, a representative of the Third from Aix-en-Provence and a traitor to his class, was first to perceive that all depended on the course followed by the lower clergy. A delegation of the Third Estate went "in the name of the God of peace and on behalf of the nation" to invite the priests to join them in the Salle des Menus Plaisirs, where they held their sessions. On the day after the Third had proclaimed itself a National Assembly (May 17), and after much hesitation and debate, about three-quarters of the clerical deputies accepted the invitation and took with them a small group of bishops. Next day (June 20), by the celebrated Oath of the Tennis Court, the National Assembly flouted the official restrictions imposed by its mandate, and swore not to separate until it had given France a constitution. Three days later, when the king tried to retaliate by ordering the three Estates to sit in separate rooms, the Third, with clerical backing, felt strong enough to defy him. Some priests, however, more conscious of their sacerdotal than of their civic status, saw reason for anxiety in the current trend of popular feeling. On June 24, Mgr. Juigné, Archbishop of Paris, barely escaped death at the hands of an unruly crowd. Similar incidents occurred notwithstanding the adherence of the lower clergy to the Third Estate, and the press was mainly hostile. On July 13, a mob attacked the venerable house of Saint-Lazare, where the sons of St. Vincent were suspected of hoarding foodstuffs then in short supply. After a night of terrible suspense, the seminary of Saint-Sulpice was spared, only because the Parisians were fully occupied storming the Bastille (July 14). Confusion was rife: the newly formed *Garde Nationale* had its colours blessed, and people knelt in the streets as the Blessed Sacrament passed; but a tide of anti-clericalism was clearly on the way.

However, on August 4, a settlement appeared to have been reached; it seemed that revolution would be accomplished in union with the Church. During an all-night session, amid scenes of wild enthusiasm, a group of liberal aristocrats proposed the suppression of feudal rights, and the clergy followed suit. One bishop offered in the name of his colleagues to surrender seignorial dues; another spoke for those prepared to forgo exemption from taxes; while a number of parish priests were ready to sacrifice occasional stipends and to vote immediately for the redemption of tithes. But on the morrow, fervour having cooled, some considered they had gone too far, especially when Mirabeau carried a law abolishing tithes without compensation. On what would priests live? What resources would be left for the upkeep of charitable and educational establishments whose expenses had hitherto been borne by the Church? Discerning minds had cause to look into the future with grave apprehension; but in fact none gave a thought to what might lie ahead. All were busy applauding, acclaiming and embracing one another; and when Mgr. Juigné proposed a vote of thanks to the Almighty for having given France so glorious a night the whole assembly agreed and betook themselves to the palace chapel, where a solemn *Te Deum* was sung.

2. FIRST CRACKS IN THE EDIFICE

AN impartial estimate of affairs at this time shows beyond doubt that the States-General were unanimous in their desire to work in harmony with the Church. In view, therefore, of what followed it may be suspected that a band of cunning politicians made use of two blind forces to strike an underhand blow at the Church: fear inspired by revolt in the provinces, and the collective excitability of crowds.

Certain decisions taken by the Constituent Assembly[3] were highly significant. First, on a motion of the Abbé Grégoire, it was decreed that "in future not a penny shall be sent to the court of Rome either by way of annates or for any purpose whatsoever." That amounted to unilateral

3. The Third Estate, which began calling itself the National Assembly on June 17, 1789, altered its name to Constituent Assembly on July 9 following. (TRANSLATOR)

denunciation of the Concordat of 1516, and would lead inevitably to conflict with the Holy See; but no one heeded the danger.

A more serious move followed soon afterwards, this time involving a matter of principle. On July 8, a committee had been appointed to draw up a constitution. Besides Talleyrand and Mirabeau, its leading members were General La Fayette, renowned for his American victories, and the Abbé Sieyès, author of a notorious pamphlet on the rights of the Third Estate. All were strongly tainted with the philosophical spirit, that same spirit which in 1776 had inspired the Constitution of the United States. The Americans had prefaced their code with a declaration of the rights of man, and the French committee did likewise. After a long debate the "Declaration of the Rights of Man and of the Citizen" was passed on August 20. That it put an end to the conception of monarchy by divine right and proclaimed the people's sovereignty was of no great importance, for both St. Thomas Aquinas and Cardinal Bellarmine could have been cited in support. Far more grave was the definition of liberty and equality in terms which, though generous, were questionable from the theological point of view. But the most alarming feature of all was the preamble. This, while recognizing the "natural" rights of man, made no reference whatever to the rights of God. True, the Declaration, setting aside an earlier draft which allowed religion its full place within the framework of society, stated in Article X that "no one shall be penalized on account of his religious beliefs"; true likewise that the preamble contained an allusion to the Supreme Being. But the Declaration was none the less atheist; the revolt of the intellect,[4] begun centuries earlier, found therein its consummation.

The vagaries of the Declaration and of the Constitution as a whole exacerbated political feeling. Towards the end of summer it was rumoured, with or without justification, that the court and aristocracy were meditating armed revenge, and the demagogues had no difficulty in rousing a few thousand starving Parisians to march upon Versailles. On 6th October the

4. *The Church of the Classical Age: The Era of Great Splintering*, Volume 1, Chapter I.

rioters, whom the king refused to have cut down, brought back the royal family to Paris, and the situation immediately deteriorated. The Constituent Assembly, which had been obliged to follow the monarch, now held its meetings in the capital, surrounded by an enormous throng ever ready to indulge primeval passions. Some of the more moderate deputies had already withdrawn, disturbed by the ominous course of events; a few had actually crossed the frontier, and Mgr. de Juigné had fled to Chambéry. It seemed that a new crisis was at hand. The threat soon became clear beyond possibility of doubt, and the Church was going to suffer accordingly.

The financial situation had not improved after six months of discussion. Two loans raised by Necker had failed, and bankruptcy stood at the gates. On October 10 Talleyrand mounted the tribune of the assembly, and coldly, with the easy manners of an aristocrat scorning rhetorical effects, proposed that the goods of the clergy be "placed at the disposal of the nation." He valued them at two billion *livres,* bringing an income of seventy million. That, claimed his lordship of Autun, would refloat the ship of state. An impassioned debate followed, during which Mgr. de Boisgelin, Archbishop of Aix-en-Provence, pointed out that the Church's wealth had been given for clearly defined purposes, among them the maintenance of hospitals and schools; and he declared that the proposal jeopardized the entire social and educational system. Realizing, however, that the Church would appear avaricious unless she herself made some sort of concession, he managed with difficulty to persuade his brethren that the State should be granted a loan of four hundred million against the property of the clergy. Le Chapelier, a deputy of the Third Estate, put the matter beyond equivocation by declaring that the Church should be relieved of her riches not only to avoid bankruptcy, but in order to "destroy the clerical order" in the name of necessary equality. By five hundred and sixty-eight to three hundred and forty-six votes a decree drawn up by Mirabeau placed all ecclesiastical property at "the disposal of the nation, which would make itself responsible for defraying the reasonable expenses of worship, the sustenance of ministers and the relief of the poor."

That vague formula, "at the disposal of the nation," betrayed some degree of embarrassment if not of hesitation; and the Abbé Maury ironically congratulated his colleagues upon their "wonderful progress in the science of embezzlement." The first step was to compile an inventory. Next an initial slice of confiscated goods (erstwhile in Crown or ecclesiastical ownership) was sold for four hundred million *livres*. Then two decrees (July and October 1790) authorized the transfer of *all* Church property. The Church thus lost at a single stroke every source of revenue, tithes having already been abolished and the remainder of her wealth despoiled. The State, however, did not thereby save itself from bankruptcy. The marketing together of so much land and other real estate caused a rapid fall in values. Buyers were of course not hard to find; they included upstart *bourgeois*, well-to-do peasants, organized groups of racketeers, but also, it must be confessed, noblemen and even members of the clergy. Future leaders of the insurrection in La Vendée (e.g., Elbée and Bonchamp) made purchases; and Queen Marie Antoinette wrote to Fersen in 1792 that the business afforded an excellent opportunity for investment. With a few rare exceptions, the bishops placed no ban on the acquisition of ecclesiastical goods. It was not until much later, in the days of the Restoration, that those who had bought national property were treated with opprobrium. But the fact remained that this huge transfer of ownership confirmed many Frenchmen (some of whom had little or no sympathy with the Revolution) in their desire not to look back, not to restore to the Church her former rights and property.

Secularization of persons went forward hand in hand with that of property.[5] In this respect the monastic orders were the hardest hit. We have already seen the urgent need of reform among the regular clergy,[6] and it appeared not unreasonable that the State should play a part therein. Unfortunately, however, the State did not confine itself to measures of reform,

---

5. A decree of December 22, 1789, secularized the field of education, taking general control of schools from the bishops and entrusting it to departmental organizations.
6. *The Church of the Classical Age: The Era of Great Splintering*, Volume 2, Chapter V, section 11.

but trespassed upon the domain of conscience. On October 28, 1789, the "pronouncing of vows in all monasteries" was suspended in the name of individual freedom. A deputy named Treilhard, an influential member of the Assembly's ecclesiastical committee, proposed a decree which suppressed them altogether, and in spite of resistance it was passed on February 13, 1790. Municipal officers visited religious houses and asked each member of the community whether he or she would prefer to leave or to stay; those who threw off the habit would receive an indemnity sufficient upon which to live, and the remainder would be housed together, irrespective of the orders to which they belonged, in a few monasteries and convents that would be spared for the purpose instead of being put up for sale with the rest. These measures, which had nothing to do with the spirit of reform, aroused protest; and the Bishop of Clermont challenged the assembly to declare whether or not it intended to "destroy the Church."

Those two decrees were on the whole catastrophic in their results, at least as concerned the monks and friars. Two out of fifty Benedictines remained at Cluny. At the Dominican convent of Saint-Honoré in Paris only one out of the thirty-one fathers decided to persevere in his state; fifteen defected, and another fifteen said they would wait and see. The Carthusians, Trappists and Capuchins, however, remained loyal with very few exceptions. As for the nuns, their stability was almost unanimous. The commissioners were told by a community of Carmelites, "The yoke of the Lord is sweet," and by some Visitandines: "We ask to live and die in the holy and blissful state which we have freely embraced, which we zealously observe and which constitutes the sole happiness of our days."

Thus, within less than a year after the first meeting of the States-General, the Church of France, the Church of the old regime, appeared to lie in ruins. Was the disaster intended by those responsible for its accomplishment? Some historians have maintained that it was not; but their conclusion is not wholly acceptable. Many parts of the Gallican Church were worm-eaten, and ominous creakings had long since begun to be heard from within its structure; it was moreover too closely linked with the monarchical system to escape involvement in the throne's collapse. On the other hand it is probable that those elements which we have already described as inimical to Catholicism contrived to exploit the shortcomings of the Church, and that too many Catholics, through indifference, levity or self-seeking, played into their hands. Irreligion was making steady progress, and while it was not the primary cause of that catastrophe which overtook the Church in 1790, it cannot be said to have been unconnected with results it had so largely helped to bring about.

Nevertheless, so strongly was the French people attached to its ancestral faith that outward appearances seemed to belie the facts. Corpus Christi 1790 was celebrated, alike in the capital and in the provinces, with remarkable pomp and fervour, many members of the Assembly taking part in the procession. Patriotism and religion were apparently on excellent terms. On July 14, all the provinces sent delegates to Paris, not only to commemorate the revolutionary events of the previous year, but also to proclaim with an outburst of fraternal goodwill that France was united by the determination of her sons; and it seemed quite natural that on this "feast of federation" a *Te Deum* should be sung and that Mass should be celebrated—though celebrated, alas, by Mgr. de Talleyrand—at an altar erected in the Champ-de-Mars. A document, however, had already been drafted which would open an abyss between the Church and the new régime: the Civil Constitution of the Clergy.

3. "THE GREATEST POLITICAL MISTAKE OF THAT ASSEMBLY"

On July 12, 1790, the Assembly passed a bill touching the reorganization of the Church in France. The fact was not surprising; as soon as the authorities determined to put the State in order it became necessary to deal with ecclesiastical affairs, for under the old regime their respective interests were closely united. The measure would have been beyond criticism if the

Assembly had confined itself within the boundaries of administration, and especially if, before deciding what steps to take, it had consulted the Pope as head of the Church. Not only had this mark of political sagacity and elementary courtesy been omitted, but the authors of the Civil Constitution showed themselves guilty, in M. Emery's words, of "an abuse of competence." A glance at the contents of this law will suffice to illustrate the truth of his words.

Least serious of the reforming measures was that which altered the map of French dioceses, making their boundaries coincide with those of the newly created *départements*. Undoubtedly it overthrew venerable traditions, and was bound to raise delicate problems in the transfer of spiritual jurisdiction and liturgical custom; but on the whole no great damage was done, and Rome, if consulted, would almost certainly have acquiesced. The eighty-three bishops were placed under the authority of ten metropolitans. Parishes also were redistributed, each being designed to contain at least six thousand souls. All titles and benefices not specified in the law were declared extinct. Moreover the Civil Constitution provided that ecclesiastics serving in a strictly ministerial capacity should receive a regular annual salary averaging twenty thousand *livres* for bishops, two thousand for parish priests and one thousand for curates.

On the other hand the law contained a whole series of outrageous stipulations. Bishops and parish priests would henceforward be chosen by the sovereign people, the former by all citizens of the *département* (Protestants and Jews included), the others by district electorates. A bishop would no longer receive canonical investiture from the Pope, but from his metropolitan or, in default, from the senior bishop of his religious *arrondissement*.[7] He would, "as evidence of unity and communion," merely send notification of his election to the Sovereign Pontiff, "visible head of the universal Church." Each bishop was to have a permanent council; it was to include the assistant

7. A decree of November 15, 1790, ordered that, in case of refusal by the metropolitan to confirm an election, recourse should be had to two notaries.

priests attached to the cathedral, together with the superior and directors of the diocesan seminary,[8] and without it the bishop might perform no act of jurisdiction. Each parish priest would appoint his curates from a list approved by the bishop. Finally, bishops and parish priests elect were obliged to swear an oath of loyalty to the Constitution of the French State.

Today it is evident that such measures could never be accepted by the Church. They were a serious blow to her discipline and her right of jurisdiction. They led to a general degradation of religious powers: the Pope lost his control over the bishops, the latter their authority over the parochial clergy, who in turn found themselves dependent on their electors. M. Emery pointed to the fundamental error of the Civil Constitution when he wrote: "To subject a power emanating from that of Jesus Christ Himself to the civil authority...[is] opposed to revelation."

Now subjection of the Church to the civil authority was the express purpose of those who drafted the new law; and here we see the damage done to so many souls by those half-heresies, errors and doctrinal deviations which bore the names of Jansenism, Gallicanism, Richerism and Presbyterianism, all then combining into a single stream. Catholic reaction was not, as one might suppose, immediate and unanimous; men were too preoccupied with coming events to grasp at once the harmfulness of such a law. The first to be confronted with a challenge to his conscience was the king. Would he sanction the decree? After consulting the two archiepiscopal members of his council, Mgr. Champion de Cicé and Mgr. Lefranc de Pompignan, he agreed to sign it, but postponed its promulgation until Rome had had time to express an opinion. Several bishops protested, but none desired a rupture, except perhaps Mgr. Asselini of Boulogne, a rigorous "integrist."

What of the Pope? What did he think, and what was he going to do? The Apostolic throne had been occupied since 1775 by Pius VI.[9] Though a

---

8. Only one seminary was allowed for each diocese.
9. *The Church of the Classical Age: The Era of Great Splintering*, Volume 2, Chapter V, section 1.

lover of pomp and isolated from the world by an unworthy court, he lacked neither intelligence nor determination. He was not well disposed towards France, viewing with grave displeasure the suppression of annates, the closing of so many religious houses and the rebellion which French agents were fostering in the papal territory of Avignon. On March 29, 1790, he had openly criticized the principles of the Revolution. In true Roman fashion, however, he was in no hurry to take a stand against the Civil Constitution, thus leaving faithful Catholics in grave uncertainty. Confidential letters were sent from Rome, begging Louis XVI, who was about to publish the Constitution, "not to drag the whole nation into schism," and cautioning those bishops who were inclined to yield. But no decision was forthcoming. It was not until the spring of 1791 that formal condemnation fell, in the shape of two briefs dated March 10 and April 13. They declared null all elections of bishops and parish priests under the Civil Constitution; but it was much too late.

On November 27, exasperated by the resistance it perceived in a large part of the clergy, the Assembly had passed a law obliging all "official priests" to swear an oath to "do all in their power to uphold the Constitution decreed by the Assembly and accepted by the king." Those who refused would be held to have resigned their duties and would be replaced; if they continued to officiate they would be prosecuted as rebels and disturbers of public order. Asked, or rather bidden, to approve this new decree, poor Louis XVI consulted Mgr. de Boisgelin, who advised him to yield. On December 26, not without grave disquiet of conscience, Louis signed. The irreparable had been accomplished.

We read in the *Memoirs* of Prince de Talleyrand: "Regardless of my own part in this affair, I readily admit that the Civil Constitution of the Clergy, decreed by the Constituent Assembly, was perhaps the greatest political mistake of that Assembly, quite apart from the dreadful crimes which flowed therefrom..."

4. THE OATH AND THE TWO CHURCHES

WHAT would the French clergy do? Above all, what would be done by those clerics (bishops and priests) who sat in the Assembly? Their decision would certainly be looked upon as a precedent. Well, in the case of a very large majority, that decision was a categorical refusal. On the first day, at the instigation of the Abbé Grégoire, whose priestly virtues were undeniable but whose revolutionary ardour was even more outstanding, sixty-two priests took the oath. It was not until January 2 that their example was followed by a bishop—Talleyrand, of course—and then by one Gobel, coadjutor of Basel. The Assembly then ordered that its clerical members be called upon by name; but it might as well have forgone its decision to have them mount the tribune one after another, for most of them expressed their refusal in terms that amounted to a profession of faith. In vain it was resolved to exclude non-jurors from the Assembly; in vain a crowd of "patriots" gathered before the Salle du Manège and threatened to hang these counter-revolutionaries. Nothing could prevail against their courage; and indeed twenty out of one hundred and nine jurors retracted, ready to lose their all rather than yield. "We have taken their property," whispered Mirabeau, "but they have kept their honour."

It is a noble story, supplying a peremptory answer to the criticism which many historians have levelled against the clergy of the *Ancien Régime* and particularly against the episcopate. In a crucial hour even the worldly prelates confronted danger in order to prove their loyalty. Out of one hundred and sixty French bishops (including coadjutors) only seven agreed to take the oath. It was, of course, inconceivable that the clergy of France as a whole should afford a like example. Thousands of priests found themselves in a terrible dilemma. Many were whole-heartedly attached to the new régime, and, though not all "presbyterians," accepted the provisions of the Civil Constitution. Most were not sufficiently expert in theology to detect its poisonous nature. Moreover the king himself had accepted it, and the Pope was silent. So why abandon the cure of souls together with the improved material conditions that were henceforth guaranteed? One hesitates to condemn those who, as the saying was, "found in their stock-pot" some justification for taking the oath. The surprising fact is, not that the French clergy was divided on this question, but that there were so many priests who, in spite of threats, official pressure and newspaper campaigns, dared to refuse notwithstanding their political convictions and private interests.

The consequences of the Assembly's vote were far reaching. "Take care, gentlemen," exclaimed the Abbé Maury, "it is dangerous to make martyrs." He was told there was no question of doing that; but indeed there was. Having set out upon its chosen path, the Revolution was led perforce to a disastrous persecution of those who would not submit to its religious decrees; it thereby alienated many who had been its ardent supporters in the early days, and enabled its opponents to represent it as unfaithful to its generous ideal of liberty and brotherhood. Paradoxically the Gallicans in the Assembly, who had done so much to create this formidable engine of war against Rome, were about to undermine the foundations of the Gallican Church, which was condemned henceforth to schism, and drive the faithful clergy to stand firm around the throne of Peter. So complete was this ruin of the Gallican Church that even the Restoration was unable to revive it, and ultramontanism emerged victorious from the revolutionary crisis. In the more immediate future the affair of the oath would hasten the course of events and bring about the fall of the monarchy; for it was in order to protect his liberty of conscience that Louis XVI attempted to leave Paris and France, thereby falling foul of the Revolution. Above all, the "political error" denounced by Talleyrand was destined to divide not only the French Church, but the French nation also, to the great misfortune of the country.[10]

---

10. Education was among the victims of the Civil Constitution and the oath. Priests and religious engaged in teaching had already been gravely affected by the secularization of ecclesiastical personnel and property; many had refused the oath and abandoned their schools. The consequent disorganization was so serious that even convinced revolutionaries began to worry.

The division was not immediate, but it became inevitable once the Roman decrees of condemnation were known. The partisans of the Civil Constitution insisted that the two briefs were forgeries, while the authorities tried hard to prevent their distribution; but all in vain—the number of retractions steadily increased. Even those bishops who had dreamed of a settlement and, in hope thereof, or as a result of Gallican sympathies, had been in no hurry to publish the briefs, realized that the rupture was complete. Moreover on March 12, 1792, Pius VI issued a third brief declaring the Civil Constitution not only schismatic but "heretical in several of its clauses," and excommunicating priests and bishops appointed under the new laws who did not retract within four months.

The fury of the revolutionaries exploded; the press launched a violent attack on the Pope, and diplomatic relations between Rome and France were suspended. Cardinal de Bernis, having refused to take the oath, had been recalled; but his successor, Count Louis-Philippe de Ségur, a colonel on his staff, had not been recognized by the Papal Court. The nuncio, Mgr. Dugnani, under pretext of taking the waters for his rheumatism at Aix-les-Bains, had left Paris without hope of return.

Meanwhile the new Church, known thenceforward as "constitutional," started to organize itself without delay. First, bishops were elected; but it was not easy to find a consecrator, because even those prelates who had taken the oath hesitated to perform such a task. Talleyrand eventually agreed to do so in a few cases—his last ecclesiastical act. Parish priests had then to be chosen, which again was no easy matter. The seminaries were empty, and holy orders were conferred upon raw youths of twenty years, some of whom had completed no more than three months of study.

Nevertheless one must not pass too hasty a judgment on the constitutional clergy, who less than two years later numbered martyrs in its ranks. Some of those who had taken the oath were tinged with Jansenism, a fact which at any rate guaranteed the austerity of their virtues. Many others were excellent priests, who chose the camp of schism merely through political conviction or in order to avoid abandoning their parishes. A careful study of the evidence leads to the conclusion that only about fifteen of the bishops were unworthy. Chief among those who deserved respect was Grégoire (1750–1831), Bishop of Blois. He never ceased to defend religion under the Convention, refusing to "unfrock" himself and insisting throughout the Terror upon wearing his episcopal cassock. It is not surprising that among the intruders there were several opportunists. Most notable was Gobel, auxiliary of Basel. Elected metropolitan of Paris, he distinguished himself for two years by his subservience to the civil authorities, going so far as to allow some of his priests to marry, before publicly renouncing his priesthood in the woeful days of 1793—a gesture which failed to save him from Robespierre's guillotine. One would prefer to say nothing of this unhappy man but for the fact that he was reconciled in prison (perhaps by M. Emery), and cried upon the scaffold: "Long live Jesus Christ!" As for the parish priests and curates, their ranks included heroes and cowards, chaste and unchaste, informers and victims of the guillotine. It would be unfair to despise them all simply because they were mistaken—often in good faith. But the faithful as a whole rejected any such distinction, and the entire constitutional clergy found itself reprobated by loyal Catholics.

The fate of the non-jurors varied. Some emigrated at once, particularly the higher clergy; not more than about twenty "Roman" bishops remained in the kingdom. Almost all the clerical deputies fled, either abroad or to the provinces. Among the parish priests, those who lived near the frontier were sorely tempted to cross it and seek refuge. But there were many others who continued to exercise their ministry, competing successfully with their constitutional rivals. Barred from their churches, they celebrated Mass in convents, chapels and even in private houses. Parents brought them their children for baptism, even though the sacrament had lost all validity as regards civil status. Many asked for their services in the hour of death. Obviously the situation could not last. What could a constitutional priest think when he saw his church empty while the non-juror drew crowds? Relations between the two groups were quickly embittered. There were, of course, exceptions; but mistrust, jealousy and before long open hostility prevailed.

Faced with this problem, the Assembly had aimed at a compromise. The authorities of the *Département de Paris* had authorized adherents of all faiths to open places of worship in private buildings; but violent disturbances had broken out when M. de Pancemont, former parish priest of Saint-Sulpice and a non-juror, attempted to make use of this right. The Assembly had intervened: Talleyrand had spoken in favour of "full and complete liberty of conscience"; Sieyès had supported him, and a decree of toleration had been passed. What results had this freedom produced? It was hardly acceptable to the new clergy, who foresaw that their churches would remain deserted. Almost everywhere, in the provinces as well as in the capital, priests who had taken the oath enlisted the support of Jacobin clubs with a view to eliminating their rivals.

Furthermore political events, themselves brought about by the religious crisis, soon rendered any form of agreement impossible. On Easter Sunday 1791 the king intended to visit Saint-Cloud and receive Holy Communion from the hands of a non-juror priest; but the mob, alerted by the tocsin of Saint-Roch, prevented him. Wounded in his deepest convictions, Louis XVI then resolved to follow the plan of escape which had long since been suggested to him. On June 20, together with all his family, he set out for the eastern frontier, where an army of refugees awaited him. The unhappy ending of that venture, ill prepared and carried out with even less efficiency, is only too well known. When the postmaster at Varennes, one Drouet, stopped the monarch's coach, the monarchy itself was ruined, and with it the cause of that loyal Church whose fate appeared so closely linked to the destiny of the Crown.

5. REVOLUTION AGAINST THE CHURCH

THE Constituent Assembly was dissolved on September 30, 1791, in an atmosphere charged with doom. Its successor, the so-called Legislative Assembly, elected to enforce the new Constitution, proved itself from the outset far more hostile to the Church. It met for the first time on October 1, and was immediately confronted with the religious question. A fortnight later (October 17) it decided to close the two great theological schools, the Collège de Navarre and the Sorbonne, whose professors had almost unanimously refused the oath. Then Fauchet, a constitutional bishop and deputy of Calvados, demanded the suppression of salaries and pensions payable to non-juror priests. There followed an impassioned debate; it lasted for several weeks until November 29, when a bill was passed extending the obligation of the oath to all ecclesiastics, on pain "of being suspect of rebellion against the law and ill will towards the fatherland." In every commune a list was to be prepared of those who would and of those who would not submit; the latter were to be kept under surveillance by the communal authorities and held responsible in case of disturbances due to religious differences. Mgr. de Boisgelin, who had remained in Paris and who, though not a member of the Assembly, exerted a good deal of influence, remarked: "What is this right which the Assembly claims, not only to make laws for the punishment of crimes, but also to create new crimes by means of laws?"

What would the king do? The Constitution allowed him a right of veto; but would he use it, and thereby suspend application of the decree against priests? Virtually a prisoner in the Tuileries since the tragic return from Varennes, Louis XVI had certainly undergone a profound change of heart. He blamed himself for having been too weak at the start of these events. On the religious plane his conscience reproached him for having approved the Civil Constitution, and all his sympathies undoubtedly lay with those priests who had refused the oath. He was strongly influenced, too, by his young sister, Madame Élisabeth, a shining figure of unyielding determination. While his brothers and aunts fled the country, she resolved to share whatever lay in store for the royal family. Her smiling grace, her goodness and her courage brought some measure of consolation into a life that was far from gay, and she constantly reminded Louis of his duties as a Christian. She wanted him publicly to dedicate his kingdom to the Sacred Heart; and although he declined to go that far, he made at least one very brave decision. On November 29, he exercised his right of veto.

Was there still time to react, and was reaction possible? The resolution of Louis XVI was undeniable; when one of his vacillating ministers suggested that it would be wise henceforward to employ juror-priests for the service of his chapel, he indignantly refused. But the good man lacked that air of royalty which enforces obedience. In vain Boisgelin implored him to appeal to the country, to pose in solemn terms the question of religion and of the peril which threatened it. The Assembly, which had at first appeared stunned by the royal veto, now recovered itself; soon it would resume its offensive against the Roman Church. The papal Brief excommunicating all clergy who had taken the oath became known in France during the month of April 1792. It caused a good deal of agitation, especially as political events both at home and abroad were on the way to creating in France an atmosphere of tension conducive to the worst excesses.

Spring 1792 marked a decisive turning-point in the progress of the Revolution. The *sansculottes* were steadily gaining influence. In March the king dismissed his wavering minister and conferred power on the "Brissotins," Roland and General Dumouriez. These men had long been planning war against Austria and other states guilty of sheltering the émigrés, with the ulterior design that a French victory would place the king in the hands of their party. The court too desired hostilities—for diametrically opposite reasons, since they calculated on defeat. On April 20, the Assembly declared war on "the King of Bohemia and Hungary."[11] Europe, which until then had shown itself completely indifferent to the peril of the monarchy and religion in France, pretended to undertake a crusade against the atheist revolutionaries. The Holy See, while observing *de facto* neutrality, found itself by sympathy and influence in the camp of the pseudo-crusaders. The Abbé Maury, now living in Rome, honoured by Pius VI with the most flattering degree of friendship, and created in turn Archbishop of Nicaea and cardinal, was going as nuncio extraordinary to negotiate with Francis II the terms

11. Francis II, who had succeeded his father Leopold on March 1, had not yet been elected emperor.

of a future peace and the reinstatement of the Apostolic See in its rights over Avignon. French Catholics loyal to Rome were thus inevitably looked upon not only as rebels against the law, but also traitors to the fatherland. And when initial setbacks in the field placed France in danger, there was quite naturally a violent outburst of anticlericalism.

On Good Friday, April 6, the Assembly had started to debate the prohibition of clerical dress and the suppression of all religious congregations. Both measures passed on the twenty-eighth. Another symptom of altered outlook concerned the Corpus Christi procession. In the previous year the whole Assembly had taken part, but in 1792 it refused official attendance. Almost everywhere, in Paris as well as in the provinces, there were violent clashes between "Roman" Catholics and the faithful of the constitutional Church. Jacobins complained to the Assembly that they had been thrashed for failing to salute the Blessed Sacrament; parish priests who had taken the oath were molested by some, non-juror priests by others. At Marseilles loyal priests were "chased like dogs"; at Lyons, in Calvados and elsewhere the vilest indignities were committed against women suspected of "fanaticism." The atmosphere was becoming explosive.

On May 27, the Legislative Assembly voted a decree condemning to "deportation" (i.e., to exile) beyond the frontier any ecclesiastic whom twenty citizens denounced as a non-juror and whom the district recognized as such. Every priest liable to deportation, if caught in France, would be sentenced to ten years' imprisonment. Henceforward priests were at the mercy of malevolent informers and the whim of authority. The text of the law ended with these words: "The present decree shall be submitted this day for the king's sanction."

So it was, and with it two other decrees for which the Brissotins had secured a vote in order to disarm the king. One disbanded his guard; the other summoned to Paris twenty thousand members of the *Garde Nationale* from the various *départements*. Once again Louis XVI stood firm. He opposed his veto to the decree proscribing priests, and also to the third, which would have introduced into the capital the worst of the "federates."

When Roland addressed him an insolent letter, the sovereign did not hesitate to send it back and to accept the resignation of Dumouriez, who, to the very end, tried hard to show him that his resistance would lead only to the ruin of religion and of the clergy. It seems that from this moment Louis XVI had offered the sacrifice of his life—he told Dumouriez so—and that he wished to make amends before God for what he called his "fault," his acceptance of the Civil Constitution. Was it this resolve that endowed the feeble monarch with sudden and unwonted strength? On June 20, the rabble invaded the Tuileries, yelling for hours on end: "Down with the veto! Death to the priests!" Trapped in a window recess, the king agreed to don the red bonnet of the revolutionaries and to drink a glass of wine "to the health of the nation"; but he refused to yield upon essentials and go back upon his veto. He would never, he said, make "the sacrifice of his duty."

The situation was tragic. The humiliation inflicted on the sovereign provoked a surge of anger in nearly all the provinces. On July 7, in the Assembly—where the riot at the Tuileries had made a bad impression—after the constitutional bishop of Lyons, Lamourette, had spoken in such moving terms that the deputies of different parties embraced one another, the king was brought to the session and acclaimed. But exasperation was mounting everywhere. Disregarding the royal veto, a number of provincial administrations were arresting recusant priests. In the south "patriots" broke into places of worship, and even, at dead of night, into the houses of those suspected of "fanaticism."

Things became much worse at the beginning of July, when the military situation deteriorated; when fifty thousand Prussians and five thousand émigrés marched on the eastern frontier; when the Duke of Brunswick (July 25) foolishly threatened Paris with destruction; and when, in an atmosphere at once of panic and of solemn fervour, the fatherland was declared "in danger." Registers of voluntary enlistment were opened, and were quickly filled with names. On August 10 the mob, behind which Danton was at work, invaded and sacked the Tuileries. The ancient Capetian monarchy was overthrown, the king and his family were imprisoned in the Temple, and a provisional executive committee was set up. France was rent in two, imperilled by invasion, and anti-religious feeling broke loose. At Paris the Commune ordered the arrest of several hundred priests who were known to have refused the oath. In the provinces—in Normandy as well as in Limousin and Provence—priests were massacred. Roux, constitutional bishop of Marseilles, tried in vain to save some unfortunate Franciscans who were lynched by a mob. The Assembly meanwhile was in the grip of such fear that it made no effort to prevent these acts of violence. On the contrary, it hurriedly passed anti-clerical measures and decrees intended to remove the Christian element from daily life. The vow of Louis XIII was annulled; orders were given for the melting down of gold and bronze objects belonging to the churches; the wearing of ecclesiastical dress was again forbidden; the law suppressing religious congregations was republished; and finally steps were taken towards a more rigorous application of the edict condemning to deportation all non-juror priests, who, if caught on French soil, were to be sent to Guiana.

It was in this climate of near insanity, a climate heavy with fears of treason and aggravated by the gradual collapse of all regular authority, that there took place an appalling episode which would set between the Revolution and the Church an impassable barrier, a river of blood.

6. THE SEPTEMBER MASSACRES

AT the beginning of September the military situation had again deteriorated. After Longwy, Verdun was falling. The Prussian invasion, it appeared, would encounter no more obstacles. Fear reigned in the Assembly: the Salle du Manège was emptying; soon it would contain no more than three hundred of the seven hundred members, all the rest having fled. Danton had practically eliminated his colleagues in the government; but as minister of justice he did nothing to soothe passions that were reaching the stage of paroxysm. Even the Commune, the insurrectional Commune of Paris led by Marat, Chaumette and Hébert, was obliged to follow those whom it pretended to direct. "All those," says the left-wing historian Gérard Walter, "who retained the smallest degree of legitimate authority yielded to a sort of general panic and allowed it to slip from their grasp." Demanding mass conscription, Marat wrote in his *Ami du Peuple*: "Citizens, the foe is at our gates. Let us not leave behind in Paris a single enemy to be gladdened by our defeats and, in our absence, to slaughter our wives and children." This was a summons to murder; it was answered all too soon.

The drama began on the afternoon of Sunday, September 2, when a platoon of the *Garde Nationale* dragged three ecclesiastics from the cab that was taking them to jail, and hacked them to pieces. This was the signal for massacres that were to last for forty-eight hours, and which occurred in most of the prisons where suspects were held.

Accustomed as a twentieth-century reader may be to the horror of massacres far worse in point of numbers, it is impossible to peruse without a shudder the narratives in which the few survivors and witnesses of those hideous events tell what they saw: Maillard, wan and lugubrious, summoning prisoners one by one to the travesty of a trial; pipes and bottles standing amid the papers on the bench of this "tribunal"; the killers drawn up in two lines at the door through which the condemned would pass, and striking them down with sabres or hatchets; distinguished victims subjected to even more revolting treatment, among them the beautiful Princess de Lamballe, whose corpse was outraged, dismembered, and the head borne on a pike to Queen Marie Antoinette. Identical scenes took place at the abbey of Saint-Germain-des-Prés, at the Saint-Firmin prison and at the former Carmelite convent. In the courtyard of what is now the Séminaire des Carmes, between the two arms of the little staircase down which the condemned walked, a laconic inscription—"*Hic ceciderunt*"—recalls their sufferings, their heroism; and their martyrdom also, for there is no doubt that many of them died for the Faith.

The victims of the Septembrists are believed to have numbered more than one thousand, perhaps eleven hundred. Among them were about two hundred and fifty priests, including the aged Archbishop of Arles, Mgr. du Lau, and the two La Rochefoucauld, bishops of Beauvais and Saintes. Can it be said that the massacres, in themselves, were directed specifically against the Church? Perhaps not. The recusant priests thrown into prison were included by the *sansculottes* in the same hatred that they bore towards all self-styled enemies of the Revolution. Moreover the determination to "empty the prisons," as advised by Marat, was such that in some places (the Salpêtrière, for example) it extended to common-law prisoners, prostitutes and ten-year-old children. One thing, however, is certain: all priests interrogated by those pseudo-courts were asked whether they had taken the oath; and not one was prepared to save his life by means of a lie. Violette, who presided at the executions in the Vaugirard section, reported on the morrow of the tragedy: "I do not understand, they seemed *happy*; they went to death as to a wedding."

The impression created by the massacres was terrible; so much so that next day the superintending committee of the Commune de Paris sent to the provinces a memorial, drawn up by Marat, in which the affair was presented as "an act of indispensable justice" and in which patriots were urged to "adopt these most necessary means." The advice met with little favour. True, there were massacres at Versailles, Meaux, Lyons, near Autun, and Antibes in Normandy; some priests, too, were put to death, among them Mgr. de Castellane, Bishop of Mende, who was executed at Versailles. But the number of ecclesiastical victims outside Paris was relatively small. Of the profound horror excited by the event we have striking testimony in a letter from Mme. Roland, whose husband was at that time minister of the interior. "If only you knew the hideous details of the killings!" she wrote to a friend. "Women brutally violated before being torn to pieces by those tigers, intestines cut out and worn as turbans; bleeding human flesh devoured.... You know my enthusiasm for the Revolution; well, I am ashamed of it." An ineffaceable bloodstain spread thenceforward over the new régime. Although soon afterwards, on September 20, the victory of Valmy had removed the fear of invasion, the Revolution moved forward to a reign of terror. Dr. Guillotin's sinister machine, hitherto little used, was now (since August 18) a permanent feature of the Place Louis XV opposite the Tuileries. And one of the most dreaded of the revolutionaries, the "communist" Babeuf, would soon write this maxim in which some historians have detected an avowal that there were invisible prompters behind the scenes: "It is essential to make the people perpetrate deeds that will prevent them from turning back."

After the decree of proscription and the massacres, Catholics loyal to Rome found themselves in a terrible predicament. Many priests went into exile; and many of them endured frightful suffering before reaching safety in foreign lands, where, as we shall see, they were not always welcome. Others, more courageous, refused to leave, considering flight as cowardice. Then began the organization of that underground resistance which was sustained throughout France and particularly in Paris during the years of terror. It was supported not only by a large number of priests who prepared hide-outs and more or less secret places of worship, but also by laymen who came from the provinces to help them in a task that became more difficult and dangerous from day to day.

As the winter ended and the reign of terror was about to start, the faithful Church was ready to confront her tragic destiny; and yet she felt herself inwardly divided. On August 14 the Legislative Assembly had imposed on all citizens—and *a fortiori* on all priests—a new oath: "I swear to be loyal to the nation, and to uphold liberty and equality or to die in defence thereof." The formula was extremely vague and it seemed that no priest, however "Roman" in outlook, could well refuse it. But did not the mere fact of taking it constitute recognition of the new régime? The situation was awkward. Maury, living peacefully in Rome, condemned the oath with vehemence, claiming to reflect the opinion of the Pope—although the Pope himself said nothing. At Paris the inter-nuncio Salamon, a prisoner in the Carmes, condemned it likewise and with more merit, but without realizing that his attitude would drive the future victims of the Septembrists to heroic intransigence. For when Maillard and his colleagues asked the priests whether they had sworn, to which oath did they refer, that of August 14 or that of loyalty to the Civil Constitution of the Clergy? On the other side some very holy priests, led by M. Emery, thought that the new oath was lawful, since it contained no reference to any constitution and was recognized as having no religious meaning. They held that by refusing to take it the faithful clergy would appear to link their cause with that of the monarchy and thus with counter-revolution (i.e., with treason), and that it would be better to provide for the future by not leaving the continuance of Catholic worship in the sole hands of the constitutional clergy. The debate on this subject lasted for years: it was acrimonious, troubling many souls and adding sorrow to confusion.

As for the constitutional Church, it too experienced an increasing sense of anxiety. Priests and bishops who had sincerely embraced the Revolution in hope of "seeing the primitive Church reborn" were disillusioned. The few citizens who attended their Masses were often by no means edifying. The authorities, whose business it was to protect them, did not hesitate to employ them as instruments of power, ordering them to justify from the pulpit any measures voted by the Assembly. The episcopal palaces were taken from their occupants on the grounds that their magnificence "was not in accord with the simplicity of the ecclesiastical state." Public processions were forbidden. Objects of worship and of piety, even crucifixes, were removed from the churches and their bronze melted down. The smallest gratuity was prohibited: woe betide a curate who accepted an offering for a baptism or a marriage! Worse still, marriage of priests was allowed in the name of liberty, and bishops were forbidden to punish those of their subordinates who took advantage of this right. The very bases of Christian society, which those who took the oath had expected to preserve, were crumbling. On September 20, the eve of its dissolution, the Assembly instituted divorce; and on the same day it established "civil status," depriving the constitutional clergy of all hold upon the faithful, since baptism, marriage and religious burial were no longer to have any legal significance. The "chastisement of schism," to quote the Abbé Sicard, fell upon the revolutionary Church, inflicted by those same individuals whom she had regarded as her allies. The hour was approaching when the Revolution would rage not against the Church alone, but against God.

7. THE INSURRECTION OF THE WEST

THE religious policy of the new régime, and more especially the punitive measures against recusant priests, led to a further result, an event that was to have far-reaching consequences. Western France revolted; not only La Vendée, as is suggested by the name usually given to the ensuing war, but more or less the entire country stretching from the north of Poitou to Brittany and the confines of Normandy, a region at that time much wilder than today, where a bitter struggle was destined to endure for four long years amid tracts of broom and furze around the little townships that dotted the landscape, and along winding roads that sheltered many an ambush. The motives of this insurrection were not exclusively religious; attachment to the royalist cause played some part in its outbreak, but loyalty to the Catholic and Roman Church constituted beyond all doubt the chief inspiration of a courage that soon became legendary. It was a terrible, frightful war, as civil strife is apt to be when it involves religious conflict; but through it shines the noblest light, that of heroic youth and sacrifice willingly endured.

The Revolution, in its early days, had not been unwelcome to a peasantry that was both poor and by temperament egalitarian. At the time of the great fear they had even attacked and pillaged the houses of middle-class citizens. The sale of nationalized property had provoked no unrest; noblemen and even priests, as we have seen, were among the buyers. Trouble began with the Civil Constitution of the Clergy and the famous oath. There were very few juror-priests in the whole of that region: scarcely more than one out of every four or five on average. And when it became necessary to replace the parish priests the ballot was repeated time after time in vain; many parishes remained without constitutional titulars, while others rejected those offered to them. The agitation began in La Vendée. In May 1792 the mayors and municipal officers of the thirty-four communes of Mauges met at La Poitevinière to discuss the situation; and in August, at Châtillon, there was a revolt of between six thousand and ten thousand men, which was suppressed by force of arms. Almost everywhere priests who had taken the oath, and were therefore extremely unpopular, had to appeal for support to the *Garde Nationale*, whom the peasants received with scythes and pitchforks. The soldiers, by way of revenge, attacked churches, chapels and processions.

The conflagration broke out in March 1793. All winter the fire had smouldered. The first proscriptions of priests had begun in the autumn. News of the September Massacres had reached the remotest villages. At the end of January that of the king's execution made a still worse impression. On March 3, a market day at Cholet, it was learned that Paris had just decided that the local lads were to be conscripted for military service. This was too much. Those peasants who clung tenaciously to their soil, those mothers who trembled for their sons at the thought of the immorality that prevailed in camp, were furious. Five hundred young people from neighbouring villages, who had come to the market, swore publicly that they would never agree to be soldiers, and next day they clashed with the *Garde Nationale*. The local authorities did not take the matter seriously, and ordered the drawing of lots for conscripts, thereby making the mistake of assembling large bodies of men in the regional centres. Incidents occurred in many places, and we are told that six hundred parishes took action simultaneously. With cries of "Long live religion!" the whole of La Vendée flew to arms.

Military operations are clearly no part of religious history. Besides, one cannot speak of military operations except in a well-defined area and for a limited period. There was no actual war in the strict sense of the word, except in La Vendée properly so called. And after the cessation of strategic movements in December 1793, there were only guerrilla operations in defence of religion. As for the Breton insurrection, which began later and continued until 1799, it never amounted to much more; the Chouans, whose ranks included dealers in contraband salt and mere adventurers along with staunch Catholics and royalists, bore no resemblance to the armies of La Vendée, nor was there ever question of a whole people taking arms.

Immediately after the events of March 1793 the Vendeans set to work with a will. A large army was formed; but the revolutionaries were taken by surprise and were slow to react. In May and June the names Thouars, Parthenay, Fontenay, Doué, Saumur and Angers marked a succession of victories. But this glorious interlude was brief, and failures multiplied. The situation deteriorated from day to day: it became critical when the Convention decided to send against the "Whites" of La Vendée part of the veteran army of the Rhine—"the Mayençais"—with Kléber at its head. A counter-attack before Cholet failed. Again, a final attempt to link up with the Bretons (and perhaps the English) failed before Granville on November 15, after a brilliant passage of the Loire at Saint-Florent on October 13. Thrown back upon Angers, Le Mans and Laval, pursued by Kléber and Marceau, the ruined army was surrounded at Savenay on December 23 and annihilated. La Vendée was left to endure the horror of those "infernal columns" which passed by leaving everything in flames, everything a heap of rubble, and corpses piled up in hundreds; but the Vendean guerrillas continued the struggle on their ravaged soil, until the government of the Republic was driven to look for a settlement.

The Catholic faith undoubtedly played a leading part in that fierce determination to fight. La Vendée may not have risen solely in order to defend its priests, but that was one of its motives. The spirit of the "white" armies was beyond all question deeply religious: their columns marched reciting the Rosary; they went into action singing the *Vexilla Regis*; and chaplains gave absolution before battle. During the seventeenth century the whole of western France had been stirred by the missions of St. Grignion de Montfort,[12] and the red badge of the Sacred Heart popularized by the saint was displayed by the rustic combatants. Nor was faith less real among those of their leaders who came of peasant stock. It may have been at the outset less

12. *The Church of the Classical Age: The Great Century of Souls* (Providence, RI: Cluny, 2023), Volume 2, p. 363.

spontaneous among the nobility, whom the peasants summoned from their mansions to serve as their captains. Officers for the most part, they doubtless estimated more clearly the perils of the enterprise, and perhaps understood the trouble in which the clergy would become involved; but having once committed themselves, all those leaders proved worthy of the firm and simple faith of their men, knowing well that they would have no earthly rewards, which in any case were beneath the sanctity of their cause.

It is certain that Christian virtue, the great law of charity, was often violated during this terrible war; nor was cruelty a monopoly of the "blues," among whom such leaders as Hoche and Marceau were almost invariably generous and humane. If the "infernal columns" committed atrocities such as have been repeated in our own day at Oradour and elsewhere, republican prisoners were tortured to death by way of reprisals; poor boys who had enlisted without conviction in the armies of the Convention were shot without trial, after a moment's grace in which to murmur an act of contrition. But it is equally true that this merciless struggle was characterized also by truly Christian gestures.

The fact is that in this fratricidal conflict two elements of the French nation confronted one another. One was Catholic and traditionalist, combining Christian with royalist convictions; the other was vaguely deist, fiercely anti-clerical, with patriotism as its sole religion. It is against this background of fundamental antagonism that the fighters of the Bocages must be judged. There were insurrections elsewhere, as when the Girondins were overthrown on June 2, 1793, and their partisans, the "federalists," rallied Lyons, Toulon and sixty *départements*. But those *bourgeois* insurrections had no religious motives; they were due to political or economic factors. La Vendée bore testimony to an inner conviction, and that hopeless struggle deserves the admiration of all who believe in the existence of realities transcending temporal interests.

The war of the Bocages had important results in the political field, obliging the Republic to acknowledge the rights of Catholic conscience thus valiantly defended. In the spring of 1795 the Abbé Bernier managed to contact the republican generals and secure freedom of worship. But the lesson had been so severe that it was never forgotten, and the revolt of the Bocages was no doubt one of the reasons that decided Bonaparte to accept the Concordat—which Bernier helped to negotiate. For the moment, however, the insurrection of the West entailed disastrous consequences for the Church; in the eyes of those tough "blue" soldiers and of their leaders the whole clergy appeared an ally of treason. The Catholics of La Vendée were dissenters; were not all French Catholics, then, potential rebels? France was passing through a crisis so grave that she could not but seek to regain her unity at all costs by crushing dissenters, whoever they might be. Thus the Catholic rebellion of the West drove the Revolution still further towards persecution of the Christian faith.

8. THE REVOLUTION AGAINST THE CROSS

THREE weeks after the September Massacres, on the twenty-first of that month, there met a new assembly known as the Convention. Before France there lay a long period of grief and suffering, destined to last for two years. Royalists and moderates had been excluded from the ballot, or had abstained from voting; all seven hundred and fifty deputies were thus confirmed revolutionaries, determined adversaries of the monarchy and, for the most part, hostile to religion.

Events moved rapidly. At its first session (September 21) the Convention unanimously abolished the monarchy; next day it proclaimed the Republic, bringing the Girondins to power. The trial of the king and his execution (January 21, 1793), which the Girondins lacked courage to oppose, marks the beginning of their decline. Although internal differences did not prevent the Convention from adopting an aggressive foreign policy based on revolutionary propaganda and the conquest of natural frontiers, that policy—encouraged for a time by the inactivity of Prussia, which was occupied with the dismemberment of Poland (January 1793)—led in March to the first coalition against France. There began a dramatic crisis, at once internal and external. In March, as La Vendée rose, the armies were falling back in Belgium and on the Rhine. Dumouriez deserted. Added to this there was an economic and financial crisis: food became short, the value of money declined and unemployment increased. Thus the Paris Commune, by threat of bombardment, easily persuaded the Convention to exclude the Girondins. But this high-handed action provoked the "federalist" insurrection of the provinces (June–August 1793), while France was invaded on the borders of Lorraine, Flanders, Alsace and Roussillon.

The Republic was nothing more than "a great city besieged," with no choice but "victory or death." It was saved by the Montagnards, who had been in power since the end of June and who established a system of dictatorship in the name of "public safety." The guillotine, now a permanent erection, became the means of government. Along with those measures to secure the Republic, steps were taken for national defence, in the shape of mass conscription and requisition (August 1793) for the purposes of total war. Held down and scourged by men devoid of pity but driven by ferocious energy, France recovered possession of herself. The rebels at home were crushed; Marseilles, Lyons and Toulon were recovered; the "white" armies of the West were overwhelmed.

Organized by Lazare Carnot, and led by captains of youthful daring, the armies of the Republic took the offensive on all fronts; Hondschoote (September 6–8), Wattignies (October 15) and Wissembourg (December 26) unblocked the frontiers and halted the invasion. But the Mountain, which had saved the fatherland, was prey to faction. At the beginning of 1794 Robespierre became director of the Committee of Public Safety, and in order to establish himself as the centre of unity he could do nothing but intensify the Terror. It was not unlikely, however, that France would tolerate the blood-bath for long, once the threat from abroad had decreased and appeared to have been finally removed by the victory of Fleurus (June 26). Loathing of the scaffold, together with a combination of fear and self-interest, was too strong for the "incorruptible" dictator. On 9th Thermidor

 (July 27) 1794 he was overthrown, and a last attempt at insurrection in Paris could not save him from the guillotine. A new chapter was about to start in the history of the Revolution.

It is against such a backcloth that we have to view those scenes in which the loyal Catholics of France served both as actors and as victims—scenes which are perhaps the most dramatic and certainly among the finest in their story. The situation developed quickly: a régime of partial toleration which had prevailed hitherto was superseded by one of outright persecution. Beginning in the autumn of 1793 and lasting until July 1794, that persecution, though not formally decreed by law, was first permitted and soon encouraged by the ruling powers. Christian France was swept by a wave of fanaticism at once cruel, despicable and absurd, such as is always experienced at times of mass hysteria. Determined atheists, loyal in varying degrees to the teaching of the *philosophes*, availed themselves of this opportunity to conduct operations whose purpose was nothing less than the suppression of all belief. It was not only against the Church that the Revolution directed its attack, but against the faith itself, against God.

Article VII of the Declaration of Rights, which served as a preamble to the Constitution of Year I (1793), stated that "the free exercise of worship could not be forbidden." But, as has long been recognized, there is often a great gulf between principles and their application. Very soon, on November 23, 1793, all churches and chapels were secularized, once more in the name of freedom and equality. Next a series of decrees—March 18, April 21, and especially October 21 (30th Vendémiaire)—inaugurated a reign of terror against priests, who, as the historian Aulard justly observes, "were all placed in a state of legal suspicion." Henceforward the deposition of two witnesses, declaring that such and such a priest had not taken the oath, rendered him liable to the death penalty. The constitutional clergy stood in equal danger with the rest. Thus, without violating the principles or even the letter of the law, the authorities were able to do as they liked. To be a priest, merely to be known as a practising Catholic, sufficed to incur suspicion of "fanaticism"—a word whose connotation was crystal clear.

The anti-religious offensive which now began was waged on all fronts simultaneously, but varied in intensity according to time and place. October–November 1793 was a period of madness: France appeared to be in the grip of frenzy against the Cross, so much so that some people were disturbed, fearing that hostility was being carried to excess and would disgrace the Revolution in foreign eyes. Among them was Robespierre, notwithstanding his distrust of "religious prejudice." He mounted the tribune to declare that violence was the surest means "of awakening fanaticism" and that "priests would continue to say Mass all the longer if forbidden to do so." On December 6 (16th Frimaire) he actually secured the passage of a bill proclaiming freedom of worship and forbidding "all violence and measures contrary to that freedom." In point of fact this laudable document remained a dead letter. Besides, it included an article which permitted all sorts of curious interpretations; for this law reserved the right to punish "all those who, under pretext of religion, attempt to compromise the cause of liberty." Persecution resumed its course before January 1794, and never ceased until July. During those months, when Robespierre himself, apparently forgetting his own promises, gave free rein to the atheists and other foes of Christianity, many priests fell victim to the guillotine. The hideous task was carried out in the provinces through "missionary agents" whom the assembly dispatched to restore the republican order by means of fire and sword. Nearly all of them were implacable enemies of the Christian faith, even (and indeed principally) those who had belonged to the Church.

The Terror which burst upon the Church of France facilitated an operation regarded as essential by anti-Christian zealots—that of demolishing the priesthood. This was to be achieved by persuading or terrifying priests into surrendering their certificates of ordination and renouncing their sacerdotal state. Furthermore ruin overtook all those elements of social life which depended on and were paid for by the clergy. Religious of both sexes were driven from the hospitals, which were thus obliged to close their doors or languish to such an extent that in several places the local authorities recalled the sisters, even while the Terror was at its height. Education, already in a bad way since the Civil Constitution of the Clergy, finally collapsed. All work in this field hitherto done by the clergy was now barred to them. The one hundred and sixteen houses run by the Brothers of the Christian Schools were closed, and the revolutionary leaders proclaimed that a child belonged (even before birth) to the nation rather than to its parents. And they went even further: the craze for secularization was carried to the point of madness. Eighteen hundred years of Christianity had left their mark on all the customs of French life; and that mark, it was resolved, must go. Every name that recalled a saint, and still more the very word "saint," was strictly prohibited. Cities, towns and villages that bore the stigma of such names were ordered to change them; for, as the departmental authorities of Taru declared, "the names of Brutus and Scaevola are sweeter to a republican ear than those of a hermit like St. John." Personal names too were altered in accordance with those principles. Patronymics that contained the slightest reference to religion were proscribed along with former titles of nobility. Names of streets and squares were likewise affected, together with the annual festivals. The most thorough undertaking of this kind was directed against the old Christian calendar. The mathematician Romme and the poet Fabre d'Eglantine devoted their imaginations to wrecking "the catalogue of charlatanism" and substituting a truly republican system (October 24, 1793). Although it had never been suggested that the old names of the months were of Christian origin, they were replaced by twelve others referring to the principal stages in the life of nature: *Vendémiaire*, *Brumaire*, *Frimaire*, *Nivôse*, *Pluviôse*, *Ventôse*, *Germinal*, *Floréal*, *Prairial*, *Messidor*, *Thermidor* and *Fructidor*. Each of these months had thirty days and, by way of tribute to the metric system, was divided into three groups of ten; September 17–21 were supplementary days, called *jours sans-culotte*, and devoted to the celebration of secular and republican feasts. As for the days themselves, little imagination was required to name them *primidi*, *duodi*, *tridi* and so on to *décadi*. The republican calendar, destined to remain in official use for nearly twelve years, was never taken seriously by the people.

These absurdities did little harm. More serious, because often irreparable, was the damage done by the revolutionaries to ecclesiastical buildings: many a stately monument of the Christian past was destroyed for ever or mutilated beyond repair. One of the most deplorable features of the Revolution was this senseless iconoclasm which destroyed a large part of the nation's artistic capital. Places of worship were seized, although they had been secularized and were therefore no longer used for religious purposes. Many great abbeys were razed to the ground, among them Notre-Dame de Montmartre, Royaumont, Longjumeau and Jumièges. The saddest loss was that of Cluny, the Benedictine masterpiece in Burgundy, demolition of which began at this time.[13] At Saint-Denis the patriots of "La Franciade" thought of destroying the abbey church; fortunately they confined themselves to exhuming the bodies of the kings, throwing those of Henri IV, Louis XTII and Louis XIV into the paupers' grave, and smashing fifty-one funeral monuments. Throughout France, or at least in most places, statues were defaced—"Gothic shams" whose mere presence was offensive to the eyes of the citizens—and there is scarcely a cathedral façade that does not bear traces of such vandalism. Movable treasures were destroyed,[14] precious vessels melted down and their gems dispersed. In some cases, as at Saint-Germain-des-Prés, monstrances, chalices and reliquaries were trodden underfoot by the Conventionals in their demented revelry. The Abbé Grégoire, an eyewitness of more than one such scene, declared: "The loss of so many works of art is enough to draw tears of blood."

But that was not the end; for the revolutionaries, finding religion determined to survive notwithstanding all their police measures, conceived the idea that substitution was the only effective means of suppression. Hence their resolve to promote forms of worship that were duly guaranteed republican and *sansculotte*. They set to work immediately, and in less than two months a good half-dozen pseudo-religions began to flourish—vagaries

13. It was continued under the Empire: the towers were pulled down in 1811.

14. A number were hidden, such as the golden statue of St. Foy at Conques.

that might amuse us, but for the recollection that all involved sacrilege. For example, there was the cult of Great Men (among them Rousseau and Voltaire), who were offered for the veneration of the masses in place of the saints. When Marat was assassinated in his bath by Charlotte Corday, on July 13, 1793, his supporters literally deified him. Montmartre was renamed Mont-Marat; for three whole days the people were made to file past the urn containing his ashes, and an unfrocked priest carried infamy to the extent of comparing the heart of "The People's Friend" with the Sacred Heart of Jesus.

There were also two cults of a more abstract nature—two cults which are sometimes identified, and both of which attempted to provide a foundation of what may perhaps be called the republican theology. On August 10, 1793, there was celebrated the feast of Nature, which was at the same time that of "the Unity and Indivisibility of the Republic." On the anniversary of the fall of the throne a huge procession wound its way from the Bastille to the Champ-de-Mars, where an enormous statue of Nature (the "Fountain of Regeneration") poured from its ample breasts, half covered by the arms, a continuous stream of water. That was thought insufficient, and on 20th Brumaire (November 10)—three days after a group of priests, led by the metropolitan Gobel, had renounced their orders before the Assembly—Chaumette proposed the solemnization of that day on which "reason resumed its rule." There was no delay in giving effect to so lofty an idea, and it was resolved to celebrate the Cult of Reason with great magnificence in Notre-Dame at Paris, which had been decorated for that purpose by the painter David. At the summit of a papier mâché mountain a little Greek temple sheltered a famous dancer, proudly representing the goddess Reason, while long lines of garlanded girls sang hymns. At the end of the ceremony, which had been attended by a meagre congregation, Reason was escorted in procession to the National Convention, whose president embraced the goddess. In the cathedral thus profaned drinking and revelry continued far into the night, and Joseph de Maistre afterwards declared (probably with some exaggeration) that a woman showed herself to the crowds clothed in raiment which mythology attributes not to the goddess Reason but to Truth emerging from a well.

Among the most ardent revolutionaries, however, there were some who did not approve of those masquerades. Robespierre, "the incorruptible," was a deist, a zealous disciple of Jean-Jacques; he believed in the existence of a Supreme Being and in the immortality of the soul. The cult of Reason, with all its affectation, disgusted him, especially as he knew it to have been inspired by such extremists as Chaumette, Hébert and the Prussian Anacharsis Cloots who styled himself a "personal enemy of Jesus." After crushing them in March 1794, he decided that his own omnipotence should rest on properly theological foundations; and accordingly he determined to crown his work by establishing a cult of the Supreme Being, of which he himself would be the high priest. On 18th Floréal, Year II (May 7, 1794) he delivered a speech on "the relation of religious and moral ideas to republican principles and on the national festivals," a speech subsequently printed by order of the Convention. In it he proclaimed that "the idea of the Supreme Being and of the soul's immortality" is a continuous summons to justice, and consequently social and republican. The new cult would be that of virtue. A decree was passed whereby the French people recognized the two axioms of Robespierre's theology, and ordered that an inscription to that effect be placed over the doorway of every church. There followed a list of public holidays; it filled two columns, beginning with the feast of the Supreme Being and Nature, which was to be celebrated on 20 Prairial (June 8, 1794). This was done. Proceedings began in the garden of the Tuileries, where an enormous pyre devoured the monstrous image of Atheism while Robespierre pronounced a fervid oration. Then the crowds, singing appropriate hymns, started in procession for the Champ-de-Mars; ahead of them went a wagon draped in red, drawn by eight oxen, and loaded with sheaves of corn and boughs of foliage, among which was enthroned a statue of Liberty. Did Robespierre honestly cherish the illusion that he had thus substituted his religion for Catholicism? In the provinces there were priests who showed themselves delighted to burn the statue of Atheism, and some of the faithful attended with their rosaries, finding in the rustic festival a faint reminder of Rogation days. Elsewhere (e.g. at Besançon), delegates assured the people that this new form of worship was simply an extension of the cult of Reason, and they burned Atheism on heaps of rosaries, holy pictures and liturgical books. But the dictator had no time to continue his work. Six weeks after the festival that had marked his apogee he was overthrown; and it may be that the secret fury felt by true Jacobins against this mummery had something to do with his fall.

9. THE TWO CHURCHES IN THE WHIRLWIND

WHAT was the attitude of Catholics towards this frantic assault upon their faith? The constitutional Church and the recusants found themselves in more or less the same situation. It was not long before the enemies of Christianity ceased to distinguish between non-juror priests and others. A sorry doom awaited those who had sincerely believed that a sort of Catholic Jacobinism was possible.

Persecuted along with her rival, and often compromised in the federalist movement, the constitutional Church never entirely capitulated. The campaign to abolish the priesthood split her in two. Through fear, weakness or self-interest some agreed to abandon their duties and even to renounce their orders; but others remained faithful. These two conflicting attitudes were embodied in the two most outstanding constitutional bishops, Gobel and Grégoire. On November 6, 1793, a delegation of Representatives requested the metropolitan bishop of Paris to resign in the public interest. After wavering for some hours and consulting seventeen of his collaborators (only three of whom advised resistance), poor Gobel uttered these lamentable words: "The people engaged me, the people dismisses me; such is the lot of a servant at the orders of his master." Next day, in presence of the Convention, he allowed himself to be capped with the red bonnet and declared that "there should be no more public and national worship but that of Liberty and Holy Equality." Then the Convention, before which four other bishops had likewise resigned, called upon Grégoire to follow suit. The Bishop of Blois, however, a convinced revolutionary but a rigid Jansenist, stoutly refused in terms such that none dared gainsay: "A Catholic by conviction and sentiment, a priest by choice, I have been elected bishop by the people; but it is neither from them nor from you that I hold my appointment.... Acting in accordance with the sacred principles that are dear to me, and from which I defy you to tear me, I have tried to do good in my diocese. I remain a bishop in order to continue doing good. I invoke the freedom of worship...."

Grégoire's courage was imitated among the lower clergy, whose eyes appear to have been opened by the persecution. On October 13, 1795, in a report addressed to the Pope, M. Emery was able to write: "Before standing trial, all the many constitutional priests who have perished repudiated the oath which bound them to the Civil Constitution and begged to be reconciled with the Church." Others did not wait until the eleventh hour to recover possession of themselves. Such men were found almost everywhere in France. Grouped sometimes around an unyielding bishop, they founded small cells of resistance, a constitutional Church faithful to its erroneous but sincere beliefs, "the Church of Grégoire" as it has been called.

As for the remainder, those who lacked the courage to stand fast, they cannot all be dismissed with equal contempt. We can hardly esteem the twenty-three bishops who apostatized, or even the twenty-four who resigned their office; but it would be unfair to execrate those many humble priests who, under terrible pressure, facing determined adversaries in complete isolation, gave way and handed in their certificates of ordination, not considering that apostasy from the clerical state was necessarily apostasy from the faith. Among the apostates there were, of course, odious men who placed themselves at the service of the police; there were also fanatics and careerists. These, however, were a minority. Even among the chicken-hearted who had surrendered their papers there were many (a majority, in fact) who stoutly refused to take the final step on the road of apostasy by marrying.

We are fully entitled, therefore, to speak of a resistance movement within the constitutional Church. She too had her martyrs. One set of figures deserves particular attention: out of four hundred and eighty-four ecclesiastics from all over France who appeared before the revolutionary tribunal at Paris, at least three hundred and nineteen belonged to the constitutional Church. Eight of her bishops perished on the scaffold, and five of them retracted their errors before dying. Those sacrifices cannot be forgotten when we pass judgment on that Church; events nearer to our own day have helped us to a better understanding of the reasons for her attitude and her setbacks.

Resistance on the part of the recusant Church was much nobler and more effective. Having gone into hiding soon after the September Massacres, she was in a position to continue her work when the Terror properly so called began. In this she was powerfully assisted by the zeal, courage and intelligence of her members, many of whom hid priests, kept secret oratories in their houses and sometimes even faced the *sansculottes* and persuaded them to depart.

Every priest of the clandestine clergy at that time led a life fraught with peril, which too often ended in blood. There was the internuncio de Salamon, who spent three months in the Bois de Boulogne, under a kiosk where the inhabitants of Auteuil danced on Sundays. There was Father Coudrin, afterwards founder of Piepus, who was known throughout Poitou as "Marche à Terre" because he was for ever on the move. There were M. Cormaux, a Breton parish priest, and his friend the ex-Jesuit Father de Clorivière, who set out each day from their lodging in the Rue de la Chaise in Paris to say Mass, administer the sacraments, hear confessions and even preach. At Strasbourg there was the Abbé Colmar, future Bishop of Mayence, who, with the help of Mme. Humann, managed to continue his apostolate by frequently altering his disguise. Some of these priests, in order to escape imminent arrest, stayed for months in a cupboard—and even in still less attractive little places. Many, in order not to attract suspicion, adopted all sorts of trades: scriveners, doctors, workers in wood or metal, water-carriers, clerks in government offices. Many too wore military uniform and took their turn mounting guard, as became good citizens. There were some, however, who did not go into hiding, but simply took care to do nothing that might offend republican susceptibilities. Among these was M. Emery, who, until an informer contrived his arrest, lived quietly in his empty seminary at Saint-Sulpice and afterwards in the house of a friend. It is also known that a few priests enjoyed the secret protection of friends in high places, and M. Emery was doubtless one of them. There is a story that one evening when M. de Keravenant sat in his lodging near Saint-Germain-des-Prés, which he thought was quite unknown to the police, he was visited by a member of the Convention who asked him to hear his confession before his marriage. The caller was none other than Danton, who was going to wed Louise Gély.

The consequences of this resistance can be summed up in a few words: despite all the efforts of those who were determined to eliminate Christianity, Roman Catholicism did not vanish from France. In Paris, at the time of Robespierre's fall, there were still more than one hundred and fifty places of worship where Mass was celebrated regularly, and at least a hundred in the surrounding countryside. Spiritual life, far from dying or suffering eclipse, became more intense; as always, persecution worked in favour of revival. Along the route to the scaffold there were always priests to give absolution secretly to those in the tumbrils; and if one of those "chaplains of the guillotine" was arrested there was no lack of volunteers to take his place.

These facts, however, do not mean that all was well with that faithful and heroic Church. It has to be acknowledged that the tragic situation of the recusants was exacerbated by disagreements and a certain lack of restraint. The affair of the "liberty-equality" oath perpetuated a conflict between men equally courageous and devoted to the cause of the Church. On one side were M. Emery and those who followed his advice, convinced that the Church should accept what was good in the Revolution, and labour to give birth to a new society instead of harking back to the dead past. The great Sulpician was strengthened in this view when, as a prisoner in Conciergerie, he had occasion to hear the confessions of many priests and even some bishops who had taken the oath, and to discover that it was easy to bring them back to the true Church. But Emery was opposed by resolute adversaries, not only by such men as Cardinal Maury in Rome and the Abbé Bernier, who were influenced by personal or political motives, but also by Lingolas, clandestine Vicar-General of Lyons, an honest and zealous priest who rejected with disdain any form of compromise and considered M. Emery's supporters as akin to renegades. Unfortunately too no superior authority was available to settle the dispute. Of the total number of French bishops in 1789, only twenty-six had not emigrated; between 1790 and December 1794 seventeen died either from natural causes or as victims of the September Massacres, or else in prison or on the scaffold. Several of those who were left went into hiding and were thus inactive, while those who struggled on lacked the prestige necessary for directing the Church of France. History poses the question whether the recusant bishops, by remaining at the peril of their lives, would not have enabled the Catholic resistance movement to organize itself more satisfactorily, to become more united, and to prepare more effectually for the future—that future of brilliant revival which was guaranteed by the sacrifice of so many of its adherents.

10. VICTIMS AND MARTYRS OF THE TERROR

WE have now to consider that sacrifice and estimate its full significance. In accordance with the age-long teaching of Christianity, it was amid insult, suffering and death willingly endured that the Church bore her witness. This is true particularly of the "Roman" Church; but it is true also of some members of her constitutional rival, who rejoined her before death in such a manner that the blood of jurors and recusants was often mingled. Thus it came about, as was realized later, that the Church, her clergy and the Catholic faith itself recovered the prestige that had faded during the Age of Enlightenment. It must be acknowledged that the spiritual renascence of the nineteenth century sprang mainly from the heroism of the victims and martyrs of the Terror.

Those victims were innumerable. There is no doubt that of the countless men and women devoured by the revolutionary Minotaur, a vast majority were Catholics, most of whom, in their last hours, remembered their baptism and died as Christians. Although they included many priests, the number of ordinary faithful (mostly humble folk) was far greater. Not all Catholics, of course, who mounted the scaffold did so for religious reasons; some were begrudged their wealth, some their fame, while in other cases petty spite was at work. It is certain, however, that many were condemned on the mere grounds of loyalty to the Christian faith. It is impossible to estimate their numbers. It must also be admitted that anti-Christian violence was not the same in all *départements*; in nine of them there is no record of a priest having suffered capital punishment; in two there was only one such sentence, and in several only two. It was in Paris and the neighbourhood that persecution was most severe.

When one thinks of this terrible period, the image that comes first to mind is that of the guillotine, a hideous instrument standing sometimes in the former Place Louis XV and sometimes at the Barrière du Trône. Numerous contemporary memoirs and prints show us the procession of tumbrils, flanked by *sansculottes* carrying pikes and loaded with the condemned, who were tied together in pairs. One imagines their long agony as, seated side by side near the bloody platform, they awaited their turn—listening to the fall of the triangular blade and feeling the planks tremble beneath its blow. And the gestures of the executioner, showing the severed head to the crowd before throwing it into the basket, add horror to a scene whose repetition it is astonishing that a civilized people should have tolerated for so long.

But in addition to this form of execution, whose rapidity might lead one to regard it as humane, the Revolution employed others whose cruelty has hardly been surpassed by the concentration camps of our own day. There were the *noyades* at Nantes, barges crammed with chained captives whom an ingenious system of trapdoors sent to the bottom of the Loire. At

Lyons and elsewhere there were mass shootings, after which the wounded and the dead were piled up indiscriminately and buried without delay. The episode of the hulks at Rochefort is still famous in the history of torture—a striking proof, alas, of the contempt in which certain revolutionaries held those "rights of man" which had been so solemnly proclaimed. From February 1784 onwards eight hundred and fifty priests, who had been arrested mainly in northern and eastern France and in Belgium, were put aboard three old ships formerly used in the black slave trade. There they were held in conditions so appalling that their detention became known as the "dry guillotine." At the mercy of so-called sailors, who formed the crews of these vessels, and quickly prey to hideous epidemics which decimated their numbers, these men still had the sublime courage to continue to live a spiritual life that was heightened by their sufferings. We possess the text of the "Resolutions" which they drew up and swore to practise; few saints have penned a nobler document. Of these eight hundred and fifty captives in the hulks, only two hundred and seventy-four were left when an order for their release was signed in February 1795, seven months after the fall of Robespierre.

Among those who went to the guillotine were the sixteen Carmelites of Compiègne, who died on July 17, 1794. They were arrested and condemned to death on a charge of having stayed together as a community after their convent had been suppressed. It is said that one of them asked Fouquier-Tinville, president of the revolutionary court, what he meant by calling them fanatics. He replied: "Your fanaticism is your foolish attachment to your stupid religious practices." Upon which she cried: "There you are, sisters: we have been condemned for our religion.... What happiness to die for our God!" At the foot of the scaffold they renewed their vows and then intoned the *Veni Creator*, which continued until the last of them was silenced.[15] Hardly less sublime were the Sacramentines of Bollène. Before dying they thanked their judges and executioners, and one of them kissed the scaffold before mounting it. There were also the Ursulines of Valenciennes, who

15. Pius X beatified them in 1906.

sang the *Te Deum* and prayed for their executioners; the Sisters of Charity at Arras, who arrived at the guillotine girt with their rosaries; and many others whom we cannot recall without emotion.

Many monks and friars were equally heroic. The Benedictines of Gravilliers proudly declared that they had never ceased to say Mass in secret. Father Imbert, a Dominican of Castres, refused to mount the tumbril: "My Master, Jesus, walked," he said, "and I demand to go on foot." The Recollects and Carmelites of Arras marched to execution singing vespers of the dead. Finally, the Abbé Fraisse, Prior of the Order of Malta, who had handed in his certificate of priesthood, subsequently repented; he surrendered himself to the revolutionary tribunal and consequently to death.

The secular clergy produced countless noble figures. Cormaux, "the saint of Brittany," refused during his interrogation to hide the least particle of truth, providing his accusers with arguments which they had overlooked. Van Cleemputte, a self-styled patriot, refused to be condemned as a royalist, but openly declared that he had been carrying out a continuous though secret apostolate. Noël Pinot, led to execution in alb and chasuble as a mark of contempt, recited the *Introibo ad altare Dei* at the foot of the scaffold. Lastly there was the Abbé de Salignac-Fénelon, founder and director of the Oeuvre des Petits Savoyards. Condemned to death despite his eighty years and the supplications of his little protégés, he preached once again from the tumbril on his way to the guillotine....

The list might be continued almost without end; nor must we omit dozens of layfolk to whom all the evidence points as having died likewise on behalf of their faith. At Lyons a merchant named Auroze was asked: "Are you a fanatic?" "Call me anything you like," he replied, "but I'm a Catholic." For that he was condemned to death. In Anjou, one Valfons, when asked his name at the start of his interrogation, stated it together with the adjectives "Catholic, Apostolic and Roman." In Seine-et-Oise Marie Langlois, a twenty-two-year-old farm-hand who had been denounced by the constitutional priest of the parish, openly laughed at her judges and their trifling questions. Elsewhere Elizabeth Minet proudly proclaimed herself guilty of a dreadful crime in having, throughout the Terror, continually distributed statuettes of the Blessed Virgin. Elsewhere again, Geneviève Goyon, a dressmaker aged sixty-six, refused to betray two Dominicans who were hiding in her house, and died along with them.

11. CATHOLIC FRANCE IN EXILE

ALL the pathos of those sufferings and sacrifices cannot be conveyed in a few pages. Catholic France, however, was not confined to that one land groaning beneath the revolutionary jackboot; she was not represented entirely by those priests and layfolk who faced the alternative of treason or heroism. Others of her members endured a fate which, though less tragic, was in many cases none the less afflicting. French Catholic émigrés, scattered in many lands, encountered numerous difficulties and bore their own witness to the Faith.

How many were these exiles? Taking account of all the successive waves of emigration, and including that of 1797 (to which we shall refer later), some historians have put the number as high as forty thousand priests and religious; but this is probably excessive. Fugitives by choice, or driven out by revolutionary decrees, their unhappy droves were continually renewed between the spring of 1792 and the eve of the Napoleonic era. Having abandoned all—family, friends, home and parish—in exchange for their security, they reached foreign lands, many of them after terrible ordeals, in a state of utter destitution. They were fortunate, too, if the countries in which they had taken refuge—Savoy, Belgium, Italy and the left bank of the Rhine—were not invaded by the republican armies, in which case they had to take the road again and flee still farther at the cost of renewed suffering.

How were God's fugitives received in the lands where they sought sanctuary? It must be acknowledged that those nations which might have been expected to show a sense of solidarity were often the least generous in their welcome. In Germany it may have seemed natural that the King of Prussia should forbid them access to his dominions; it was more surprising that the King of Bavaria and a number of minor sovereigns, who were also Catholics, should do likewise.[16] His Majesty of Austria closed his frontiers, dreading the revolutionary contagion which might be transmitted by Frenchmen as such. "Our ecclesiastics," wrote the Bishop of Nîmes, "are dying of hunger beneath the walls of twenty millionaire abbeys in Swabia." Some deplorable incidents are on record. The celebrated abbey of Fulda refused French émigré priests a decent place in which to sleep; Fussen, in Tyrol, forbade them to say Mass; Weingarten set watch-dogs on all who tried to enter its cloister. Outside the papal territories, how many Italian states admitted refugee priests? Neither Milan, nor Parma, nor Modena, nor the Serene Republic of Venice; they were all too scared of attracting the revolutionary thunderbolt. In Piedmont the situation was unstable and its welcome precarious; Naples would receive none but bishops, vicars-general and other dignitaries. The reaction of wealth to the cry of distress is invariable.

There were, however, some noble exceptions, particularly in Rome and the Papal States. On this occasion Pius VI behaved with the utmost generosity, and it was with good reason that in 1795 a medal was struck showing him with arms wide open to the French priests. He received five thousand of them into the Papal States, created a charitable fund for their support and ordered the bishops of his dominions to behave in brotherly fashion towards them. But in order to avoid overcrowding in the Eternal City, which might have provoked anti-French demonstrations, he settled the refugees in four towns: Viterbo, Perugia, Bologna and Ferrara. Monks and friars were distributed among the houses of their respective orders. The Pope's generosity, of course, did not meet with unanimous approval. The pontifical authorities obliged French priests and religious to take an oath that they were neither Gallicans nor Jansenists; those who had formerly adhered to the constitutional Church were made to retract and even to do

16. The only parts of Germany that extended a welcome were Westphalia, Silesia and Constance.

penance. As for the French religious, various memoirs suggest that their life in the monasteries which had given them shelter was often far from happy.

Other Catholic countries proved themselves faithful to the duties of hospitality. In Spain the bishops were remarkably generous in their welcome. The Spanish Government, however, was less warm-hearted, fearing that a dangerous revolutionary might lurk beneath the tatters of a refugee priest, and also that the émigrés themselves might be contaminated with Jacobinism, Jansenism or Gallicanism. A decree forbade them to engage in any religious activity apart from celebrating Mass.

The Catholic cantons of Switzerland were as spontaneously generous as the faithful in Spain. Despite their meagre resources, they welcomed no fewer than four thousand priests, raising charitable subscriptions on their behalf, while the famous abbey of Einsiedeln spent enormous sums to help them.

Still more touching is the fact that certain Protestant countries displayed a generosity that does them the highest honour. Calvinist Geneva extended its charity to six hundred priests who sought asylum within its walls. Nor did Holland fall short of her duty: many priests of Jansenist tendencies found shelter there, and in 1794 the Jansenist news sheet *Nouvelles ecclésiastiques*[17] reappeared in Holland, having ceased publication at Paris in December 1793.[18] But it was England that proved herself above all others the home of kindly hearts; she was publicly thanked by Pope Pius VI, who offered her as an example to the whole of Europe. Nearly ten thousand priests and thirty-one bishops made their home in England. Later Pitt spoke of them in these words: "Few will ever forget the piety, the irreproachable conduct, the long and dolorous patience of those men, cast suddenly into the midst of a foreign people different in its religion, its language, its manners and its customs. They won the respect and goodwill of all by a life of unvarying godliness and decency." Thanks to this contact many prejudices

17. *The Church of the Classical Age: The Great Century of Souls*, Volume 2, p. 519.

18. Pichegru's invasion of Holland obliged the émigré priests to take refuge in England.

vanished; the presence of French priests helped in large measure to obtain for English Catholics full equality of rights, and also pioneered the renascence of English Catholicism in the nineteenth century.

The virtues to which the English prime minister paid such striking tribute appear all the more remarkable when we consider the difficult circumstances in which a large majority of émigré priests had to live. Having been unable to take money in their flight, most were obliged to earn a living by practising some trade. Among them were schoolmasters, scriveners, clerks, hatters, tailors, candle-makers, even coachmen and farm workers. In these situations they retained their dignity; only a few ex-courtier abbés, who had managed to escape with substantial funds, continued to live in the elegant surroundings of Coblenz the same lives they had led before 1789.

The bishops too remained steadfast in adversity. Many of them had suffered equally with the humblest priests. Despoiled of their wealth, the majority declared themselves happier in poverty, closer to their priestly vocation. Even the notorious Cardinal de Rohan, forced to flee his ostentatious mansion at Strasbourg, recovered his good name by an exemplary life. Surrounded by the priests and seminarists whom lie sheltered in his house at Ettenheim, he wished to be simply "a priest of Jesus Christ" and "a poor man."

One of the most attractive features in the lives of these French exiles is the glow of mutual charity with which many of them were inspired. In the hour of misfortune men too often obey the motto *Sauve qui peut*; but the generosity of those outcasts towards their brethren in distress amazed the foreigners among whom they dwelt. In England, an unassuming Breton bishop, Mgr. de La Marche,[19] founded a Committee of Subscribers for the Help of the French Clergy. From Constance, Mgr. de Juigné and Mgr. de la Luzerne arranged for collections to be made throughout the Catholic world in order to assure their priests an indispensable monthly sum of nine

19. The same whom his flock had once nicknamed "Bishop Potatoes." *The Church of the Classical Age: The Era of Great Splintering*, Volume 2, Chapter VI, section 3.

livres. At Rome, until his death in 1794, Cardinal de Bernis spent all that remained of his income on board and lodging for his fellow countrymen. At Turin, and later in Tuscany, the Abbé Madier, former chaplain to the king's aunt, Madame Victoire, organized an energetic body of workers for the relief of the clergy.

All those facts bore witness to the Faith, even though such witness was not sealed with blood like that of the victims of the scaffold. The émigrés, of course, had the shortcomings of refugees in every age: they judged the situation solely in terms of the past, and thus deceived themselves in many respects. At the beginning of 1793 a meeting of French ecclesiastics, held at the abbey of Saint-Maurice-en-Valais, passed a manifold resolution determining the conditions which appeared necessary for the complete restoration of Catholicism in France. The Church, it declared, must recover her entire patrimony; the registers of civil status must be restored to her; throne and altar must once again form an unbreakable alliance; and so on. Those illusions were to prove very dangerous in 1815, when an attempt was made to give them effect.

12. RELAXATION AND REVIVAL IN THE THERMIDORIAN ERA

ON the morning of July 26, 1794—8th Thermidor according to the new calendar—nothing seemed to indicate that the regime of which Robespierre had made himself absolute master was in the slightest danger. But next evening, 9th Thermidor, a warrant was issued for the arrest of Robespierre and his supporters. On the evening of the 10th they in turn journeyed through Paris in the tumbrils amid a joyous throng exulting in their fall.

Yet those who brought about that fall were no less revolutionaries than Robespierre and his friends. They had no intention whatsoever of changing the régime, even of modifying its orientation, and still less of returning to a policy of religious leniency. They were, however, straightway swept aside, borne along on the torrent of joy that followed the tyrant's fall. Robespierre became the scapegoat, as though he alone had been responsible for the Terror. The same blow that had struck him down put an end to fear. The whole of France was nauseated by the scaffold; she wished to live, and the regime was obliged willy-nilly to align itself with public opinion.

Quite suddenly there was an outburst of faith. Little more than a week or so after the fall of Robespierre, Mass began to be celebrated once again in several parts of France. During the winter émigré priests reappeared in the frontier provinces, disguised as tinkers, pedlars, gunners and so forth; and those who had remained in France boldly emerged almost everywhere from their hiding-places. In the spring this flood increased. Police reports showed that individuals armed with a small bell were parading the streets, summoning the people to religious services. In some localities, for want of priests, laymen celebrated "white Masses." At first the revolutionaries had not understood the significance of these events. They had continued for some while to guillotine priests both in Paris and in the provinces; some delegates had even raised to five hundred francs the reward promised to anyone who denounced a refractory priest. But these final acts of persecution meant little. Local administrations were no longer anxious to apply measures intended to destroy the Christian faith, and their agents often forewarned those whom they should have arrested. What was to be done against a whole people determined to recover its religion? M. Emery tells us that in Paris, on Easter Sunday 1795, it was necessary to celebrate open-air Masses and repeat the singing of Vespers. Authority was thus compelled to sanction an accomplished fact.

Between 1795 and 1797 a series of new religious laws was published, revealing in no uncertain manner the political instability of France. The regime wavered between a desire to separate Church from State, which corresponded to the philosophy of most Thermidorians, and a nostalgia for Jacobin severity. On September 18, 1794, six weeks after the fall of Robespierre, the Convention hallowed that separation by means of a financial decree: "The Republic will no longer pay the expenses of religious worship or the salaries of its ministers." The system established by the Civil Constitution was thus abandoned, and with it the constitutional Church. At the same time a number of delegates took it upon themselves to offer an amnesty to refractory priests and declared that they would no longer regard as suspect those parish priests who continued to perform their duties. This daring policy was an important factor in the pacification of La Vendée, which was accomplished on February 17, 1795. Four days later (February 21; 3rd Ventôse, Year III) the Assembly, urged by Grégoire, passed a decree completely separating Church and State. True, it subjected the exercise of worship to offensive restrictions; but even so it enabled religion to regain a footing in the city. Consequently there was a new leap forward, a spate of chapels and oratories, an outburst of devotion. Anxiety mounted in the Jacobin camp; constitutional bishops and priests were among the first to complain, rivalled as they now were by the non-jurors. Three decrees of this period indicated a stiffening of attitude, especially that of September 29, 1795 (7th Vendémiaire, Year IV), which laid down rules for the exercise and control of religious worship, and also exacted a new oath of submission to the laws of the Republic. Tension was further increased by two foolish conspiracies on the part of some royalists, with whom a number of priests unfortunately associated themselves. Before breaking up, the Convention ordered that all laws against priests which had been passed since 1792 must continue to be strictly enforced.

When the new government, known as the Directory, came to power on October 27, 1795, the situation was hopelessly confused. Was religion acknowledged, tolerated or proscribed? Were priests considered suspect, or did the law ignore them? In point of fact Catholics had become once again a force in the land. On 14th Frimaire (December 4, 1796) the law which had re-enacted terrorist measures against priests was repealed. The clergy now had only to take the Liberty-Equality oath in order to secure recognition; there was no longer any question of the Civil Constitution. The Catholics, who, under cover of philanthropic societies, had carefully prepared for the elections of Germinal, Year V (March 21–April 9, 1797), achieved notable success: ninety-five percent of the former members of the National Convention were defeated. New measures were immediately passed (7th Fructidor—August 24) abrogating the proscriptive decrees and restoring all rights to those priests who would declare that they submitted to the laws of the Republic. The Church appeared to be on the eve of regaining control of France when, on 18th Fructidor (September 4), another jolt on the stony path of the Directory again imperilled the Church's peace.[20]

Meanwhile, thanks to political fluctuation and uncertainty, the Church regained a firm foothold in France. I refer mainly to the Roman Church, though what remained of the constitutional Church made a courageous effort to profit by circumstances and revive its strength. The head of this latter movement was Grégoire, constitutional bishop of Cher-et-Loir, who acted so to speak as Pope, or at any rate patriarch, of that poor body now three parts ruined and deprived of its very grounds of existence. Gathering around him a committee of bishops, he published in quick succession two "encyclicals" aggressively Gallican in tone and intended to give fresh impulse to religion in France. He also founded a newspaper, *Les Annales de la Religion*, to defend his views; and as soon as the law permitted he reopened churches and chapels one after another. His committee had the good sense to associate the laity with this revival by creating "cultural societies" whose elected heads were to direct the material life of the parishes. It likewise concerned itself with education, drawing up a regular code of instruction and opening many schools. Lastly, with that fearlessness which had always been one of his outstanding characteristics, Grégoire harassed the government and spoke from the tribune in order to obtain for his Church confirmation of her rights.

In the event his efforts came to nothing. The constitutional Church was attacked from all sides. Everywhere the rivalry of recusant priests kept people away from its services. "Roman" schools were reopened throughout the country, especially after a law of 3rd Brumaire, Year IV (October 25,

20. Cf. the present chapter, section 14.

1795), had granted freedom to teach, and they were far more popular than those of the constitutional clergy. Furthermore many priests who had taken the oath retracted under the influence of Roussineau, parish priest of Saint-Germain-des-Prés, who started the movement. Their return to the bosom of the Roman Church was facilitated by M. Emery, who took care to avoid hurting self-respect in the formula of retractation. Finally, the constitutional Church suffered a very grave internal crisis. Some of its most intelligent and most active parish priests thought that the time had come for them to assert their own rights and diminish those of the bishops, in accordance with the theories of Catholic "presbyterianism" which had played a part in the working out of the Civil Constitution and which no ordeal had managed to destroy. The result was keen tension between Grégoire's committee and the "presbytery" of Paris—a tension that gave rise to disagreeable incidents, as on the occasion of the reopening of Notre-Dame for Catholic services. The constitutional Church did its best to counter these difficulties by summoning a national council on August 15, 1791; but its days were clearly numbered.

The future evidently belonged far more truly to its rival, to that Church which had resisted the revolutionary Moloch for five years and had purchased with its blood the right to live. Each day witnessed an increase in the number of priests returning from exile; Catholics were reopening churches and chapels one after another; and the religious revival was so rapid as to scare the last of the Jacobins. The bishops were in no hurry to leave their new-found homes and return to France; but Mgr. de Maillé de la Tour-Landry ordained a number of priests in private houses, and his example was soon followed by others. Nursing sisters began to resume their work in the hospitals, and Camille de Soyecourt settled a small community of Carmelite nuns in the half-ruined convent of their order at Paris, while Father de Clorivière was organizing the Priests of the Heart of Jesus and the Daughters of the Immaculate Heart of Mary, two congregations which he had founded in secret. At the height of the Terror, Father René Bérault had founded the Daughters of the Holy Heart of Mary at Bougé, chiefly for the care of incurable diseases; and after his death in 1795 his work was continued by Anne de la Girouardière.

Moreover the Church, having emerged as it were from the catacombs, was remodeling her own life. The home missions, developed now on lines adapted to contemporary circumstances, took on fresh energy and discovered new methods of approach. During the Terror a number of priests had voluntarily taken to the road, carrying with them altar linen, sacred vessels, etc., and celebrating Mass in a different place each day. The Abbé Linsolas, Vicar-General of Lyons, was outstanding among several men who conceived the idea of systematizing the work and continuing this apostolate once religious peace had been virtually restored. Missioners would go from parish to parish, evangelizing those who had left the Church, bringing back to the Roman obedience juror-priests and their flocks. The parochial pattern was temporarily ignored, and the diocese broken up into a number of sectors known as "missions," within which it was intended that the priests (usually in charge of several villages) should carry out their apostolate with the greatest possible flexibility. In this way, it was hoped, a better distribution of spiritual resources would be secured, and risks would be fewer in the event of danger. Arrangements were also made for a certain number of lay organizations in each locality to reinforce and continue in many different ways the activity of the missioners, as "forerunners," "heads of the parish," or catechists. The idea seemed an excellent one: among the several benefits it conferred was that of establishing an efficient Catholic organization against the ever-present possibility of renewed persecution. The example of Lyons was soon followed by other dioceses, and the undertaking as a whole revealed an extraordinary vitality in the bosom of French Catholicism.

Nevertheless all was not well in that renascent Church. Tendencies which we have already noticed were still at work, and led to something like open antagonism. Priests who had returned from exile or emerged from hiding took advantage of the altered situation to wreak their revenge, as indeed was only human. Some of them advised their parishioners to urge their sons to desert from the army, to refuse payment of taxes and even to expel juror-priests. The more intransigent encouraged attempted landings on the coast of France. Many regarded restoration of the monarchy as going hand in hand with that of religion. And, of course, when the decree of 7th Vendémiaire, Year IV (September 29, 1795), required all citizens to take an oath of "submission to the laws of the Republic," the extremists declared themselves hostile to any such measure. On the other hand the moderates, guided by the sage advice of M. Emery, counselled prudence. "Religion," said the great Sulpician, "is an end, not a means; it must not be used to further the interests of a political régime." Some bishops recommended their clergy to accord a large-hearted welcome to former constitutional priests who had returned to the fold; but in many cases they spoke to deaf ears. And when the Pope twice declared that he could see no difficulty in the formula, "I promise to obey the government of the French Republic," the extremists denounced the papal brief as an undeniable forgery.

It was, however, none the less certain that the Church in France witnessed at that time a reversal of the religious situation which no one would have dared to prophesy four years earlier. Towards the end of 1796 the republican general Clarke, afterwards Duc de Feltre, wrote from Italy in a report to the Directory: "Our revolution, so far as religion is concerned, has proved a complete failure. France has become once more Roman Catholic, and we may be on the point of needing the Pope himself in order to enlist clerical support for the Revolution, and thereby the support of those districts which the clergy again controls."

13. ROME, THE CHURCH AND THE VICTOR OF ARCOLI

SINCE his effigy had been burnt in the gardens of the Palais-Royal, the Pontiff's shadow had never ceased to hover over French policy. His will had been at work in the course of events far more actively than the revolutionaries had imagined. It was in his name, and through loyalty to him, that so many Catholic priests and laymen had faced prison and death. Now, in the new atmosphere of lowered tension, a word from him was of capital importance; and Bonaparte, the young victor of Arcoli, laboured to give effect to what General Clarke had written.

While France lived through those tragic years that began in the spring of 1789, Rome had not ceased to concern herself with the rest of mankind and to guide the footsteps of the Catholic world. Indeed, as he grew older, Pius VI seemed to acquire a heightened sense of his responsibility. As early as Christmas 1775 his Encyclical *Inscrutabile divinae sapientiae* has shown that his intellect was fully alive to the great problems of the age. An allocution delivered on learning of the death of Louis XVI, and another at Christmas 1793, were couched in even graver terms. The Eternal City, it is true, despite the thunderbolt of the Revolution, remained preoccupied with petty intrigue, aristocratic or popular festivals, rivalry both ecclesiastical and secular, questions of precedence and brilliant cermonies, just as she had been throughout the eighteenth century. Disquiet, however, had been steadily mounting, increased by the arrival of an incessant stream of French émigrés and outlawed bishops. In 1792 the governor of Rome had banned celebration of the Carnival. Anxiety had begun to furrow the handsome countenance of Pius VI.

Indeed, in whatever direction the common father of all Catholics turned his gaze, the events he witnessed could cause nothing but distress. A tragedy had just occurred more serious in some respects than that of France: a great Catholic country had vanished from the map of Europe. Following the partition of 1772, which deprived her of two-fifths of her territory, Poland had made a strenuous effort to improve her system of government: a new constitution, adopted in 1791 and modelled on that of France, abolished the most flagrant vices, particularly the absurd *liberum veto*. Unfortunately this policy of reform was opposed by some discontented nobles, to whom the Czarina Catherine II was only too willing to lend the support of her troops. After Valmy, Frederick William II, King of Prussia, disappointed at having failed to extend his depredations westward, withdrew his forces from the Rhine to the Vistula. Then, on January 23, 1793, under pretext of stifling at Warsaw "the influence of horrible tendencies emanating from the frightful Parisian sect, together with the spirit of French demagogy which threatens the peace of Europe," Russia and Prussia proceeded to a second dismemberment. The Polish Diet, known as "the dumb Diet," was obliged to withhold its protest in face of Russian bayonets which guarded all exits from its hall of session, and its silence was taken as assent.

Polish patriotism reacted with the violence of despair. Kosciuzko led a formidable rising which managed to drive Catherine's troops from Warsaw and Vilna. But Russian revenge was not long delayed. Suvorov's victory at Maciejowic (October 1794) and the capture of Praga (November), which was followed by terrible massacres, restored order—Muscovite order. Austria and Prussia then claimed their share. The final treaty was signed in October 1795, and Poland was erased from the map of Europe.

This unpardonable operation resulted in the disappearance of one of the oldest bastions of the Roman Church. About two-fifths of Polish Catholics found themselves henceforward subject to Austria; worse still, the remainder were handed over to Protestant Prussia and Orthodox Russia. No Catholic heart can be anything but deeply moved by these outrages. They afflicted Pius VI, as appears from letters addressed by him to the emperor Francis II; but he failed to strike a note of keen indignation, or to find the right words for an effective appeal to world opinion. Maybe he felt too weak, too helpless and lacking in authority.

Assuredly there were clouds on all horizons. Even in countries where the Church was not directly menaced, the Pope found little cause for satisfaction. In Italy itself the situation was far from reassuring. Subversive ideas had been filtering into the peninsula ever since the outbreak of the French Revolution. True they were not widespread; but this flow was combining with another, more secret and more dangerous—that of Italian Jansenism, which had made considerable headway even among the episcopate and members of the Curia,[21] and in which an inclination to rigorist reforms

21. *The Church of the Classical Age: The Great Century of Souls*, Volume 2, p. 525.

mingled with strongly anti-papal currents. The Synod of Pistoia had miscarried,[22] and its leading spirit, Scipio Ricci, had resigned his see in 1791; but he would not retract until 1805, and his partisans remained numerous. The condemnation of the synod's theses by the Bull *Auctorem fidei* (1794) had not been unanimously accepted; some bishops, among them Mgr. Solari of Noli, had even refused to publish it. Several bishops had openly declared themselves in favour of the Civil Constitution, and the arrival of French troops in Italy won for these quasi-rebels a good deal of support.

In Austria Josephism had not been buried with its founder, and Francis II was equally determined to control the Church. In Catholic Germany episcopal opposition to the Pope had not ceased with the submission of Febronius. Rome therefore welcomed the news that a rebellious people, by sweeping away its mitred lords, had put an end to those wretched quarrels, and that the German peasantry, glad to be able once more to hear Mass in Latin (which certain bishops had forbidden), had helped in the expulsion of their masters. As for Spain, power was now in the hands of the queen's favourite Godoï, an atheist anti-clerical resolutely set upon bringing the Church to heel.

Strangely enough, the only bright spots in the landscape were England, where the small body of loyal Catholics was moving with firm step towards equality of rights, and the United States, where the Catholic Church was becoming ever more firmly rooted, thanks to the work of Mgr. Carroll[23] and the influence of a team of Sulpicians sent by M. Emery, as well as to many French refugee priests.

Finally, the unhappy Pope could not avert his gaze from those tragic scenes of which France was the theatre, particularly as the course of the Revolution affected Italy and the Papal States. In August 1789 there were "patriotic" riots at Avignon, and the people of Carpentras asked for a meeting

22. *The Church of the Classical Age: The Era of Great Splintering*, Volume 2, Chapter V, section 5.

23. Ibid., Chapter VI, section 13.

of States-General. Members of the Constituent Assembly demanded the annexation—they called it restitution—of the Comtat. In March 1790 Carpentras obtained its States-General, and Avignon elected a revolutionary municipality which adopted the French Constitution. On June 11 the vice-legate Casoni was expelled; and when the counter-revolutionary Haut-Comtat flew to arms, France sent troops to re-establish order. Pius VI protested in vain, and on September 14, 1791, after a year's hesitation, the assembly voted the reunion of Avignon with France. The Pope was greatly distressed. Tension between the Republic and the Holy See had steadily increased since that date, and the campaign against priests loyal to Rome had been intensified.

There was an abrupt change of situation in Italy in the spring of 1796, when the Directory gave Napoleon Bonaparte command of an army with instructions to pin down an Austrian force in the valley of the Po and thus facilitate the offensive of Jourdan and Moreau on the Rhine. Napoleon, a brilliant strategist, carried out the operation with unexpected dash. The Sardinians were separated from the Austrians at Millesimo, crushed at Mondori, and forced to sign a peace which involved their evacuation of Nice and Savoy. Then, having routed the Austrians at Montenotte and obliged them to retreat northwards, Napoleon pushed on towards Lombardy and occupied Milan. Mantua, head of the famous quadrilateral, stood firm; within a period of six months four armies were sent to relieve the town, but Napoleon compelled every one of them to retire. After Arcoli (November 15, 1796) and Rivoli (January 14, 1797) the whole of Italy was at his mercy.

The significance of these lightning events was not lost upon the Holy See. Pius VI was overwhelmed by the fall of Milan; and as Godoï had allied Spain with the French Directory, he asked the Spanish ambassador Azara to mediate between the invader and himself. The support he had given to the combined enemies of France had not been very effective, but it was notorious and he might therefore expect reprisals. He did not as yet know that the Directory, which was still strongly Jacobin and anti-Christian, had ordered Bonaparte not only to march on Rome and "topple the tiara," but also to establish there "a form of government that will render that of the priests odious and contemptible." Augereau had already invaded Romagna and was approaching Ancona.

For the time being Napoleon made a show of obedience to instructions from Paris; he even promised "to polish off the old fox in no time." The conditions of the armistice of Bologna (January 23, 1796) were extremely harsh: the Holy See was to pay twenty-one million francs and hand over five hundred precious manuscripts, one hundred pictures, together with statues, busts and vases; Roman ports were to be open to the French fleet and closed to enemy shipping. The Pope accepted all without demur; he even drew up a Brief, *Pastoralis sollicitudo*, recommending French Catholics to submit to the Republic. However, negotiations for peace broke down, and on September 14 the Pope announced that he had decided to reject the conqueror's demands, even at the peril of his life. Napoleon was still engaged before Mantua, which was one reason for not risking a march on Rome. Besides, he had a very different policy in mind. He called on Cardinal Mattei, Archbishop of Ferrara, and addressed him in these words: "My lord Cardinal, the Directory does not want war with Rome. I myself wish to be not the destroyer but the saviour of the city."

Cacault, the French Government's diplomatic representative, was ordered to arrange a settlement; and he would have done so had not both sides made mistakes. The Directory, instead of being satisfied with the pacificatory Brief signed so willingly by the Pope, went so far as to demand from him the revocation of all Bulls published since 1789, in other words approval of the Civil Constitution of the Clergy, which Pius VI, with unanimous support of the Sacred College, refused. The Pope, on the other hand, badly advised and believing that the siege of Mantua would prove fatal to Bonaparte, entered into secret negotiations with Naples and the Emperor, and recruited an army which he placed under the command of an Austrian. As soon as Napoleon heard that negotiations were afoot between the Holy See and Austria, he acted with lightning speed: he resumed war against the Pope, occupied Ancona, carried off the treasures of Loreto and marched on Rome. Pius VI was defenceless against the victor of Mantua, the fall of which succeeded in opening his eyes and striking terror into his heart. Even so, in those early weeks of 1797 the Directory became aware of the Catholic reawakening in France and was not anxious for a definitive break with the Pope. Bonaparte himself, too, thinking perhaps of his own future, was still less eager. He told the Archbishop of Milan: "Everyone will be able to confess his own God, and practise the form of worship that his conscience dictates, without fear of not finding it respected."

Accordingly, after the defeat of the papal troops, while Italy expected to see Rome invaded and the Pope in flight to Naples, the conqueror assured Pius VI through the abbot of Camaldoli: "Bonaparte is no Attila." Finally, agreement was reached by express wish of the youthful victor. Bonaparte again promised Cardinal Mattei: "I shall take particular care to prevent any change being made in the religion of our fathers." As for the Pope, he instructed his representatives "to make every sacrifice except in matters concerning religion." The condition proposed (and imposed) by the conqueror seem relatively moderate, when we consider that it was in his power to do and to take anything he pleased. But they were burdensome all the same: a further indemnity of sixteen million, the handing over of additional works of art, and the surrender not only of Avignon but also of rich provinces beyond the Apennines. Some members of the Directory would have liked to heap worse humiliations on the Pope and crush him completely. Bonaparte, however, turned a deaf ear. The Treaty of Tolentino, signed on February 19, 1797, marked in theory the end of conflict between France and the Holy See.

It was no doubt during the summer of 1797, while in residence at Mombello, that the young Caesar brought his plan to fruition. He too realized the importance of the Pope's collaboration, which Clarke had declared necessary. Having secured the appointment of his brother Joseph as ambassador to Rome, he resumed the idea of a papal Brief which would help towards the religious pacification of France, and contemplated "measures that might bring back a majority of the French people to the principles of religion." Pius VI entered into his views and took steps in the direction of appeasement. The Church in France was entitled to foresee an end to the crisis that had tormented her; but one more ordeal awaited.

14. FRUCTIDOR, YEAR FIVE

DURING the summer of 1797 it was rumoured that a group of determined politicians, among them Barthélemy and General Pichegru, was preparing to overthrow the régime and restore the monarchy. The Republicans were alarmed, especially those who had voted for the king's death and consequently feared reprisals. Three members of the Directory, former Jacobins, decided to forestall any such move. Since the Constitution afforded them no recourse to legal measures, they appealed to Bonaparte, who, despite his fame, was detested alike by royalists and moderates. He dispatched his lieutenant, Augereau, from Italy to Paris with orders to direct the operation. On September 4 (18th Fructidor, Year V) Barthélemy was arrested in bed; the great Carnot, suspected of unreliability, was obliged to flee; one hundred forty deputies were deprived of their seats, and Pichegru was apprehended. Naturally enough the new masters of France were led by force of events to resurrect the policies of the Jacobins and Montagnards.

On the morrow of the *coup d'état* (19th Fructidor) they repealed the law of 7th Fructidor, which in turn had abrogated that of 3rd Brumaire. Thus, in effect, were re-enacted the terrible decrees of 1792 and 1793: priests who had remained in or returned to France became liable to the death penalty. Nevertheless the whole climate had changed, and it seemed no longer possible to execute priests. A vote of the deputies even decided to "apply to existing laws such modifications as humanity and the Constitution shall suggest." But the Church's adversaries hypocritically arranged to substitute for the guillotine a new form of "dry guillotine" in the shape of deportation to Guiana. Potential victims of this penalty included priests who had emigrated after refusing to take the oath to the Civil Constitution, those who had refused the oath of liberty and equality, those who had been driven from France but had returned—in fact all ecclesiastics vaguely held to be unpatriotic, counter-revolutionaries or trouble-makers.

To these already formidable measures there was added another, which, without having the clergy directly in view, placed not a few of its members in grave difficulties of conscience. In order to put a stop to royalist intrigue, it was decided on September 5, to exact from all electors a new oath as follows: "I swear hatred of royalty and anarchy, devotion and obedience to the Republic and to the Constitution of Year III." Many priests who had returned to France from abroad, or who had emerged from hiding, considered that the reinstatement of religion should rest upon that of monarchy. Even among those who were not royalists many would not allow that a priest might swear to hate. Others, having carefully studied the wording of the decree, concluded that the oath did not oblige one to hate kings *in person*, or even the monarchical regime *as such*, but only to reject the latter as contrary to the *de facto* government—that is, to the Republic. Now the Church, as is well known, teaches submission to the *de facto* government. This theological exegesis reduced the oath of hate to a mere act of submission to established authority, thus enabling priests to take it and remain in office. Many agreed to do so, urged by such bishops as Mgr. de Juigné; though M. Emery, a royalist at heart, would not submit. A number of others also publicly refused and incurred legal penalties. Thus began a new period of persecution. It varied in intensity from one region of France to another; for such anarchy prevailed that in many places the decrees were a dead letter. But a mere handful of anti-Christian fanatics in any district was sufficient to start a priest hunt.

Nor was the persecution directed only against priests. Public oratories were closed, and parish churches which had been legally reopened were immediately banned for worship. Sisters who had returned to care for the sick were molested, and some communities were broken up. The notorious "observers," lately employed by the Convention to supervise the task of de-Christianizing France, were again seen at work. The police had orders not to strike openly, but to employ a continual succession of pinpricks—a game at which police forces everywhere have always been expert. Catholic schools, both Roman and constitutional, were subjected to strict supervision, and some were closed on the grounds that they were not sufficiently "in line." The Black Band, which had pillaged the national property of the Church, dismantled the abbeys and destroyed masterpieces of art; the cathedrals of Arras and Cambrai were pulled down at this time, and that of Orléans only just escaped a like fate. Many convent chapels, too, were turned into ballrooms, for there was much dancing under the Fructidorian régime.

These measures affected not only the Roman Church, the erstwhile recusant clergy: it was not long before the constitutional Church also felt the sting, although she had welcomed the revival of Jacobinism. At a national council which happened to be in session when the *coup d'état* occurred, some hot-heads had proposed that a *Te Deum* be sung. The oath of hatred, however, so disturbed the consciences of other members that the council confined itself to professing unqualified submission to the Republic and a desire for appeasement. Such moderation was not to the liking of the Fructidorians; still less were certain protestations of loyalty to the Pope uttered by a number of well-known constitutionalists. Indeed that unhappy Church was fast falling to pieces; certain quite large parishes rendered obedience to no one—neither to Grégoire's committee of bishops nor to the "presbytery." The most sensible among the constitutional bishops, including Grégoire himself, would have liked to attempt reconciliation with Rome; but a dry declaration signed by fifty émigré bishops reminded them of their position as schismatics and condemned their blindness. The constitutional clergy was losing ground at all points.

Lastly, to complete the lamentable scene presented by France at this date, we must recall the final attempt made not only to annihilate Christianity, but to find a substitute. For this purpose the authorities set about creating not one but two religions. The first, intellectually superior and more or less esoteric, was called Theophilanthropy. It affirmed the existence of God, the immortality of the soul, a morality based on self-interest, solidarity and tolerance—in fact the teaching of Rousseau in dogmatic form. The sect had its priests (laymen, of course), who held services before an altar adorned with foliage. Dressed in white tunics, blue togas and red girdles, they led the initiates in prayer and exhorted them to examination of conscience. It also had its own schools—one might almost say its own seminaries. For the benefit of the common people who were unable to penetrate the mysteries of Theophilanthropy, the poet François de Neufchâtel revived the *culte décadaire*, which the Convention had managed to endow with no more than the feeblest energy. Every tenth day the churches would be open, and officials wearing the most dazzling uniforms would hold patriotic and secular services, during which citizens would be married, newly born infants would be received into the community and—no doubt by way of entertainment—the laws would be read. Both these religious experiments ended in one vast fiasco.

Resistance gathered force against the Fructidorian terror; priests went into hiding, and clandestine Masses were celebrated. In some parishes the bells too were hidden, in order to prevent their being confiscated and melted down for the purposes of war. Clandestine schools also began once more to function. But the political character of this movement was strongly marked. In many places the clergy openly invited their flocks to take part in the struggle, and even exhorted them to armed revolt against tyranny. It is therefore hard to tell how much of the agitation that disturbed the country at that time sprang from religious motives, and how much was due to political ideals. In Brittany the Chouans, helped by English money and led by that great captain Cadoudal, joined hands with the peasants of Normandy under Frotté and with those of Maine and Anjou. A formidable insurrection, moreover, broke out at Toulouse.

The most serious troubles occurred in Belgium and Switzerland. Before the *coup d'état* of Fructidor the revolutionaries had been slow to apply the anti-religious laws in Belgium, where the introduction of civil status and divorce had not been well received. When lack of funds led the Directory to suppress the religious orders, and thus lay hands on their enormous wealth, there were angry complaints. After Fructidor these grew louder, when the French Government, laying aside all restraint, arrested Cardinal

Frankenberg on October 9, 1797, for having refused to take the oath of hatred, and closed the University of Louvain on the twenty-fifth. The storm was finally precipitated by some ridiculous measures against street crucifixes and wayside calvaries. Indignant at seeing their priests arrested, the peasants devised an original demonstration of piety. Assembled in the open air, they celebrated "white Masses," at which the congregation, reading aloud the liturgical text, associated themselves with a Mass offered simultaneously by a priest in hiding. Returning from those Masses, they attacked French republicans. The rebellion, which had started on religious grounds in the territory of Waes, spread throughout Belgium on 18th Fructidor, Year VI, when the Directory decided to enroll twenty thousand conscripts. A whole army was required to put an end to this "peasant war," and, of course, the priests were held responsible. Nine thousand were included in the lists of proscription; about nine hundred were apprehended. Similar causes produced similar effects in the Catholic cantons of Switzerland. A first peasant revolt broke out in the spring of 1798 in Valais and Fribourg, where the French authorities declared the priests responsible on pain of death for the preservation of order. A second, in September, included Unterwalden.

The religious policy of the Fructidorians, however, was as great a failure as the rest of their policy. Nor had a forced loan of two hundred million francs improved the economic and financial situation. In order to maintain themselves in power, the victors of Fructidor had been obliged in the following year (22nd Floréal, Year VI—May 11, 1798) to effect another *coup d'état,* after which, a year later (30th Prairial, Year VII—June 18, 1799), Sieyès forcibly established himself as head of the government. The foreign situation was no better. Bonaparte's Italian victories and the brilliant Peace of Campo Formio (October 17, 1797), so far from terminating the war, had greatly extended it; for the Directory's policy of annexation and "vassal republics" had alarmed the European sovereigns. The second coalition, led by Russia and Britain, won victory after victory, hurling its armies against all the French frontiers and recovering northern Italy, while the Egyptian expedition, planned and led by Napoleon, came to nothing.

Towards the end of summer 1799 France herself and the French Church were both in painful situations. Though the enemy offensive had been halted by the victories of Masséna and de Brune, invasion was expected. No one believed any longer in the régime, not even those who derived profit from it. Moral decadence reached unimaginable depths: prostitution was rife; so were official corruption and banditry on the roads. Catholics themselves appeared to have lost heart; it might have been said that, while they were still capable of resisting police interference, they could no longer attempt the Christian restoration of that moribund society. Indifference was gaining ground. What unforeseeable shock, what tragic event, would occur to end the march of death? None knew.

15. THE "LAST POPE"

EVENTS in Rome were not encouraging. After the Treaty of Tolentino it might have been expected that peace was assured between France and the Holy See. Both sides had given cause for such a hope. Pius VI had appointed as secretary of state Cardinal Doria Pamphili, a man of strongly irenic disposition; he had also placed at the head of the new "military" Congregation Mgr. Consalvi, a young prelate of outstanding ability and discretion, who was destined to a brilliant career; and lastly he had given official recognition to the Republic of the Directory. The new French ambassador, Joseph Bonaparte, had displayed the utmost courtesy: Romans were flattered by the magnificence of the ceremonial with which he presented his letters of credence, and "black" society was entertained with princely magnificence at his residence, the Palazzo Corsini, where his wife (formerly Julie Clarie) had a friendly word with everyone.

This honeymoon, however, was of short duration; too many grounds of conflict still remained. The carrying out of the financial clauses of the Treaty of Tolentino had quickly turned into shameless pillage. Enormous convoys laden with priceless art treasures had moved through Italy on their way to

France, arousing the most understandable wrath, which was aggravated by private spoliation on the part of French soldiers from the highest to the lowest rank. On the other side political passion had risen to white heat; the *gelanti* of the papal party, choking with indignation, had gone about declaring that the Treaty of Tolentino was null and void, and the French Republic a collection of gangsters. The Italian Jacobins, especially at Milan, had poured out invective against the Pope. At Rome even the French embassy had become a resort of agitators. The affair of the Cisalpine republic had impaired relations between the Holy See and Bonaparte himself, despite his friendly attitude; only an ultimatum from the young Caesar at Mombello secured recognition for that "sister republic," half of which consisted of territory wrested from the Papal States. Upon whom could the hapless Pius VI rely, enfeebled as he was by age[24] and bitterly disappointed? Certainly not upon Austria, which was about to sign the Peace of Campo Formio (October 17, 1797). Certainly not upon Naples, which was awaiting a favourable opportunity to snatch a few shreds of the Church's dominions. At Rome "papal fever" was raging; men were discussing the succession even before Pius VI was dead.

The *coup d'état* of Fructidor aggravated the situation. Joseph Bonaparte informed Paris that the Holy See appeared ready to negotiate a general settlement of "religious matters," only to be told by Talleyrand, the foreign minister, that the new government "attached no importance to the priests," and that he knew how "to keep them in order" without the intervention of Rome. Napoleon himself, who was highly indignant over the affair of the Cisalpine republic, rallied—or made semblance of rallying—to the Fructidorian views. On September 29 he wrote to his brother that if the Pope died he must do all in his power "to see that another was not appointed and that there was a revolution"; if in spite of everything a conclave did meet, he must use every available means, including threats, to prevent the election of Cardinal Albani. If that enemy of France were chosen, declared Bonaparte, then he himself would instantly march on Rome.

24. Pius VI was already more than eighty.

 A single incident was enough to fire the train. On December 28, 1797, some Italian "patriots," helped by young artists from the Académie de France, demonstrated before the Palazzo Corsini with cries of "Long live the Roman Republic!" Papal troops hurried to restore order, and a scuffle ensued. Young General Duphot left the embassy to calm the enraged mob and prevent the irreparable. As he advanced, gesticulating with his sword towards the papal soldiers, a nineteen-year-old corporal, believing himself in danger, shot him dead. Notwithstanding the apologies offered by Cardinal Doria and Mgr. Consalvi, Joseph Bonaparte asked for his passport and left Rome, vowing terrible reprisals.

The Directory's answer was not long delayed. On February 10, 1798, General Berthier arrived from Ancona with ten thousand men and invested Rome. An officer preceded by a trumpeter appeared at the Porta Angelica and demanded the immediate surrender of the castle of Sant' Angelo. At midday the French troops occupied the Quirinal, Pincian and Janiculan heights and entered by all the gates. General Cervoni, the newly appointed commandant of the city, called on the Pope with a request for an indemnity and hostages. The aged Pontiff, who had refused to flee and seek refuge in Naples, saw that resistance was futile and gave way.

There followed ten days which hovered between farce and tragedy. The clergy and nobility trembled, foreseeing the scaffold erected in the public squares; the workpeople of Trastevere grumbled; liberals shrewdly threw open their mansions to the French officers. Meanwhile the streets of Rome witnessed political demonstrations that resembled a carnival. Brandishing tin eagles which they had taken from theatrical property shops, crowds went in procession to the Forum to demand a republic. The leading citizens, however, in order to avoid a republic created by the common people, asked General Berthier to visit the Capitol on February 15 and authorize proclamation of the Roman Republic. Administration of the city would be entrusted to seven consuls in place of the Pope's officials; but the Holy Father's spiritual authority was declared inviolable. Berthier, in a fervent speech that was wildly applauded, represented the shades of Cato, Pompey,

Brutus, Cicero and Hortensius offering warm welcome to "the sons of the Gauls," who had come to restore the altars of liberty at Rome, and amid the enthusiasm of that splendid demonstration two cardinals threw off the purple, "a symbol of fanaticism and servitude."

But the comedy was soon transformed into tragedy. On February 20 a French officer named Haller—a Protestant from Zürich, and son of the great naturalist—accompanied by General Cervoni, called at the Vatican before dawn with a demand for the Pope's abdication. There followed an outrageous scene: Haller bullied the unfortunate old man, and even tore the Fisherman's Ring from his finger. When Pius VI begged at least to be allowed to die in Rome, Haller retorted: "I assure you, one dies the same way everywhere." Forced into a carriage, "like an undesirable foreigner being deported," he was escorted by a troop of boorish soldiers to Siena and thence to the Charterhouse of Vai d'Ema. But as the French occupants of Tuscany were frightened of a popular revolt, it was decided in April 1799 that he was much too near Rome and must be sent across the Alps.

This insult to the Holy Father provoked some reaction. From October 1797 onwards risings occurred in various parts of Italy, where French administrators had tried to introduce anti-clerical regulations. The Neapolitans made a surprise attack on Rome itself, and the French troops were obliged to withdraw; but they returned a few weeks later, and then pushed on to Naples. When the successes of the Second Coalition had shaken French domination in Italy, the French army began to retreat, and evacuated the Eternal City on September 29, 1799. But nothing on earth could any longer avail the unhappy Pope.

Removed to Florence on March 28, Pius had travelled stage by stage the dolorous road into exile. After Turin and a rough journey through the pass of Mont-Genèvre, he had reached Briançon. Then, for fear of an Austro-Russian raid to rescue him, he had been transferred to Valence, the place appointed for his residence—his prison. Throughout the journey into France, both the myrmidons of the Directory and the Roman prelates of the papal suite had been greatly surprised at the immense prestige still enjoyed by the helpless and humiliated old man among the common people. All along the route crowds had come to see him and implore his blessing. His once handsome face had become like a waxen mask, in which only the eyes now lived, revealing both his anguish and his goodness. Suffering did much to enhance the character of Pope Pius VI. In the days of his glory he had been considered unequal to his destiny; but in adversity he proved himself a saint.

Imprisoned at Valence, where he arrived on July 14, and guarded by implacable jailers, the "one-time Pope" moved slowly towards death. Completely paralysed, but with mind still lucid, he watched it approach with a courage worthy of the vocation which the Holy Ghost had laid upon him. In his last moments, after receiving the *Viaticum*, he made a final gesture of blessing and forgiveness, and was heard to murmur on behalf of his ferocious enemies: "*Domine, ignosce illis*"—"Lord, be not hard on them." It was August 29, 1799 (12th Fructidor, Year VII). Barras, Sieyès, Talleyrand and Roger Ducos were for the time being masters of France. Citizen Jean-Louis Chauveau, municipal officer of the commune of Valence, certified the decease "of the said Giovanni Angelo Braschi, exercising the profession of pontiff." Then he sent to Paris a report in which, playing the prophet, he declared that the dead Pope would certainly be the last. And indeed, from the human standpoint, that petty prison warden appeared to speak the truth.

CHAPTER II

The Sword and the Spirit (1799–1815)

1. AN ISLAND CONCLAVE AND A MILITARY CONQUEROR

ON the evening of November 30, 1799, the entrance to the Grand Canal at Venice was a scene of intense excitement, unusual at that humid season. There was continual coming and going of gondolas and market-gardening boats between the Molo dei Slavi, where thirty-five cardinals were assembled, and the monastery of San Giorgio Maggiore. Hundreds of clerics, officials, menservants and guards had already taken possession of the small island on which the convent stood. Next day (December 1) the conclave, summoned to elect a successor to Pius VI, would close its doors, and well-informed persons were assuring their friends that it would be a long time before those doors reopened.

Why had Venice been chosen for the meeting of the Sacred College? Because of decisions made by the late Pope.

> Foreseeing the difficulties that would beset the holding of a conclave, and anxious to guarantee its freedom, Pius VI, by three successive acts, had altered the rules laid down by his predecessors. A Brief of February 17, 1797, while urging the speedy choice of the Pope's successor, extended the period allowed between his death and the meeting of the conclave; a Bull of December 30 in the same year empowered the cardinals to decide the place and date of that assembly; and a

> third document (November 13, 1798) specified that the most senior member of the Sacred College was to select a meeting-place in the territory of a Catholic ruler and to summon the conclave.[1]

A Catholic ruler—but which one? Spain indeed had offered her territory, but the older cardinals were frightened at the prospect of so long a journey; moreover Godoï's government, having been in alliance with revolutionary France for five years, gave cause for anxiety. Ferdinand of Naples was closer; but he was suspected, rightly or wrongly, of preparing rather to confiscate certain papal territories than to restore them to their rightful owner. The Emperor Francis II appeared more reliable. One could pretend to overlook his impenitent Josephism and his manifest desire to annex the Legations, and—since the conclave must be held somewhere—accept his offer of Venice, which he had held since the Treaty of Campo Formio. Cardinal Albani, dean of the Sacred College, was already there, together with the sub-dean, the aged Cardinal-Duke of York.[2]

To Venice, accordingly, he had summoned his colleagues in the purple. The Sacred College at that date consisted of only forty-six members. No more than thirty-five had been able to reach the City of the Doges, and thirty of those were Italians. Only one was French—the famous Cardinal Maury, whom Louis XVIII had officially appointed as his representative and who, with supreme confidence (particularly in himself), promised his master that, since the affairs of the Holy See were "daily acquiring a new affinity with those of the king," he would secure formal recognition of the fact. As for Cardinal Herzan, he said nothing to indicate what orders the Emperor of Austria had given him.

Twenty days before the meeting of the conclave, on November 9 and 10 (18th and 19th Brumaire according to the revolutionary calendar), the

1. J. Leflon, *Pie VII*, vol. 1, p. 532.
2. Since the death of his brother, Charles Edward, he had been Pretender to the crowns of England, Scotland and France, calling himself Henry IX.

Directory had suffered yet another violent shock. It was the fifth or sixth such occurrence in four years, but it appeared to be decisive. Contrived by Sieyès and his moderate friends against the last of the Jacobins as well as against the royalist peril, the military *putsch* had been led by General Bonaparte, who had lately returned from Egypt. A new and provisional régime had been proclaimed, in which, under the disguise of a three-headed consulate, all power was bestowed upon the First Consul, Bonaparte. Remembering this, together with the young general's Jacobin past and the curious policy he had adopted towards the Holy See after his lightning victories in Italy, the cardinals and other churchmen at Venice hardly knew what to think.

But before long the Sacred College, shut in the monastery of San Giorgio, were sufficiently preoccupied with papal affairs to forget those of France. The conclave quickly proved to be sharply divided. The *zelanti*, who wanted a fighting Pope acceptable to Austria, favoured Cardinal Mattei; the *politicanti*, who advocated more pliant methods, supported Cardinal Bellisomi. Standing apart from those two groups were the *volanti*, who would decide the issue as soon as they chose to come down on one side or the other; but they hesitated for a considerable while. Amidst all the reefs and eddies one man quickly showed himself a first-rate pilot: Ercole Consalvi, who, though not a priest, was an official of the Holy See, a canon of St. Peter's and a Monsignor. A master of diplomacy, he had been chosen as secretary to the conclave.

The early scrutinies produced no result. Moreover the situation was complicated still further by the meddling of two secular powers: the Austrian Emperor, to whom Cardinal Herzan, his representative at the conclave, insisted that he must refer before taking any decision; and the King of Spain, whose envoy Mgr. Despuig, Patriarch of Antioch *in partibus*, was an extremely able prelate. Days, weeks and then months passed. The French diplomat Cacault had predicted that the Holy Ghost would "intervene for the sake of peace"; but it was not until March 14, 1800, that He did so.

In point of fact it was a secret understanding between Mgr. Consalvi and Mgr. Despuig that freed the Sacred College from their dilemma. The

Spaniard had orders to preclude the election of Mattei, Austria's candidate; Herzan in turn threatened to veto that of the Savoyard Cardinal Gerdil, who might have been chosen as a caretaker Pope; and the votes in favour of Bellisomi fell from twenty-two to nineteen. At this juncture the secretary of the conclave whispered the name of a cardinal whose election was said to be desired by the people of Venice but who had been completely overlooked in the first scrutinies—Mgr. Barnabo Chiaramonti, Bishop of Imola. A former monk of San Callisto at Rome, he had continued to lead the Benedictine life. Deeply pious, and friendly towards all, he had more often been found praying in the church than taking part in the conversation of the various cliques. But beneath this irenic exterior lay the firmness of a rock, an absolute intransigence on matters of fundamental concern. Such objections as others raised were swept aside by Mgr. Consalvi, and eventually Cardinal Chiaramonti was elected almost unanimously. He took the name Pius VII, and quickly proved himself an inviolable repository of divine truth.

Immediately after his coronation Pius VII declared his intention of returning to Rome. Austria tried to dissuade him, arguing that the situation in the Eternal City was as yet far from stable. Then, when she realized that nothing could shake the Pontiff's gentle obstinacy, she attempted to secure her own recognition as mistress of the Legations of Bologna, Ferrara and Ravenna, which her troops had occupied; but Pius VII refused with equal firmness. In order to avoid a journey through disputed territories, the Pope set out on board ship and landed at Pesaro, which was still a free port. Travelling thence by way of Ancona, he reached Rome on July 3 accompanied by Mgr. Consalvi, whom he hastened to appoint secretary of state.

It was on this homeward journey that he received some stupendous news. Master of France since December 13, Bonaparte had crossed the Alps by the Great St. Bernard Pass, despite heavy snowfalls; and having taken Melas in the rear, he had defeated the Austrians in the plain of Marengo on June 14. Henceforward, for fifteen years, the destinies of the Church depended on the relations of these two men: the monk Chiaramonti, Pius

VII, and the victorious soldier Bonaparte, who was soon to become Napoleon, Emperor of the French.

2. AN ADDRESS AT MILAN AND A VISIT TO VERCELLI

ON June 5, 1800, four days after reaching Milan, Bonaparte struck a mighty blow altogether in keeping with his technique. Two hundred priests, among whom were a couple of bishops, met at his invitation in the archducal palace. Their anxiety turned to astonishment when, instead of the blasphemies that most of them had expected to hear, they found themselves listening to a most charming and apparently quite sincere address. "I wished to see you all assembled here," the speaker declared, "in order to have the pleasure of letting you know in person the feelings which inspire me as regards the Catholic, Apostolic and Roman religion. Now that I enjoy complete authority, I have decided to take whatever steps I may deem most suitable to secure and guarantee that religion...." The young general spoke many other words of encouragement, criticizing the *philosophes* and their errors; stigmatizing "that cruel persecution to which the French Republic had subjected religion; and asserting that experience had undeceived the people of France, that Catholicism was capable of serving as the foundation of democratic and republican government, and that France now recognized that the Catholic religion was like an anchor which alone could save her from the violence of the storm." The priests and prelates of Milan looked at one another in amazement. Were they dreaming? No indeed, for the conqueror then made a solid proposal: "As soon as I am able to get in touch with the new Pope, I hope to have the pleasure of removing all remaining obstacles to a complete reconciliation of France with the head of the Church."

A week later Marengo was fought and won. It remained to be seen whether Bonaparte would persevere in his good intentions once free of the Austrian menace. The Lombard clergy, however, were not left long in doubt. On June 18, in Milan Cathedral, which had been illuminated and adorned as for the greatest feasts, Napoleon had a *Te Deum* sung in thanksgiving for his victories. He attended in person, seated on a dais in the choir amid serried ranks of the Milanese clergy. "The atheists of Paris" might well be indignant, as the First Consul predicted in a dispatch addressed to his two colleagues giving them the news. He was manifestly following his plan.

The working out of that plan in France had been evident since the morrow of the *coup d'état*. One of the first measures of the Consuls—and the plural, as we know, scarcely hid the singular—had been to publish three decrees putting an end to religious persecution (December 28—7th Nivôse). Freedom of worship was solemnly guaranteed. Churches which had not been alienated would be restored; Mass might be celebrated on a day other than *décadi*; the earlier oaths of loyalty, among them that of hatred for monarchy, were suppressed in favour of a simple promise of "obedience to the constitution." Next, there appeared in *Le Moniteur* a liberal proclamation to the peoples of the West, together with a commentary on the new oath, explaining that it was purely civil and imposed no obligations in the religious field.

The sense of relaxation, however, was lessened by the fact that Fouche, Talleyrand and Lucien Bonaparte were members of the French Government, and also by the attitude of the police. The latter continued to pester the Catholics, and were in no hurry to recall deported priests or to free their prisoners. But Napoleon was biding his time. "One victory will enable me to do all that I wish," he had told his brother Joseph when setting out for Italy; and Marengo would open the door to every possibility.

The six months which the First Consul had devoted to governmental affairs, before resuming command of his army, had convinced him that one of the first problems he would have to solve was the religious question. Amid the terrifying disorder in which France stood at that time, a prey to anarchy, bankruptcy and brigandage, the Church afforded a sorry spectacle. Not that faith was absent: quite the contrary—it showed itself in many ways. But ecclesiastical organization was in a deplorable state; nay, in utter confusion.

One of the Nivôse decrees, by reimposing the oath of loyalty, had aggravated the discord instead of preparing the way for a return to order. The

"Roman" Church, forty-three of whose dioceses were without bishops, was once again divided on the subject of the new oath. Inoffensive as were its terms, it proved unacceptable to the intransigents, and it was regarded as scandalous, particularly in the provinces, where many good priests linked the cause of Catholicism with that of royalty. To the more prudent, such as M. Emery, who advised submission in the interest of souls, the zealots—among them Linsolas, Vicar-General of Lyons—answered with a vehement refusal. In their eyes it was useless to re-establish the normal system of parishes; the missions[3] would suffice. But not a few missioners themselves believed that it was time to rebuild stable institutions and, for that purpose, to reach an understanding with the government.

Confusion reigned likewise in the constitutional Church. Though it was supported by a number of influential men, and though its indefatigable leader Grégoire did his best to reorganize it, the constitutional Church was more of a façade than a reality. The movement towards retractation emptied the ranks of its clergy; the "presbyterian" elements were becoming less and less obedient to the bishops; and owing to lack of seminaries few, if any, joined the priesthood. In order to defend and revitalize itself, the constitutional Church attempted one last manoeuvre: the Jansenist elements, with Grégoire at their head, renewed their links with the many small Jansenist movements in other countries. But the effort achieved very little. Moreover the republican and democratic tendencies of those movements were not altogether pleasing to the ambitious First Consul, who never failed to show his mistrust of the constitutional "intruders."

The key to the situation was clearly in Rome. Bonaparte was well aware that, no matter how great his power, he could never by himself lead the Catholics of France from their state of anarchy; and the attitude he had adopted at Milan was inspired by no other ultimate motive. It was impossible without the Church to rebuild France on solid foundations, impossible to reorganize the Church without the Pope. Hence the spectacular offer

3. See Chapter I, section 12.

to negotiate. This operation was heralded by a significant gesture. On 9th Nivôse 1799 a fourth decree, even more unexpected than the three on religious appeasement, was published in *Le Moniteur*; it directed that in the name of "the human dignity of the French nation some marks of respect be shown to a man who had occupied one of the highest ranks on earth," the late Pope Pius VI. And the authorities at Valence, who had triumphantly declared that that Pope would be the last of the series, had been obliged on January 31, 1800, wearing full uniform and *crêpe* armbands, to follow the hearse drawn by caparisoned horses, which bore the Pontiff's body to its temporary resting-place while the cannon of the garrison fired salvoes in its honour.

One question remained: what attitude would Pius VII adopt towards Bonaparte's proposals? Whilst hurrying to Rome by way of Pesaro and Ancona, he considered the situation. His city was still occupied by the Neapolitans, but under the terms of an armistice signed after Marengo the Austrians were to evacuate the papal Legations in favour of the French. How decide between the two? He could look for no other support; must he then reach agreement with the French general? What was known of Bonaparte remained disquieting: a former adherent of Robespierre, he was a revolutionary who, two years earlier, had boasted before the Muslims in Egypt of having "destroyed the Pope." There was yet another reason why His Holiness could not feel altogether confident: he had sent notification of his election to Louis XVIII instead of to the government at Paris. If the Consul knew that, what must he think?

It was in such a frame of mind that Pius VII, before entering the Eternal City, received news of the declarations and *Te Deum* at Milan.

At the same time letters reached him from Bonaparte's lieutenants, who, in order to settle some local incidents, wrote to him in terms which even the strictest Catholics would not have disowned: "His Holiness, Our Most Holy Father Pope Pius VII." Was the future brightening? Did the victor truly desire reconciliation? No sooner had the Pope settled in his new home than he received another and more sensational dispatch. On his way back to France after Marengo, the First Consul had stopped at Vercelli, where he had had a long and cordial interview with Cardinal Martiniana, one of the most respected members of the Sacred College. He had formally notified the cardinal of his wish "to settle ecclesiastical affairs in France," and had even suggested a plan for the reorganization of the Church, a plan whose two main features appeared far from unacceptable—the creation of a new episcopate in place of both the émigrés and the intruders, and an arrangement whereby the State would undertake to support the clergy and pay them a pension in compensation for their confiscated property. The cardinal, after praising the "great" general, his sincerity and moderation, ended by quoting this typically Napoleonic phrase: "Go to Rome and tell the Holy Father that the First Consul would like to make him a present of thirty million French Catholics."

3. DIFFICULT NEGOTIATIONS

A few days after receipt of Martiniana's letter Pius VII replied agreeing to begin talks with the First Consul of France, and adding that he would forthwith send to Vercelli a representative empowered to conduct negotiations. This unusual promptitude on the part of Rome showed clearly that the Sovereign Pontiff himself was anxious "to settle ecclesiastical affairs in France." But he was under no illusion as to the obstacles which the negotiators might encounter on the way to such a settlement.

Difficulties arose from a conflict both of personalities and of principles. At Paris Bonaparte alone was determined to reconcile the Revolution with the Church; he was surrounded by men who would have liked to sabotage the undertaking. At Rome the secretary of state, Consalvi, discerned the importance of what was at stake; but he was opposed by a group of cardinals hostile to the Revolution, and by a number of émigré bishops. More serious than the clash of personalities was their difference in outlook. However sincere on either side may have been the wish to arrive at an understanding, it was none the less true that their respective theological systems were diametrically opposed. The First Consul, heir to the erstwhile Gallicans and Erastians, meant to secure recognition of the State's supremacy over the Church, which was to be an element of his policy; and as heir to the *philosophes* he wanted all religions on an equal footing in the service of the State. As for the papal diplomats, they were going to rely upon the unalterable doctrine of the Church. And by insisting on complete freedom of Catholic worship or extinction of the constitutional schism they would do far more than embrace a system of religious toleration which would have been limited to that doctrine; they were going to assert, as they were entitled (and indeed bound) to do, the primacy of the spiritual.

Pius VII's chief negotiator, Mgr. Spina, was accompanied by Father Caselli, formerly superior general of the Servîtes. At Vercelli the papal delegates learned that the victor of Marengo had returned to France and that he wanted the talks to be held in Paris. So they travelled onward, not without a sense of foreboding.

Mgr. Spina arrived in the French capital on November 5, 1800. Five days later he was visited by a florid little man with coarse features and a squint, who, though still young, bore traces on his countenance of premature exhaustion. The caller was Bernier, former parish priest of Saint-Laud at Angers, ex-agent general of the royal Catholic armies and one of those who had inspired the insurrection of La Vendée. Summoned by Bonaparte on the morrow of 18th Brumaire, he had laboured for the appeasement of the West with a zeal which some of his companions in arms had regarded with suspicion, but which the First Consul had learned to appreciate. A shrewd diplomat? A prudent courtier? An adventurer? Perhaps he was something of all three. His ways were crafty; they went hand in hand with the pliancy of a mind ready to adapt itself to all circumstances, and perhaps with a degree of ambition ready to covet everything. Why had Bonaparte chosen him? "Bernier," he once said, "is a scoundrel, but I need him and make use of him." This eloquent and able man, a good theologian and trained in the arts of diplomacy, had appeared to him capable of handling the difficult enterprise. Indeed the Abbé Bernier was destined to be associated from first to last with the negotiation of an agreement between France and the Holy See; it earned him a mitre instead of the purple of which he had dreamed.

Those negotiations formed as it were three acts of a highly complicated drama. The first act took place between November 1800 and the end of January 1801—a succession of mere preliminary scenes. Proposals and counter-proposals followed one another, neither of the two camps entirely disclosing its positions. On December 24 there was great excitement: Napoleon had narrowly escaped death at the hands of assassins. It is not known whether the culprits were Jacobins or Chouans; but it is quite certain that the attempt was part of a royalist plot in which Catholics were implicated. Mgr. Spina, on Bernier's advice, sent a well-timed letter dissociating himself from the criminals; but little headway was made in the direction of the hoped-for agreement. Talleyrand accused the papal envoy of "sending France to sleep." Mgr. Spina replied by insisting that he must submit to the Pope the proposal—it was indeed the fourth—which the First Consul had just drawn up. The situation was tense, but no one desired a breakdown.

And now began the second act. Determined that the talks should make some progress, Bonaparte took matters into his own hands. He resolved to send a personal representative to Rome, and selected for this post Cacault, the shrewd and highly intelligent Breton diplomat who had already proved his worth in the Eternal City, where he counted a number of friends. When Cacault asked what attitude he should adopt towards the Holy Father, Bonaparte replied in words both splendid and cynical: "Treat him as if he disposed of two hundred thousand troops." Napoleon himself could have immediately thrown half a million into Italy.

The shifting of the scene from Paris to Rome boded ill for the negotiations. Mgr. Spina took account of many factors. In the Quirinal, the cardinals still talked of demanding from the French Government compensation for the crimes of the Revolution, notwithstanding the presence of French troops encamped at the city gates. The debate hinged upon all sorts of points: recognition of Catholicism as the official religion of France, which

Bonaparte would not allow; compulsory dismissal of émigré bishops, which the Pope rejected; the status of married priests; the conditions upon which priests who had taken the oath should be reconciled with the Church; and so forth, interminably. On May 18, after a terrible scene during which the First Consul threatened the hapless Spina with the creation of a schismatic Church or his own conversion to Protestantism, Talleyrand sent an ultimatum to Rome: the Pope must accept the French proposals within five days, or diplomatic relations would be broken off and Cacault would leave his post. This ultimatum was received in Rome on May 28; it had crossed a papal message declaring, after months of hesitation, that the Holy See would accept certain parts of the French plan.

The third act began on a dramatic note. Cacault, who saw through the manoeuvre, countered with another which he knew would please his master. "There is some misunderstanding," he told Consalvi. "Go to Paris. The First Consul does not know you; you will get on well together and understand one another. He will see what an intelligent cardinal is like; you will make the Concordat with him." Pius VII, uneasy though he felt, agreed to part with his treasured collaborator. Cacault and Consalvi entered a single carriage, the one bound for Florence, where he would await instructions to return to Rome, the other for Paris.

Things turned out as Cacault had predicted. On arrival in Paris the secretary of state was immediately summoned to the Tuileries by the First Consul—"Let him come in full canonicals," he told the messenger bearing the invitation—and was received by him with a magnificence and a degree of courtesy that were equally significant. Discussions were resumed, though not without frequent delays. Bernier employed all his astuteness to oil the wheels. There was a succession of proposals and counter-proposals. The question of married priests, so dear (and with good cause) to Talleyrand, continued to be a stumbling-block. Bonaparte became exasperated and once again attempted a five-day ultimatum. Then he risked a fresh manoeuvre, presenting for the Cardinal's signature a text different from that which had been approved. But all to no effect. Subtle and firm, Consalvi played a more skilful game. Joseph Bonaparte, whom his brother had entrusted with the final stages of the negotiation, knew not what to say or do. On July 14, during a dinner for two hundred guests, the First Consul in threatening tones called upon Consalvi and Spina to yield, making an allusion to Henry VIII of England that was full of innuendo. The Cardinal was inflexible: he invited his host to re-read the prepared text and tell him if it was unacceptable. Bonaparte, taken by surprise, did so. Only one point for discussion remained: the question whether the government would have a right to authorize or supervise religious worship. They talked it over in presence of the Austrian ambassador, Kobenzl, and the text was eventually reduced to a state which the irascible First Consul was able to accept. Next day, July 15, official announcement was made of the agreement between the Republic and the Holy See. Cardinal Consalvi, Mgr. Spina and Father Caselli signed on behalf of the Pope; Joseph Bonaparte, Councillor Cretet and Bernier for France.

4. THE CONCORDAT OF 1801

It mattered little that the word "Concordat" was not used; for the agreement was in fact a Concordat, similar to that which had governed relations between the kings of France and the Holy See, which had been torn up by the Revolution, and which the new diplomatic instrument was going to replace. This renowned "covenant between the French Government and His Holiness Pius VII" formed a very brief document, well within the compass of two octavo pages. Drawn up according to protocol in the names of the Pope and the First Consul, each acting in the plenitude of his sovereignty, it consisted of a preamble in the form of two declarations (one French, the other papal) and seventeen concise articles. In the declarations, which were at least as important as the articles, France acknowledged that "the Catholic, Apostolic and Roman religion" was that of "the majority of French citizens," which meant that the endeavour to establish a national religion in the spirit of the Civil Constitution of the Clergy was abandoned. The Sovereign Pontiff, while congratulating himself on the agreement, recognized *ipso facto* the French Republic, which had never yet been done.

A closer study of the document as a whole shows the concessions made by Rome to have been the most important. The Pope allowed that Catholicism was not the declared religion of the State, that the map of dioceses should be adapted to the new administrative divisions, and that the prerogatives of the monarchy had devolved upon the First Consul—who, incidentally, became forthwith a canon of St. John Lateran! He promised, with a view to the creation of a new episcopate, to request the former titulars to accept "every kind of sacrifice, even that of their sees"; and it was agreed that if they refused they should be ignored and replaced. The new bishops were to be nominated by the First Consul, the Pope conferring their spiritual powers. The bishops, in turn, would appoint parish priests from a list approved by the government. Before consecration they would take the oath to obey "the government established by the Constitution," not "to foster any league harmful to public tranquillity," and even to report any intrigue that might be hatched "to the prejudice of the State." Finally, "in the interests of peace," the Pope undertook not to protest against the nationalization and sale of former Church property which had been alienated, and not to disturb its purchasers.

In return for these advantages the French Government placed at the bishops' disposal all churches and chapels which had not been alienated, undertook to pay the clergy "a reasonable salary," allowed Catholics the right to make foundations in land or money for the benefit of the Church and guaranteed freedom of public worship. The First Consul refrained from any specific reference to the "constitutional clergy." Nothing was said about religious congregations, nothing on the subject of education, nor anything concerning Christian morality and its practice.

As a treaty concluded between two powers the Concordat of 1801 was intended to put an end to a situation injurious to both parties rather than to effect a return to the old Christian order. It caused a good deal of surprise and indignation. In France royalist and Catholic traditionalists regarded it as an act of treason; and the bishops of the old régime, who had emigrated or remained in hiding, were understandably furious that their loyalty should be thus repaid. Full-blooded revolutionaries were no less angry, and elected bodies showed their wrath by placing themselves under the leadership of notorious atheists. There was murmuring in the army. The Institute, which officially adhered to Theophilanthropism, proposed "The Influence of Luther" as a subject for their examinations. The First Consul was unmoved by this opposition, which he had foreseen. "I know what I'm doing," he said. "I'm working for the future."

The atmosphere in Rome was no better. A commission of twelve cardinals appointed to study the document was far from enthusiastic: the rigid Cardinal Antonelli drew up a veritable indictment of the text, which, he declared, re-established in France a mere "phantom of religion." Moreover nothing definite had been laid down regarding the temporal rights of the Holy See, for Pius VII had tactfully abstained from introducing political matters into the negotiations. He himself was greatly distressed by the measures he would have to take against those bishops who had remained loyal. Yet no one dreamed of rejecting the treaty; Rome was wide awake to the triumph for the Holy See represented by the signing of the Concordat. The Revolution had set out to implant Gallicanism and erect a Church virtually independent of the Pope. It was now asking the Pope to create a new episcopate and to give an authoritative ruling on a number of outstanding problems. Gallicanism was thus failing, root and branch; ultramontanism, with the aid of revolutionary France, was embarking on what was destined to be a brilliant career. That is why it was not very difficult for Consalvi, in four days of discussion, to obtain the approval of the commission of cardinals. On August 15 the Encyclical *Ecclesia Christi*, supplemented by three Briefs, was signed by Pius VII.

Some thought that these events were preliminary to an era of great calm and peace. French troops had evacuated papal territory, with the exception of Ancona; the constitutional clergy were ordered by the First Consul to close the national council, which had been in session for some weeks; and Fouche, who had addressed a circular to departmental prefects, ordering them to "deport seditious priests," was directed to withdraw it. A minister of cults was about to be appointed, and Portalis was talked of as a likely candidate. It was announced that the aged Cardinal Caprara had arrived in Paris as legate *a latere* at the express wish of Bonaparte. On September 8 the First Consul signed the definitive text, and two days later the ratifications were exchanged.

This honeymoon lasted throughout the winter of 1801–1802. February 1802 may be said to have marked its apogee; in that month the mortal remains of Pius VI were handed over to Mgr. Spina, who took them back to Rome. But an event was soon to take place that would do worse than chill relations between the new friends. Under pretext of laying down simple police regulations for giving effect to the Concordat, the First Consul had directed Portalis to draw up seventy-seven Organic Articles—a regular code of ecclesiastical law. Whether through negligence, lack of intelligence or senility, the cardinal-legate did not reject them when they were presented to him. The fact was that this addition to the Concordat was intended to restrict the rights of the Holy See in France. Some examples will show that Bonaparte was overstepping his own authority. According to Article I all acts of the Holy See required government approval before publication in France. Article II forbade bishops to leave their dioceses, and obliged them to submit to the State the rules of their seminaries, in which moreover the Four Articles of 1682[4] would have to be taught. Article III imposed a liturgy and a single form of worship for the whole of France, forbidding the celebration of feasts other than Sundays and traditional days. There were also pages of meddlesome regulations; parish priests, for example, were forbidden to perform a religious marriage without a certificate from the mayor. One article even dealt with bishops' dress, going so far as to prescribe the colour of their stockings!

4. See *The Church of the Classical Age: The Great Century of Souls*, Volume 2, p. 282.

On receipt of this extraordinary document Pius VII was overwhelmed with grief. What could he do about it? He refused to recognize the Organic Articles, and maintained this attitude to the bitter end. Bonaparte, however, in accordance with his carefully laid plan, had obtained control of the French clergy, and could therefore allow himself to take liberties with the Holy See, knowing full well that Pius VII could not afford a rupture without discrediting himself in the eyes of Christendom. Moreover the desired effect had been achieved: Catholics rallied unanimously to the new regime.

But in that spring of 1802 the atmosphere was one of joy, reconciliation and peace. At Amiens, on March 25, a treaty was signed terminating the war with England. On April 8 a draft bill, passed by the Legislative Body and the Tribunate, and recognized as constitutional by the Senate, received force of law; cleverly drawn up to allay the mistrust of republicans, it included the Concordat and the Organic Articles in a single document. On the eighteenth, Easter Sunday, it was published in *Le Moniteur des Lois*. On the same day the great bell of Notre-Dame, which had been silent for ten years, summoned the Parisians to a solemn service. Wearing the magnificent robes designed by David, the three Consuls were received on the threshold by the new archbishop-elect, Mgr. de Belloy. All Paris crowded beneath the age-old vaults. The great organ and the trumpets of the consular guard mingled their notes with the rhythmic salvoes of artillery. Cardinal Caprara celebrated the Mass, surrounded by twenty-seven bishops who, with hands on the Gospel, took the oath of loyalty to the regime.

5. DIFFICULTIES OF ORGANIZATION

It was now necessary to apply the Concordat and organize the new Church. Some extremely delicate questions had been settled between the signing of the Concordat and the ceremony of April 18, among the least serious of which was the rearrangement of dioceses. Far more difficult both in theory and in practice was the problem of the bishops. The Concordat provided for a clean sweep of the two episcopates, the constitutional and that which had remained faithful to Rome. How would the deprived titulars react? Of the three documents which supplemented *Ecclesia Christi* the first, *Tam multa* (a Brief), was addressed to the legitimate bishops. Its drafting had caused the Pope agonies of mind, for he was called upon to do nothing less than ask his own supporters to resign their sees. But Pius VII bravely set his hand to the task. After showing them that the superior interests of the Church required their resignation, he warned them that in the event of refusal he would be unhappily obliged "to take the necessary steps to remove all obstacles." The one truly Catholic reply to such an order was expressed (after a good deal of shuffling) by Mgr. Juigné in these terms: "If His Holiness considers my resignation necessary for the conservation of religion in France, I resign." The eleven bishops who had remained in France or returned from exile, understanding more clearly the needs of the situation, submitted without delay. But among the eighty-four who were living abroad some did not follow the example of obedience provided by the former Archbishop of Paris. There were ultimately fifty-eight resignations and thirty-seven refusals. Pius VII then issued the Bull *Qui Christi Domini vices*, which announced the suppression of the one hundred and thirty-five ancient bishoprics of France together with those of Belgium and the left bank of the Rhine. As a result the bishops, whether they had resigned or not, no longer possessed any territory and lost all jurisdiction.

Events took a different course in the constitutional Church. Sensing the approach of a storm that would sweep it away, Grégoire and his committee had begun by attempting discussion with the envoys of Pius VII, but the latter declined to recognize them as bishops. Then, in order to assert their existence as such, they had summoned the "national council," of which they had been talking for a year. It met at Paris in June 1801, immediately after the arrival of Cardinal Consalvi for the final negotiations. The assembly included forty-three bishops and fifty-five priests representing various dioceses, not to mention a number of delegates sent by Jansenist-Gallican parties in Italy. The chief concern of this council was to give evidence of its loyalty to the government, hoping that the latter would defend the constitutional clergy against the Holy See, which had determined to crush the "schismatic" Church. The desired result was not forthcoming. In an audience obtained by Fouché for Grégoire and Périer, Bishop of Clermont, the First Consul did no more than declare that all the bishops of both Churches should hand in their resignation, and that there would be constitutionals at the head of some dioceses—of some, but not of all. After this setback the council tried to negotiate with the "incommunicant" clergy—that is, with those who had not taken the oath; but in vain. It then lost itself in the sands of idle discussion as to the reciprocal rights of bishops and parish priests.

The eventual signing of the Concordat filled the constitutionals with anguish. Their astonishment knew no bounds when they learned that it was the Pope himself who, by a second Brief (*Post multos labores*) and in manifest agreement with the First Consul, demanded their resignation. Grégoire no doubt voiced the opinion of all when he suggested writing to the Pope a letter of protest, explaining that they had taken the revolutionary oaths simply in order to maintain the exercise of religion in France; that they had suffered much in consequence at the hands of the Terrorists; and, moreover, "as a worthy recompense for their energy in confessing the faith," they had been the victims of another persecution "with all the refinements of hitherto unknown barbarity"—that of the royalist Chouans. "What we did in 1791," added Grégoire, "we would do again today. The oath for which we are blamed hallowed our duties to religion and justice." If a demand for their resignation in the name of the Pope meant that they were "bound by everything Pius VII had done and taught," they refused. All Bernier's marvellous cunning was again required, this time in order to interpret the formulas, to weaken opposition and to dress the wounds of proper pride. Moreover the constitutional bishops were far too dependent on the government to be able to offer serious resistance to its orders. All resigned, though some (Grégoire among them) raised a bitter but vain cry of protest.

The way was now clear; the next step was to create the episcopate foreseen by the Concordat. True to his principle of abolishing the past and effecting, if necessary by force, a fusion of the old and the new France, Bonaparte chose sixteen of the sixty bishops from the episcopate of the *Ancien Régime*, and twelve from among the constitutionals; the remainder were new men. He also took care to have all social classes represented. The arrangement was skilfully devised; but it did not please the Pope, who learned with indignant astonishment that schismatic constitutionals were going to keep their mitres. His legate Caprara had bowed to Napoleon's decision. Ten of the twelve intruders refused to obey an order from Rome requiring them to disavow in writing their attitude towards the Civil Constitution of the Clergy; and in doing so they enjoyed open encouragement from Bonaparte himself, who declared that "a man who goes back on his word disgraces himself." Bernier tried to work out a formula whose terms would deceive the Pope; but it was not until Pius VII went to Paris for the coronation that the Church was able to consider the ten as reconciled on the strength of a somewhat equivocal declaration. Bonaparte, however, had his episcopate.

The reorganization of the Church in France raised problems at a lower level. It had been decided that instead of the thirty or forty thousand parishes into which the country had been divided under the *Ancien Régime,* there should be only one to each canton (i.e., about three thousand in all), having a parish priest paid by the government, together with chapels of ease. In many cases there was strong opposition from the people, who remained deeply attached to the old order. The situation was fraught with difficulty, and remained so until the end of the Napoleonic era when the new system was abandoned.

The most disturbing aspect of the whole affair was the lack of priests. A great majority of those who had taken the oath submitted to papal authority, and most of the non-jurors who had returned to France agreed to take the obligatory though inoffensive oath of loyalty to the regime. But there were numerous vacancies. Many priests had died, either naturally or on the scaffold or in the galleys, and there had been virtually no recruitment for more than ten years. Appeal was made to ex-monks and friars—even to apostate and unfrocked priests who declared themselves repentant.

The small salaries—one thousand francs to fifteen hundred francs for parish priests, five hundred francs for curates—was not a great inducement to those who wished to take part in this reorganization of the French clergy. Nevertheless the effort proved so successful that the indispensable number of about twenty-five thousand priests was found within a few years. Seminaries were reopened.[5] Between 1800 and 1815 they produced six thousand priests—a very small total, no doubt, and insufficient, but one that promised well for the future. It was a long, wearisome task, which did not bear fruit until after the Restoration. The Church in France still had difficulties to overcome; even when the framework had been set up, a gigantic effort was still required in order to make sure that Catholicism, once reinstated, was not a mere outward semblance, "a dummy without stability," as the intransigents and royalists declared it to be. But if we recall the state of religion three years earlier, we may wonder at the astonishing reversal of the situation from the end of 1802. Yesterday proscribed and persecuted, the Church was henceforward honoured, revered and protected by authority against those who persisted in their secret determination to do her harm. It is possible to understand why, despite the bitterness he might feel at certain aspects of the imperious Consul's behaviour—the Organic Articles and the appointment of twelve constitutional bishops—Pius VII remained forever grateful to him. In January 1803 he expressed his gratitude by creating four French cardinals. Among them was a former archdeacon of Ajaccio who had once been unfrocked for having served as an inspector of transport under the Convention, but had later been reconciled to the Church and had just been appointed Archbishop of Lyons: Mgr. Fesch, uncle of Napoleon Bonaparte, who made him his minister plenipotentiary to the Holy See.

5. See section 9 below.

6. BONAPARTE, PATRON OF CATHOLICS?

BOTH signatories of the Concordat derived from it an increase of strength. The Pope immediately recovered his prestige: it was remarkable with what haste the Lutheran King of Prussia and the schismatic Czar of Russia sent him their ambassadors. Even those Catholic states which, as Cacault wittily observed, had "beaten and ill-treated the Holy See worse than a Negro does his fetish," would doubtless hesitate from now onwards to show the least discourtesy.

The First Consul also knew full well that he himself had gained by the reconciliation. France was pacified, the Catholics had been won over to his regime, and the clergy were on the way to becoming an instrument of power as they had been in the time of Louis XIV. These were splendid fruits; but the operation was capable of bringing other advantages which the victorious general undoubtedly had in mind as he looked towards the future. As an ally of the Holy See, the new France appeared to the Catholic peoples of Europe very different from atheist France of the Terror. Might not the revolutionary message, associated henceforward with religion, be propagated wherever his victorious arms had enabled France to obtain a footing? This European policy had certainly not been absent from Bonaparte's thoughts while negotiating the Concordat.

Various symptoms quickly revealed these secret designs. In Italy, where the defeats of 1799 had overthrown the "sister" republics, Marengo empowered the conqueror to revive those that he elected to re-establish; and from January 1802 he styled himself President of the Italian Republic, that is to say, of the former Cisalpine republic now greatly enlarged. After the Peace of Amiens he reunited the island of Elba with France, then Piedmont, then the duchy of Parma, while the Ligurian republic became nothing more than a protectorate.

In the countries which he thus controlled he at once applied a religious policy based upon that of France. In Piedmont, former kingdom of Victor Emmanuel, the ecclesiastical organization was quite simply that of the French Concordat. Confronted with the equivalent of an ultimatum (February 17, 1803), and fearing nationalization of Church property in Piedmont, Pius VII yielded in order to avoid more fatal consequences. His meekness was ill repaid by the imposition upon Piedmont of the Civil Code (including divorce) and by the appointment of notoriously Jansenist and anti-Roman priests as heads of the commissions entrusted with religious affairs and education.

As regards the Cisalpine republic, immediately after its restoration Bonaparte announced his intention of securing religious peace, threatening to "go and break the heads of all those good-for-nothings" who continued at Milan and elsewhere to practise anti-clericalism. He arranged that Article I of the Constitution of the Republic of Italy should contain a clause recognizing Catholicism as the State religion—a thing he had refused to do in France. This was not to the liking of many Italian republicans who were hostile, if not to religion, at any rate to the Pope. Nor did Pius VII welcome the prospect of a concordat with a republic whose tendencies he knew all too well and which remained in unlawful possession of the Legations. Nevertheless he found himself obliged to negotiate. Melzi, vice-president of the republic, had imposed on the clergy an organic law, which, though somewhat more liberal than the French Organic Articles, claimed to regulate the fortunes of the Church without seeking the Pope's advice. Pius VII therefore agreed to the working out of a concordat in place of the organic law, and in November 1803, after fourteen months of negotiations, a text was settled that gave the Pope full satisfaction. The importance of this new concordat was immeasurable: Catholicism was declared the religion of the State; the clergy were confirmed in possession of their goods, and it was stated that all litigious questions were to be settled "in conformity with the discipline of the Church." These clauses were much more favourable than those of the French Concordat, and they provided Pius VII with an answer to those who accused him of having been too weak in his dealings with Bonaparte in 1801.

Unfortunately the Holy See's adversaries were wide awake. They included a swarm of Jansenists and Josephists, most of whom came from the

 University of Pavia, a bastion of anti-papalism. Under their influence Melzi published (January 25, 1804) two decrees which directed that the laws of the Republic should apply in all cases where the Concordat had not expressly stipulated otherwise, and that presidents of the Italian Republic, as successors of the ancient emperors and dukes of Milan, should enjoy all their privileges. The Pope was gravely disturbed. France was in theory a friend and ally of the Holy See; but it might have been said that wherever she wielded influence disagreeable incidents occurred one after another as if of set purpose.

How far would Bonaparte's dreaded arm reach? To what extent would he act as arbiter of the Catholic world, a part he seemed determined to assume? Troubles approaching a state of civil war had broken out in Switzerland. The cantons, having now become the Helvetic Republic, had proscribed Roman Catholicism, expelled the nuncio, and now talked of setting up a constitutional schismatic Catholic Church. In order to quell the consequent unrest, Bonaparte drew up an Act of Mediation (February 19, 1803). Its most notable result was to impose on the Swiss military co-operation with France; but religious clauses were not lacking. A nuncio returned to Lucerne in the person of Mgr. Testaferrata, though restoration of order in the dioceses was a very slow process.

The situation in Germany was equally confused, and for similar reasons. There Bonaparte played one of the major cards of his policy. The Treaty of Lunéville, by extending the French frontier to the Rhine, dispossessed a number of German princes on the left bank, but stipulated that they should receive compensation. The First Consul took steps to control these indemnities. He came to an arrangement with the King of Prussia (who lost the duchy of Cleves), the Elector of Bavaria (who ceded Frankfurt) and other interested parties, and rewarded them handsomely with gifts of ecclesiastical territory. At the political level the treaty resulted in the famous Congress of 1803 (February 25), which reorganized "the Germanys." These were streamlined by suppression of the very small states—particularly the ecclesiastical principalities—and enlargement of the greater, which were invited to become clients of France.

Pius VII protested against this flagrant spoliation; he was bound to do so, even though in the depths of his heart he considered that the mitred princes of Germany, adherents of Febronianism who had caused his predecessors so much trouble,[6] were receiving just punishment from heaven. But his protests were fruitless, and in desperation he tried an appeal to Mgr. Dalberg,[7] arch-chancellor of the Empire. That enlightened prelate answered that he must be more realistic and accept an accomplished fact, suggesting that the affairs of the Church in Germany should be regulated by a general concordat. Pius VII was quite willing to fall in with this idea, for the Italian Concordat then in process of negotiation led him to hope for a settlement of the points at issue on similar lines. The attempt, however, raised insuperable difficulties. Vienna stood firm on the principles of integral Josephism; Bavaria and Württemberg were unwilling to sign a general agreement, but proposed a number of separate concordats. Mgr. della Genga, nuncio at Munich and later Pope Leo XII, concluded from all this dissension that "in order to escape the wolves we must surrender to the lion."

Thus it came about that when Pius VII arrived in Paris for the coronation he found himself confronted with a plan for a concordat drawn up by Dalberg. But having foreseen the danger, he refused outright to discuss German affairs in Paris. The concordat, if there was to be a concordat, would be negotiated at Ratisbon; it would be general, applying to the whole of Germany; and it would affirm the rights of the Holy See in such a way that they could not be defied by another Melzi. This was tantamount to saying that the Concordat signed with France in 1801, and so lenient towards revolutionary ideas, would not serve as a model for those which other States might wish in future to obtain from the Holy See. In any case the Third Coalition and the Confederation of the Rhine were about to eclipse the

6. *The Church of the Classical Age: The Era of Great Splintering*, Volume 2, Chapter V, section 4.

7. Ibid., section 10.

 affair of the German Concordat, which remained in abeyance until after the fall of Napoleon.

Pius VII then gained a point: Napoleon Bonaparte was not to win recognition as universal patron of Catholics as he had planned to do. Thus at the very moment when agreement seemed complete between the Sovereign Pontiff and the master of France, the conflict that would soon set them one against the other was stealthily approaching.

7. THE NEW CHARLEMAGNE

EVENTS since the Concordat had unrolled an endless carpet of glory before the First Consul. His popularity had increased from day to day. In May 1802 the Senate had proposed that the consulate should be guaranteed to him for another period of ten years. Cambacérès and the Council of State, going still further, had suggested that a plebiscite should confer the consulate on Napoleon Bonaparte for life; and France had favoured this proposal by three million five hundred thousand against eight thousand three hundred votes. Two decrees of the Senate had inaugurated the new regime within the framework of the Constitution of Year X, and thereby greatly increased the powers of the head of State. The government had forged in quick succession two fresh instruments of authority: the Legion of Honour, which would surround it with a new and loyal nobility, and the high schools, which would train the youth of France to sound principles. The regime had also strengthened its position by promulgating the Civil Code and by a remarkable economic recovery.

Bonaparte, however, wished to go still further. He was well aware that the majority of Frenchmen, and the clergy in particular, retained an instinctive preference for the monarchical system. An abortive royalist conspiracy of March 1804, followed by the execution of the young Duc d'Enghien, snapped the last links with the Bourbons and their adherents, who were compelled to face the fact that Bonaparte was working not for the king but for himself. The Consul had already adopted a quasi-royal way of life: a regular court had been instituted at the Tuileries. Amid the excitement caused by the conspiracy it was easy for Fouché and the more zealous servants of their master to obtain from the Tribunate on May 3 a motion inaugurating the Empire. This motion became law by vote of the Senate on the eighteenth, and Napoleon Bonaparte became Emperor of the French.

Eager for legitimacy and filled with the lessons of history, he knew that the title he had just assumed would not be irrevocable in the eyes of his subjects until he had become "the Lord's Anointed," like the kings of France. Even before the legal establishment of the Empire by the Senate, Napoleon had confided to Cardinal Caprara during a reception at Saint-Cloud that he wished to be crowned by the Pope at a ceremony which would take place in Paris. This request placed the Curia in a very difficult position: must they confer on a man who was giving so much cause for complaint a privilege that would set him above all the Catholic princes of Europe? There was only one precedent, and even then, when Stephen II came to crown Pepin the Short, the latter had promised to fulfil the Pope's "every demand and request." Moreover it was doubtful whether the Sovereign Pontiff was entitled to absent himself from Rome for several months in order to please a single ruler; and those members of the Curia who would accompany the Pope to Paris did not enjoy the prospect of visiting a country which was represented to them as atheist, impious and even worse.

No fewer than five months of negotiations were required before Napoleon's ambition was achieved, and more than once it seemed that they would come to grief. For example, the constitutional oath which the Emperor had to take at his coronation appeared to include the Organic Articles, and was therefore unacceptable to the Holy See. There was also difficulty over the possible presence of former constitutional bishops at the ceremony. But Pius VII decided on his own to accept the invitation. What was his motive? Gratitude towards the signatory of the Concordat, or the wish to seize an opportunity of direct talks with Napoleon on a number of outstanding questions? At all events, the "capital interests of religion" seemed to demand a favourable reply. On the French side the Emperor was so determined that the coronation should proceed in the manner he desired that he was ready to take all steps necessary for the attainment of his goal.

Pius VII left Rome on November 2 with a retinue of forty persons, after delegating his powers to Consalvi. He had reason for anxiety: how long would he be living far from Rome? His absence was in fact destined to last for nearly five months. Again, what sort of reception would he get in France? As things turned out, the warmth of his welcome among the rank and file exceeded anything that could have been expected; but the Emperor received him with somewhat less cordiality, and Pius VII quickly realized that the haughty sovereign he had come to crown was prompted by hidden motives in his dealings with the Holy See. The Pope, however, was prepared to overlook much for the sake of being able to discuss matters which he regarded as of paramount importance, and difficulties were resolved in a spirit of magnanimous conciliation: the Pope would not be present while the constitutional oath was sworn; the Emperor would be dispensed from communicating at the Mass, and, of course, from prostrating before the Pope as Louis XVI had done before the Archbishop of Rheims.

At the eleventh hour an incident occurred which nearly wrecked the whole proceeding. On the eve of coronation day Napoleon's wife Josephine asked for an audience of the Holy Father, and informed him that she had been through no more than a civil marriage with her imperial spouse. Distressed by the discovery that he had been wilfully deceived, Pius VII acted with firmness: he demanded that the religious marriage should be performed at once, failing which he would take no part in the coronation. He gave permission, however, for a quasi-clandestine ceremony at which Cardinal Fesch would officiate alone, in a room in the Tuileries. And so it was done. Through the guile of a woman who hoped to assure her future, the all-powerful emperor was driven to "forced marriage."[8]

8. A marriage not performed in presence of the parish priest of one or other spouse was tainted with a defect that would later enable the ecclesiastical court to annul it. See section 12 below.

Next day, December 2, the coronation took place with a degree of splendour and magnificence worthy of the Capetians. The weather was fine, albeit cold; the thunder of salvoes and the peal of bells echoed in the keen pure air. In front of Notre-Dame David had erected an elaborate triumphal arch. Inside, tapestries and velvets hung from the galleries and vaulting. Pius VII arrived on time, but had to wait two hours before the procession entered. Then Mass began; the ceremonial in broad outline followed that used at the coronation of the kings of France, but the unctions had been simplified. During the Introit the sword, sceptre, orb and hand of justice were blessed by the Pope, who handed them to Napoleon with a reminder that the powers thus granted him should be employed to protect the Church of God and her members. Then the Emperor himself took the crown from the altar and set it on his head, as had been previously arranged[9]; after which he placed a diadem on Josephine's brow while the choir intoned *Vivat Augustus in aeternum.*

For the moment all was triumph. But what had the Pope gained? And what would he gain during the four months he spent in Paris hoping to succeed in negotiations that he had so much at heart? In vain the theologians of the Curia made representations on the subject of the Organic Articles; they met with an absolute refusal even to discuss the matter. As regards Melzi's decrees, their overtures were equally fruitless; the Emperor replied that he wished to respect the freedom of the Italian Republic—an altogether fatuous answer, since he was preparing to make a kingdom of that republic with himself upon the throne. The only important point on which the Holy See made any progress was the situation of constitutional bishops who had been nominated by Napoleon but had not retracted. Persuaded by Napoleon himself of the uselessness of their resistance, they yielded.

When the long list of planned festivities was ended Pius VII started for home. His return journey was even more triumphal than his arrival; but he

9. This point is now certain, contrary to a tradition that Napoleon "seized" the crown from under the Pope's eyes. The story was given credit by some incorrect editions of Consalvi's memoirs (ed. Cretineau-Joly, 1884, and Brochon, 1895). Mgr. Nasalli Rocca di Comeliano's edition (Rome, 1950) corrects the error.

 was not the only one to take the road for Italy. On March 18, 1805, the Italian Republic became a kingdom, and shortly afterwards Napoleon arrived in Milan to assume the Iron Crown of the Lombard kings. Would he now settle the question of Melzi's decrees? He limited himself to a declaration that the Italian Concordat would be given full effect, and to the publication of two new "organic" decrees which regulated the affairs of the Italian Church in Napoleonic style, without reference to the Pope. Napoleon's Italian game was beginning; Pius had cause for terrible anxiety.

8. A CHURCH UNDER FIRM CONTROL

THUS, with the Pope's blessing, the great adventure of the Napoleonic Empire was about to write a new and legendary chapter in the pages of history. For ten long years the Eagle would trace the orbit of its flight over Europe—Europe at first stricken with amazement and then gradually devoured. Twice the ancient continent would be redesigned according to the sole will of the victor; after 1808 the enormous task would appear more difficult, but a long time would elapse before the monstrous genius of strategy was conquered.

This domination of the world was linked with the domination of France, the latter being the means to the former. Strengthened year after year by military success, a despotism was established compared with which that of Louis XIV would have seemed light. The Constitution of Year XII[10] had laid the foundations of a monarchy more absolute than that of the Capetians. Its very trappings were taken over from the old royal house, and made more sumptuous to the point of vulgarity. The Church's place in that system had been carefully planned. More of an "outside bishop" than Constantine, Justinian or Charlemagne, more of a "viceroy of God on earth" than the Sun King, Napoleon I regarded the Church merely as a means of government.

10. This was the approximative name given to the senatorial decree of May 18, 1805.

When he agreed to spend considerable sums on public worship—sixteen million francs in 1809—he intended that the outlay should pay dividends. The necessary alliance of political and religious institutions became one of the favourite themes of official eloquence, while successive ministers of cult took pains to put the clergy at the service of the régime. Meanwhile, however, Napoleon always behaved as a Catholic sovereign, signing himself "your devoted son" in letters to the Pope, ending those addressed to bishops with the traditional formula, "I pray God to have you in His holy keeping," asking public prayers for the Lord's blessing on his armies, having the *Te Deum* sung after his victories and ordering that military honours be paid to the Blessed Sacrament.

The bishops nominated by the Emperor were eager to prove their gratitude by serving him. We find them not only exhorting their flocks to tranquillity and respect for authority, which was still more or less within the limits of their function, but issuing pastoral letters to secure the acceptance of conscription and even collaborating with the police to neutralize the activity of hot-heads. This unreserved submission to the civil power was a shameful attitude on the part of God's representatives, and it was destined to have some deplorable consequences. The bishops appointed under the Concordat, though otherwise deserving of esteem, were too much like civil servants; they long remained aloof from the preoccupations and anxieties of their people, and were very slow to grasp the movements of the Christian conscience—facts that would weigh heavily on the fortunes of the Church in the nineteenth century.

Perhaps the best example of the French episcopate's subjection at this date was its acceptance of the *Imperial Catechism*, which Napoleon sought to impose on the Empire and whose chief purpose was to explain to His Majesty's good subjects that God wished them to obey him. The man chosen to prepare this extraordinary document, in collaboration with Bernier, was d'Astros, a young canon of Notre-Dame, a cleric of subtle intelligence and unlimited ambition. D'Astros cleverly took cover in the shadow of Bossuet, basing his own work on the catechism used in the diocese of

Meaux, but expanding Bossuet's remarks on the duty of subjects towards the monarch. Lesson VII, commenting on the fourth commandment, was particularly elaborate: the Emperor had cause for satisfaction when he read that, as the Lord's anointed and defender of order, he manifestly held his Empire by the will of Providence and that the faithful were obliged to obey him in the same way as they were bound to obey God, "whose image he is on earth." Duly approved by the master, the *Imperial Catechism* was published by decree on April 4, 1806.

More dangerous was Napoleon's educational policy, which proceeded from the same intentions and with which the Church found herself likewise associated. On May 10, 1806, a decree of alarming brevity inaugurated the imperial *Université*.[11] The framework of the new institution was well planned in three main sections. Primary education was represented by the junior schools, secondary by the grammar schools and colleges, superior by the senior schools (including the École Normale Supérieure for teacher training) and faculties. *L'Université* was divided territorially into *académies*. At its head was a grand master, assisted by a chancellor and a treasurer, along with whom sat the *Conseil de l'Université*. Each *académie* was governed by a rector. The decree of 1808 laid down that "public instruction is entrusted exclusively to the *Université*. No school or any educational establishment whatsoever may be constituted apart from the imperial *Université* and without the authority of its head."

There indeed, and in the strictest sense, was a monopoly of education. But in what spirit did Napoleon conceive it? "My principal aim," he said, "in setting up a teaching body is to possess the means of guiding political and moral opinions." Since religion was already at his disposal for the fulfilment of those designs, it was natural that education should be entrusted in large measure to it. Hence the choice as Grand Master of Fontanes, a former

---

11. Its organization was completed by two additional decrees in 1808 and 1811. [The name *Université* denotes simply the central educational authority. It is left in French throughout this volume in order to avoid any confusion with the University of Paris. (TRANSLATOR)]

pupil of the Oratory and a staunch Catholic; of Mgr. de Villaret, Bishop of Casale in Piedmont as chancellor; of many good priests and devout laymen as rectors or inspectors-general; and of other worthy clerics and seculars (including M. Emery and Bonald) as members of the *Conseil.* Hence also the prominence of religion in the Napoleonic scheme of education. The catechism was part of the curriculum; bishops were entitled to make pastoral visitations of lay establishments, and no reference to atheist or ill-disposed philosophers was allowed.

In practice, free institutions were able to grow up side by side with those of the State, but always under the latter's control and completely subject to it. The Brothers of the Christian Schools were fully integrated with the *Université,* they were required only to pass an examination in order to prove themselves qualified. The Fathers of the Faith (former and future Jesuits) reopened colleges where they offered a more traditional and classical brand of education than could be had in the grammar schools; but it was no less dedicated to the regime and hardly less military in flavour, with rolling drums and lessons in civics and patriotism. In a word, the monopoly implied a regular organic union of education and the Church, so true was it that Napoleon felt sure of "his Church."

The French Church behaved with utter pusillanimity when confronted with this attempt to domesticate her institutions by means that had never been employed under the *Ancien Régime.* She stooped to the last degree of sycophancy. The "modern Cyrus," the "new Alexander," the "Constantine of our age" and "Charlemagne" were the least flattering metaphors that occurred in the pronouncements of her bishops. "You are the most perfect of heroes that have yet come from the hands of God," wrote Mgr. Le Coz, a one-time constitutional bishop who had later retracted. And Prince de Rohan, chaplain to the court, improved on his lordship's outburst by declaring that "The Great Napoleon is my tutelary god." Finally Mgr. Charrier de la Roche summed up the lessons of imperial history in these words: "All is supernatural, all is miracle." One day Napoleon reminded a close friend that in China the emperor was God, and added: "That is as it should be." Nor can we deny that the Church of France had done much to establish him in his conviction.

It could hardly have happened otherwise. We must remember the condition of that Church—three parts ruined, split until recently into several factions and powerless in so many respects. The mass of the clergy were naturally indifferent to dangers they could scarcely perceive. They were grateful to Napoleon for having restored religious peace, for having enabled them to resume their task, and for having by a decree of January 1, 1806, suppressed the revolutionary calendar which had been in force for fourteen years, and thus having brought back Sunday and the good old traditional feasts. What more could a country priest desire? What was likely to disturb him far more than the threat of caesaropapism was military conscription, which took so many lads from his parish; but he could say nothing against that.

The only considered protest raised against the intolerable ascendancy of Napoleon's empire over the Church is found half uttered in a book published in 1808 by a young Breton priest, Félicité de La Mennais, with the title *Réflexions sur l'état de l'Église en France pendant le XVIII*e *siècle et sur sa situation présente.* Setting forth his views on the necessity of reorganizing that Church, and suggesting a well-thought scheme for training of the priests, he showed his dislike of a salaried clergy and of a hierarchy subject to the State. But an apostle of liberty, who was at the same time a champion of ultramontanism, had little chance of a hearing at that date. His book passed almost unnoticed—except by the police, who confiscated it.

9. A SPIRITUAL AWAKENING

THE docility of the French Church to the new Charlemagne may be excused to some extent by an incontestable revival that was due to the peace he had secured. The stirring of devotion, noticeable since the early days of the Consulate, was no mere flash in the pan. It continued under the Empire; and at any rate during the first part of his reign Napoleon encouraged it by measures that revealed a true breadth of mind. Doubtless he intended not so much to re-Christianize France as to use for her benefit the stored strength of Catholicism; but that policy enabled the Church to recover her vitality together with certain means of performing her duties, all of which had been adversely affected by ten years of proscription. How then could the clergy have failed to express gratitude to one who was giving them another chance?

The Napoleonic Empire, therefore, corresponds to a period of religious awakening whose importance must not be underestimated; for the Church would not have become what she did in the nineteenth century if that awakening had not occurred. Its symptoms were many. Perhaps the most important feature was the reopening of seminaries. Most of the bishops realized the necessity of taking action first at this level. M. Emery, who at the beginning of 1800 had assembled a few students in temporary lodgings in the Hôtel de la Vache Noire, and had then installed them in a house on the Rue Notre-Dame-des-Champs, managed to restore Saint-Sulpice. Thanks to his initiative ten senior seminaries were established by the Sulpicians in the provinces, though not without difficulty, since teachers were hard to find. The Lazarists erected seven, and many others were founded by bishops with their own diocesan priests. Not everything, however, was perfect in those houses, especially from the intellectual point of view. They turned out an eminently respectable body of clerics, but one that had an extremely limited understanding of its role, taking little or no part in the intellectual renascence of the country and refusing to become involved in the problems that beset the people.

Nevertheless pastoral activity was resumed. History has not learned to appreciate the apostolic work carried out by simple *curés* in their parishes; but results achieved show the effort made by hundreds and thousands of unknown priests to reconvert their little flocks. Episcopal activity is better known, and is altogether worthy of praise. Nearly all the bishops spent themselves generously in their dioceses, making numerous visitations and travelling long distances to give confirmation.

The imperial episcopate, indeed, deserves comparison with that of the seventeenth century.

Missions also were resumed. The kind instituted during the Terror by the Abbé Linsolas[12] and his rivals was outmoded, because the normal institutions of religion were once again in operation. But the older type, organized by such men as Vincent de Paul, John Eudes and Grignion de Montfort, was needed more than ever before. Individual missioners applied themselves to this task; but before long a number of congregations were formed to bring it to fulfilment. Father de Clorivière's Society of the Heart of Jesus emerged from hiding; while Father Tournely's Society of the Sacred Heart, the Carthusian Society and the Society of St. Irenaeus (the two last at Lyons) all did good work.

More surprising was the Emperor's readiness to permit revival of the religious orders, though his own view of them was one of unqualified disapproval. "The abasement of monastic life," he declared, "is destructive of all virtue, of all energy, of all government." During negotiations leading to the Concordat Pius VII had pleaded their cause in vain. "No monks!" the First Consul told his representatives. "Give me good bishops and good parish priests; nothing else is required." Thus the Concordat made no mention of religious orders. One of the Organic Articles even appeared to ban them, and a decree of 1804 made their existence dependent on government approval, which might be withdrawn at a moment's notice. It is ironical that in such circumstances the Empire witnessed the birth or rebirth of so many orders and congregations that in 1809 it became necessary to give them a sort of combined status.

The fact was that while Napoleon considered monks as "unprofitable creatures" he recognized that there were religious of both sexes who were extremely useful and whose services the government would be foolish to reject. By virtue of this criterion the female congregations received better treatment. There was need of teaching and nursing sisters; they were

12. See Chapter I, section 12.

already at hand, prepared to resume their work in the full light of day, a work that many of them had never ceased to carry out in secret. On December 22, 1800, "citizeness Duleau, formerly Superior of the Sisters of Charity" was authorized "to train pupils for service in the hospitals." She made such good use of the permission that by 1805 the daughters of M. Vincent had two hundred and sixty houses in France. One after another the Nursing Ladies of St. Thomas of Villanova, the Sisters of St. Charles (Nancy) and the Sisters of St. Maurice (Chartres) took their places once again at the bedsides of the sick, to the great joy of the common people. At La Rochelle the Sisters of Wisdom were escorted back to the hospital by the mayor and commanding officer of the garrison with military honours. Teaching nuns followed. First came the Ursulines: in 1789 they had three hundred and fifty houses; in 1808 they had five hundred, with seven thousand religious. As for the contemplatives, whom Napoleon judged "lazy," they overcame the difficulty by opening small schools within their enclosures; and the bishops, notably Bernier, helped them in this pious ruse. The Carmelites, whom Mother de Soyecourt had managed to reassemble at the height of the Terror,[13] reopened convents almost everywhere; Visitandines, Poor Clares and Calvarians followed their example. In 1814 there was a total of eighteen hundred houses of female religious in France alone. On one point, however, Napoleon failed completely. Scared by the number and variety of these congregations, he tried with his logical mind to unify them, starting with the nursing sisters, whom he placed under the lofty protection of his mother, Her Imperial Highness Mme. Laetizia. But where no pope had ever succeeded, the all-powerful Emperor was doomed to equal failure: the female congregations, large and small, remained jealously distinct.

Napoleon was more suspicious of the male orders. Those which confined themselves to prayer did not interest him in the least; nor was the Benedictine Pius VII able fully to revive his order, which in 1814 had only

13. See Chapter I, section 12.

 thirty of the fifteen hundred houses it possessed in 1789. The Franciscans of the three observances, and the Dominicans for whose reform and reorganization the Pope laboured so strenuously, were no better treated by the French authorities; they received no permission to re-establish themselves.

Nevertheless the Emperor made a few exceptions to his rule of "No monks!" Some monks, after all, were useful. While crossing the Alps before Marengo, Napoleon was thankful for the services rendered to travellers by the famous Canons of St. Bernard, and he therefore decided to establish hospices on the great Alpine passes. In 1801 Mont-Cenis was entrusted to the Trappists of Tamié, and it was they who, in 1805 when Napoleon went to Milan for his coronation as King of Italy, welcomed him and saved his legs from the consequences of frostbite. The Emperor also heard tell of Dom Lestrange, formerly novice master of the Trappist monastery at Soligny, who had resettled his community at Val-Sainte in Switzerland, together with a convent of Trappistines and a kind of school. Fleeing from the revolutionary invasion in 1798, Lestrange had led his little group as far as Russia. Obliged to leave that country, he had taken the opportunity to found several Trappist houses in various countries as far afield as America, and had just returned to Val-Sainte after countless adventures. Full of admiration for such a man, Napoleon offered him the hospice of Mont-Genèvre and allowed him to reopen several monasteries of the order in France, notably that of Saint-Valérien. His esteem for Dom Lestrange remained unaltered until the latter took sides against him in the great conflict with the Pope and ordered the prior of La Cervera to retract the oath of loyalty which he had incautiously taken. From that day the Trappists were no better than "dangerous ultramontane fanatics."

Meanwhile other congregations won the Emperor's sympathy, especially those engaged in education; for, as Cardinal Fesch observed, "the national economy would profit considerably by entrusting them with the work of free education." It was thus that in 1804 the Brothers of the Christian Schools were officially re-established, and we have seen the part they played in the imperial *Université*. Another class of most useful religious were the missionaries,[14] who disseminated French propaganda in distant lands. Accordingly the Lazarists, Fathers of the Holy Ghost and Priests of the Foreign Missions were not only authorized, but actually subsidized.[15]

More curious is the fact that Napoleon, who was a disciple of the *philosophes* and therefore hated the Jesuits, did not interfere for some time with the Fathers of the Faith, a fairly flourishing congregation closely akin to the Society. Various elements had fused to give it birth, including Father de Clorivière's disciples and those of a strange Italian named Niccolo Paccari who called themselves the Company of the Faith of Jesus.[16] But Napoleon's tolerance was short lived: anxious though he was to have good teachers, he became suspicious. Might not the Pope, who had restored the Society of Jesus in Russia (1801) and then at Naples (1804), do the same everywhere?[17] A decree of June 1804 attempted to suppress the Fathers of the Faith, who once again went into hiding; and during the struggle with the Pope the imperial government was to have no more dangerous adversaries than these elusive men.

The reappearance of the old orders and congregations was in itself a sign of extraordinary vitality, confirmed by yet another symptom. The Church in France did not confine herself to the revival of earlier formations, but created new ones. Immediately after Napoleon's re-establishment of religious peace there was a flowering at many points. The few foundations which heroic men and women had ventured to undertake at the height of the Revolution took advantage of the new situation to strengthen their positions. Among them were the Sisters of the Holy Heart of Mary (Baugé) and the Sisters of Charity (Besançon). Military service resulted in the creation of fewer male institutions.

---

14. See Volume 2, Chapter VII.
15. In 1809, accused of being pro-English, they were suppressed.
16. The Fathers of the Faith were introduced into France by Father Varin de Solmon and opened a number of colleges.
17. See Volume 2, Chapter V, section 6.

Nevertheless Father Coudrin, after many adventures during the Terror, dreamed of thanking Jesus and Mary by founding in their honour a new bodyguard of prayer. He met Henriette Aymer de Chevalerie, who had earlier been imprisoned by the revolutionaries, and their united fervour gave birth on Christmas Eve 1800 to the twofold Congregation of the Sacred Heart, vowed to adoration of the Blessed Sacrament and afterwards celebrated under the name of Piepus. Less famous perhaps, but no less worthy, were the Sisters of the Cross (founded in 1807), known also as the Sisters of Saint-André of La Puye from the place where they settled during the Restoration. Their aim was "to comfort the poor and instruct the ignorant." Education too—or rather the education of upper-class girls and according to the spirituality of St. Ignatius—was the calling of the Ladies of the Sacred Heart, founded in 1800 by St. Sophie Barat and destined to a glorious future. Teachers likewise, and disciples of St. John Baptist de la Salle, were the followers of Julie Postel, who in 1807 founded the Poor Sisters of Mercy at Cherbourg. In the same year Mother Anne-Marie Javouhey founded a teaching society known as the Sisters of St. Joseph of Cluny, who soon afterwards dedicated themselves to the foreign missions.

Thus, despite the subjection in which he kept her, and despite the precarious situation of the religious orders, the Church experienced under Napoleon a wonderful reawakening. To what extent did it affect the average man and woman? It is extremely difficult to say, for documentary evidence is slight. Complaints of bishops and police reports suggest only that the faithful did not communicate frequently, or indeed often enough, though attendance at Mass was good. One question, however, may reasonably be asked: to what extent did attendance at church services indicate true progress of the faith? "At Paris, even more than in the rest of France," wrote Grégoire in his memoirs, "there are religious services, but very little religion"; but Grégoire, as is well known, was a Jansenist. Picot, whose *Mémoires pour servir à l'histoire ecclésiastique* (1815) are by no means favourable to the Napoleonic era, was more optimistic: "It cannot be denied that the Concordat was for a fairly large number of people the opportunity and occasion of a sincere return to religion.... The instruction given by parish priests, the administration of the sacraments and attendance at public prayers gradually recalled many of the faithful to religion." What is quite certain is that we can already see the emergence of a new Catholic élite, forerunner of that which was to play an important part in the history of the Church right down to modern times—a young body of laymen of which the eighteenth century had had scarcely an idea.

All these facts give an impression of obvious vitality, but the revival was undoubtedly limited. The middle classes continued to follow the teachings of Voltaire and other *philosophes*. The "ideologists" still dominated the French Academy, the Academy of Sciences, some fields of higher education, many learned societies and even some organs of the press. The court itself, and even more so the army, remained fundamentally irreligious; the upper ranks of the civil service became progressively hardened in the same attitude as the conflict between the regime and the Pope grew more violent. The Church was far, very far, from having won the day.

It is none the less true that a transformation had begun, that new habits had taken root. The change was noticeable in the sphere of morals, which had reached a very low ebb towards the end of the Directory. In some *départements* of France zealous prefects made regulations for dances and the sale of drink. Fashion itself was involved: women ceased to dress—or rather to undress—in the manner of the ancients; they adopted high stiff collars, and it was considered elegant to wear a rosary as a necklace. In some circles to miss Mass came to be looked upon as a lack of good taste. If we consider the state of affairs ten years earlier, we can understand why, even at the worst moments of their struggle, Pius VII always retained a measure of heartfelt gratitude to the man who had made such a change possible.

10. CHATEAUBRIAND

LITERARY history preserves a trace of that astonishing reversal in the fortunes of religion. One book is its most impressive testimony, a book which, moreover, itself did much to effect the transformation of minds and hearts. I refer to *Le Génie du Christianisme*, which appeared most opportunely four days after the solemn proclamation of the Concordat, and which was praised by Fontanes in *Le Moniteur*, the most official of all French papers.

It is perhaps a somewhat disconcerting paradox that François-René de Chateaubriand (1768–1848), a monument of pride, a monster of egoism, a man, too, whose conduct was by no means beyond reproach, should appear in French literature as the pre-eminent witness of Christianity, the most outstanding herald of the Catholic cause in that age. Such, however, is the case.

He was slow in assuming the role of religion's fervent champion, just as he was slow in acquiring the calculated rhythms of a prose style that was to be his glory. His first book, *Essai sur la Révolution* (1797), written while he felt his way as a needy exile, is on his own admission "a book of doubt," full of contradictions, a "veritable chaos." The death of his mother in 1798 brought him suddenly face to face with stark reality and completely changed his outlook. "I never yielded to a blinding supernatural light," he afterwards said; "my convictions grew from the heart—I wept and I believed." Returning to France in 1800, thanks to his friend Fontanes, he was welcomed by the First Consul's sister Élisa and her circle. How far did his profound conviction coincide with the Master's aim as he saw it at that time? How far was his literary work, in answer to the political operation of the regime, associated with his act of faith? It is hard to say. Heralded by *Atala*, a simple piece of writing calculated to touch sensitive hearts, *Le Génie du Christianisme* burst upon France in a blaze of glory. It is said that Napoleon wept when he read those burning and pathetic pages. But he was delighted with their preface, which sang the praises of "the mighty man who has snatched us from the abyss." The coincidence is too strong not to have been intentional.[18] The

18. Chateaubriand, however, did not confine himself to the role of Emperor's eulogist. Appointed secretary to the embassy in Rome, dismissed by Cardinal Fesch, and then sent as minister-plenipotentiary to the Valais, he abandoned his diplomatic career after the execution of the Duc d'Enghien. Three years later, on July 4, 1807,

splendid volumes of the *Génie* have a place in the work of Christian revival directed by Napoleon.

Their author required no fewer than five volumes in order to unfold a plan worthy of his stature. His aim was to produce something better than a mere theological treatise. It was "to summon all the powers of imagination and all the interests of the heart in support of that religion against which they had been armed." Noble as was his design, it was not entirely original; the subject-matter of his apologetic had been in the air for some considerable time. But all his predecessors had lacked the rhythm, the inspiration, the orchestration—in a word, the genius of his style. It is there that Chateaubriand excels; it is not so much his method of demonstration as the flow of his thought that catches us up and carries us along. He deals in succession with dogma and doctrine, and then with the poetics of Christianity (so much more lofty and persuasive than that of the pagans). Turning to literature and the fine arts, he exalts the work of Pascal and restores Gothic architecture to its rightful place after the long period of its eclipse. Finally, in the section on aesthetics, he paints a splendid picture of Catholic worship with its festivals, its vestments, its bells and tombs, and all the services rendered by Christianity to human society.

It would be a serious exaggeration to claim that the plan is carried out to perfection. Side by side with passages of undeniable sublimity there is much that can only be described as dismal and even platitudinous. As to the apologetic value of the work, specialists have found no difficulty in showing it to be frivolous—and worse. But, in a sense, what does that matter? The enchanter wins the day; the magic of his style prevails over the arguments of his critics. His is the triumph of Pascalian apologetic adapted to the pre-romantic sensibility of the masses. There was born a neo-Christianity, which

---

he published in *Le Mercure* an incendiary article which moved Napoleon to fury. The rupture between those two geniuses was now complete, and henceforward René hardened in his opposition to the regime. Elected to the French Academy in 1811, he refused to modify his inaugural address, which was considered too liberal by the government, and waited until the fall of the Empire before taking his seat.

 was to be served later by Ballanche, Camille Jordan, Michaud and Ampère, and which would water the soil whence Victor Hugo, Lamartine and others would one day derive their nourishment.

Literature was thus associated with the Christian revival initiated by Napoleon. What of the arts? They too played a part, though in much less striking fashion. The Revolution had witnessed a total disappearance of Christian art; worse indeed than a disappearance—a systematic ruination of innumerable ancient monuments. It was the age in which the great abbey churches, when not transformed into temples of Reason or Theophilanthropic cult, or used as warehouses, were simply pulled down; the age also in which David, appointed *de facto* director of fine arts, resolved to make them contribute "to the progress of the human mind." With the new Napoleonic regime Christian art received back its dignity and rights—upon condition, of course, that that dignity should yield pride of place to the arts whose business it was to exalt the Master, and that those rights should be subordinate to the claims of State. Within such limits, however, Christian art recovered its vitality. It expressed itself perhaps not so much in masterpieces of painting, sculpture and architecture as in the lively debate of ideas[19] and in numerous writings that were to exert considerable influence later on. This was the period when the "Roman Circle" and Overbeck's "Nazarenes" discovered the Primitives and early Renaissance painters, and when the influence of Chateaubriand and a few German authors led to the defence of Gothic. Architecture, however, produced few churches; about the only notable achievement was Vignon's completion of the Madeleine, begun in the reign of Louis XV and very nearly dedicated to St. Napoleon. Sculpture was responsible for still fewer Christian masterpieces; even in the work of Canova (1757–1822) religious inspiration is hardly discernible. But painters gave increasing prominence to biblical subjects and scenes from Christian history, while music also became associated with the

19. The problem of style, the influence of antiquity and the Gothic revival will be studied in Chapter VII.

reawakening of souls through the compositions of Gossec, Méhul, Cherubini and Beethoven.

11. THE PRIESTHOOD AND THE EMPIRE

THE light of religious peace which had irradiated the era of the Concordat was only a fleeting dawn. The sun had not yet risen when clouds began to gather. The Organic Articles added to the treaty by Napoleon had saddened Pius VII, not so much because of their content as the lack of respect which they showed towards the Holy See. Nevertheless their content rendered "the Church's eldest son" absolute master of the clergy and arbiter of French Catholics. How far would the new Charlemagne decide to meddle in religious affairs? It was quickly apparent that his intention in this respect knew no bounds. "He has already seized the thurible," murmured the Archbishop of Bordeaux; "if we allow him, he will soon mount the altar steps." The Pope was inevitably alarmed by this authoritarian ascendancy. In Italy itself the governors of the Cisalpine republic seemed quite capable of imitating Paris.

Some minor incidents helped to disturb the atmosphere. During a visit to America in 1803 Napoleon's youngest brother Jérôme Bonaparte married a young Protestant, Miss Elizabeth Patterson, in presence of the Bishop of Baltimore, but without asking the permission either of his mother or of the First Consul. The latter, who was anxious that the marriages of his relations should serve his own policies, had the union dissolved by the civil courts for lack of parental consent, the husband being only nineteen, and then asked the Pope to declare it null and void. After studying the case himself, Pius VII refused on canonical grounds.[20] Napoleon therefore had

20. Napoleon invoked three grounds of nullity: lack of consent, marriage with a heretic and absence of the parish priest from the ceremony. But lack of parental consent is not an impediment that invalidates marriage; union with a heretic is illicit, but not invalid; and the presence of the parish priest has been obligatory only since the Council of Trent and in countries where its decrees have been promulgated—which was not the case in the diocese of Baltimore.

recourse to the ecclesiastical court of Paris, which proved more obliging.[21] At about the same time he learned that brother Lucien had just married his mistress, Alexandrine de Bleschamp, before the mayor *and* the parish priest; that the offender had taken refuge in Rome; and that Cardinal Consalvi, appreciative of his good taste, was treating him as a friend.

These were but the preliminary events in a libretto of which, to quote Madelin, "the denouement had already been written."[22] There was something far more serious. By assuming the Iron Crown of the Lombard kings Napoleon had revealed his interest in Italy. Moreover he attempted no concealment of his desire to possess the whole peninsula as far as Sicily and to be in reality, as was stated on the medal struck after his coronation at Milan, *Rex totius Italiae*. What place would Rome and the Holy See occupy in such a scheme? On this point also he spoke with the utmost frankness: "The Pope will be my vassal," he told a confidant. He subsequently wrote to Pius VII: "Your Holiness is sovereign of Rome, but I am the Emperor." In support of this highly equivocal statement appeal was naturally made to the case of Charlemagne. Since his coronation Napoleon was legitimate heir not of the French kings, but of the Emperor. Now Charlemagne had included Italy in his possessions; therefore if his successor allowed the existence of sovereign princes in the peninsula, it was only by courtesy and on condition of their remaining under his tutelage. Swear as he might that he would not lay hands on the Pope's spiritual power, it seemed that Napoleon had already determined to be Emperor of Rome and there to demonstrate his power.

In the autumn of 1805 Napoleon began his struggle with the Third Coalition. Learning that Britain was massing troops at Corfu, probably with the intention of landing on the Adriatic coast of Italy, he ordered General Gourion Saint-Cyr to occupy the papal city of Ancona. This was a

21. He married Jérôme to a daughter of the King of Württemberg, who was a Protestant!
22. Louis Madelin, *La Rome de Napoléon, la domination française à Rome de 1809 à 1814* (Paris, 1906).

shameless violation of the States of the Church. Pius VII protested, refusing to admit that the operation was intended to ensure his own safety. Moreover when Anglo-Russian forces disembarked at Naples and expelled the French, it was expected that the Emperor would suffer defeat in Austria; but the challenge of Europe was answered with the lightning victory of Austerlitz. Pius VII was not overwhelmed by the news: three weeks later there was dispatched from Rome a letter couched in forthright and solemn terms, protesting against the occupation of Ancona and reasserting the rights of the Apostolic See. Pius VII did nothing to mitigate its effect.

Conflict now appeared inevitable. In vain the Pope, sorrowful but still most fatherly, reminded Napoleon that scarcely a year had elapsed since his return from Paris after the splendours of the coronation, and that he might have expected a better reward for his indulgence. Napoleon, deeply committed to his Italian policy, annexed Venice to the kingdom of Italy, of which his stepson Eugène de Beauharnais was viceroy, and installed his sisters at the head of two principalities. He also created his elder brother Joseph King of Naples, but without consulting the Pope, who was theoretically overlord of that realm and who declined to recognize the appointment. The situation deteriorated from day to day. An ultimatum was sent from Paris requiring the Pope to expel from Rome all subjects of governments at war with France, and to forbid the entry of their ships into his ports. The dispute thus began to turn on something more fundamental than the occupation of papal territory; Pius VII was now bidden to renounce his position as universal father and his spiritual authority, which transcended all political antagonisms.

The march of events accelerated, hastening with ever more rapid strides towards a struggle between the priesthood and the Empire such as had occurred during the Middle Ages. On one side stood the most powerful figure in the world, incomparably stronger than any of the Holy Roman and Germanic emperors had ever been. On the other a frail old man in white, whose only weapons were of the spiritual order, who knew his liberty and perhaps his life to be in danger, but who never for a moment dreamed of capitulation to tyranny. Few episodes in the history of the papacy command so much respect and admiration.

On May 6, 1806, Joseph's troops occupied Civita Vecchia, the port of Rome, still under pretext of defending it against the English. Ten days later Fesch was replaced as French ambassador by Alquier, a former member of the Convention, but reasonable and moderate. On June 5, by way of reply to the Pope's refusal to recognize Joseph as King of Naples, there were fresh spoliations: the principalities of Benevento and Pontecorvo, both papal enclaves on Neapolitan soil, were conferred on Talleyrand and Bernadotte. Consalvi protested; but on June 17, threatened with arrest, he was obliged to resign the secretariat of state and was replaced by Cardinal Casoni. On July 8 a new ultimatum ordered the Pope to close his ports to British shipping and hand over his fortresses to French troops. Pius VII again refused. There followed a few weeks of respite. The Fourth Coalition had just been formed, and Napoleon employed his troops in a lightning attack which overwhelmed Prussia at Jena and Auerstaedt (October 14) and opened the road to Berlin, which the conqueror entered on the twenty-seventh while Frederick-William's last regiments surrendered.

At Berlin, on November 21, Napoleon signed a decree initiating the Continental Blockade: all trade with Britain was forbidden, and neutral ships that had called at a British port were to be barred from all ports of the Empire. His aim was to starve the British people; but so far from yielding they hit back with a total blockade of France and her colonies. The Holy See now stood in even greater peril. Napoleon, of course, would never allow the Papal States to remain an open breach in the "system," any more than he would allow Portugal or Spain to do so. He was more than ever determined that the Pope should be the enemy of his enemies. Once again Pius VII refused. Napoleon sent another threatening letter in which he spoke of depriving the Pope of his temporal power and setting up a French government at Rome. The difficult campaign in Polish Prussia (1806–1807) afforded a fresh lull; but the two bloody victories of Eylau (February 8) and Friedland (June 14), and the Treaty of Tilsit (July 7 and 9) which eliminated the Russian menace, enabled Napoleon to return to his Italian preoccupations. The conflict was resumed. On July 12 Pius VII again refused to adhere to the Continental System. On the twenty-second Napoleon wrote to Eugène de Beauharnais: "Perhaps the time is not far distant when I shall recognize the Pope merely as Bishop of Rome." He had no wish, however, to break with the Holy See; he was by no means anxious to provoke a schism. Tentative negotiations were begun at Paris, led by Cardinal de Bayane; but they came to nothing, since the purposes of both sides were irreconcilable. During the autumn, while the kingdom of Etruria was in process of annexation to the Empire, French troops overran the duchy of Urbino and the provinces of Macerata and Spoleto, completely isolating Rome. Alquier was recalled and replaced by an ordinary *chargé d'affaires*. Napoleon gave out that he might summon a council, but Pius VII stood his ground.

On January 10, 1808, Prince Eugène received orders to dispatch troops to Rome "under pretext of passing through the city on their way to Naples, but in reality to occupy the place." The operation was entrusted to General Comte Sextius de Miollis, who, it must be said, used the utmost tact in carrying out instructions of which he did not at heart approve. On February 2, while the Pope and cardinals were celebrating the feast of Our Lady's Purification, French troops entered Rome by the Porta del Popolo, surrounded the papal palace, compelled the papal soldiers to join their ranks and arrested their officers. Calm in this hour of ordeal, Pius VII issued a declaration: "I leave to God my cause, which is also His." Miollis did his amiable best to win the hearts of the Romans—and of the Roman women; but he had more success with the latter than with their menfolk. Incidents continued: cardinals subject to the King of the Two Sicilies were expelled from Rome; others followed them, and hostile prelates were placed under arrest. Pius VII remained unperturbed—courteous to French soldiers and officials, but always resolute. Even the annexation of Ancona failed to shake his determination—on the contrary. Napoleon chose this moment to become involved in Spain—a regular hornets' nest. He sent his brother Joseph to Madrid, to replace the last Bourbon sovereign, and difficulties began. The

 Pope appointed Cardinal Pacca as secretary of state—a provocative gesture in Napoleon's eyes, for Pacca was well known as a *gelante*. Then, in order to show that he could fight on the spiritual plane also, he refused to confer investiture on Mgr. de Pradt, the new Archbishop of Malines, in accordance with the Concordat. The situation had now grown so tense that rupture was certain.

Once again, however, war brought respite. Napoleon was checked in Spain throughout the winter of 1808–1809. The Fifth Coalition, in April, tried to lay him low, but once again his reply was terrible: Eckmühl (April 19–23), Wagram (July 5–6) and then the entry into Vienna with Austria on her knees. What could the unhappy Pontiff do? On May 17, 1809, in the palace of Schönbrunn, Napoleon signed a decree annexing the Papal States to the Empire. Rome was to be "an imperial and free city"; she would be governed by an "extraordinary administrative assembly" presided over by Miollis; the Pope would receive an annual salary of two million francs. On June 10 the tricolour was hoisted on the castle of Sant' Angelo in place of the papal banner.

Pius VII, however, had foreseen the blow. After consultation with Pacca he had prepared two Bulls. One provided for the election of a new pope in case of necessity; the other, *Cum memoranda illa die*, excommunicated the despoilers, their accomplices and their advisers. Despite the French police this second Bull was posted on the walls of Rome by night. On learning of the sentence Napoleon made a show of laughter, though he was inwardly disturbed.[23] By that time, however, in a fit of rage, he had ordered Murat, his lieutenant in Rome, to bring "this crazy fool" of a Pope to reason.

During the night of July 5–6 four hundred French soldiers and gendarmes supported by two Neapolitan battalions undertook a grand military operation. It amounted to nothing less than an attack on the Quirinal, that ancient building where two platoons of Swiss mounted guard over an aged

23. Napoleon was not publicly named in the Bull, but he was notified of his excommunication by a personal Brief.

priest whose only weapon was his breviary. The commanding officer of this exploit was General Radet, who set to work with hopeless inefficiency and almost failed to reach his objective. He had taken care to ensure that the operation was conducted in silence, so as not to rouse the fury of the Roman mob; but the scaling ladders used by his brave warriors broke and thus gave the alarm. The tocsin began to sound from a neighbouring bell-tower, while Radet, hatchet in hand, was hacking at the heavy entrance gate. He would never have reached his goal had not one of his officers, more agile than himself, obtained entry through the window of a privy and admitted him indoors.

Radet and his men rushed through the vast halls in search of the Pope, while an undisciplined gang of scoundrels looted the Quirinal. Suddenly they came face to face with Pius VII. Awakened by the uproar he had dressed hurriedly in his white cassock, mozetta and stole, and was now seated at a table, grasping a crucifix. Cardinal Pacca and the Spanish Cardinal Despuig stood on either side of him. Radet, finding himself in presence of Christ's vicar, was momentarily bewildered. He and his officers removed their hats.

Invoking orders received, which he attributed directly to Napoleon, Radet called on the Pope to renounce his temporal sovereignty. Pius VII answered in French: "We must not, We will not." Radet then genuflected and kissed the Pope's hand. A carriage was waiting in the Piazza Monte Cavallo, and the Holy Father was bustled into it along with Cardinal Pacca. Once again the prisoner blessed Rome, the crowd and even those who were committing this outrage. Radet took his seat beside the coachman, resolved to do his best to mitigate the bleakness of the situation. Passing through the Porta Pia and following the Aurelian walls they set out along the Via Flaminia in the direction of Florence. The whole thing had been done with sordid precipitation, as though the central figure were a violent criminal. In the carriage Pius VII asked Pacca whether he had thought of bringing money. They fumbled in their pockets, and burst out laughing: the Pope had one *papetto* (twenty-two French *sous*) and the cardinal three *grossi* (fifteen *sous*).

Rarely has the transfer of a prisoner been so badly carried out. The imperial orders had been vague and contradictory, and those whose business it was to give them effect were so apprehensive of failure that they overstepped their instructions and their powers. The authorities through whose territory the carriage passed had but one idea—to see the back of so embarrassing a guest, and the farther away the better. Thus, having journeyed stage by stage through half the length of Italy and across the Alps, Pius VII reached France. He had, however, one consolation in the welcome given him by the people of Savoy and Dauphiné, who crowded the roadsides along which he passed in order to receive his blessing. Pacca relates that at Grenoble his reception was not that of a prisoner but of a father "upon whom a beloved family pours out the most touching expressions of its love and respect."

Where was he to reside? Napoleon had originally ordered that he should be left in Italy; but hearing that he was at Grenoble, the Emperor countermanded his own instruction and designated Grenoble as the place of his detention. Communications, however, were slow in those days, with the unfortunate result that the local authorities sent the Pope back to Italy. Meanwhile Cardinal Pacca—"that rascal" as Napoleon described him—was imprisoned in the fortress of Fenestrelle, to contemplate the disadvantages of securing the excommunication of a mighty emperor. Travelling by way of the Rhone valley and Nice, where an enormous crowd welcomed him with joyous enthusiasm, Pius VII at length arrived on August 17 at Savona, a small city on the Italian Riviera about twenty-five miles from Genoa and chief town of the new *département* of Montenotte.

On learning what had taken place in Rome, Napoleon sent a dispatch to Fouché declaring himself "annoyed at the Pope's arrest." He went so far as to add: "It is an act of clear stupidity." On several occasions, too, he insisted it had been done without his orders and contrary to his wishes. But that was mere quibbling. He may not have given express instructions that the Pope should be abducted; but he had written more than once to Murat or Beauharnais in vague and angry terms which were clearly responsible for the ultimate decision. Did he really regret what had happened? At the time most certainly not. General de Montholon, in his memoirs, observes: "All General Bonaparte's dreams, all the Emperor's plans in Italy, became possible of fulfilment through the abduction of the Pope." For the moment they did; but later...?

Talking one day with Fontanes, Napoleon uttered some words that seem now like a prophecy: "There are only two powers on earth, the sword and the spirit.... In the long run the sword is always beaten by the spirit." Subsequent events were to prove him right.

12. CANONICAL AND MATRIMONIAL AFFAIRS

"I don't want him to look like a prisoner," said Napoleon when giving instructions as to how the Pope was to be treated. One wonders whether he was jesting. Pius VII remained at Savona for three years, a captive in the strictest sense, confined to the bishop's palace, almost completely isolated from the world, his household reduced to three or four menservants and secretaries, subjected periodically to what can only be described as a search of his apartments, and eventually deprived of ink and paper. In that painful situation, his heart swinging between distress and boredom, the Sovereign Pontiff retained his vigorous determination. Napoleon's plan was clear: the Pope, separated from his evil counsellors, receiving alternate marks of veneration and terrorism, would eventually yield by surrendering his temporal rights. To every suggestion and to every argument Pius VII opposed a smiling constancy, in presence of which the most resolute of opponents felt disarmed. Seclusion, privation of ordinary amenities and solitude could not unhinge a Benedictine trained to the cloister. The Pope's bearing passed the understanding of General César Berthier, who had charge of the material arrangements of his detention.

Nevertheless Pius VII was a worried man. Before his arrest, which he had foreseen, he had been able to hand the Fisherman's Ring and entrust the apostolic delegation to Cardinal di Pietro. A certain number of cardinals had remained in Italy, ready to meet in case of necessity. But the imperial police quickly busied themselves with those "leaders of the opposition," as Radet described them, and firmly "invited" them to leave Rome. The oldest and those who were sick received permission to stay, but forty-two were sent to France. Thirty-nine of the latter reached Paris, where they formed a miniature Sacred College. The heads of the great religious orders were lodged in the castle of Sant' Angelo. The Roman Congregations no longer had superiors or staff, and most were deprived of their archives. The Church was indeed stricken and disorganized.

But what Napoleon had not foreseen was the fact that a situation created by himself was going to cause him endless trouble. For the moment it may have seemed that the loyalty of the Church in France to her protector was a complete answer to suppression of the Pope's temporal power and the imprisonment of Christ's vicar. A number of bishops expressed in no uncertain terms their sorrow at the treatment inflicted on Pius VII. Some let it be clearly understood that the situation might imperil the very unity of the Church. None, however, protested against the spoliation of papal territory.

The Pope still possessed his spiritual authority. He had also at his disposal a weapon that Innocent XI had employed against Louis XIV[24]—he had only to refuse investiture to the bishops nominated by the Emperor, and the Church in France would eventually be disrupted. Nor need he go so far as to brandish this weapon like a sword. If it were objected that, in order to defend his temporal interests, he was going back on his signature by refusing to carry out a clause of the Concordat, he had only to reply gently that he was refusing nothing, but that as a prisoner cut off from the entire Church he was unable to make inquiry into the qualifications of nominees, an inquiry that was obligatory under canon law. Napoleon found himself caught in his own snare. If he decided to go ahead and forcibly install

24. *The Church of the Classical Age: The Great Century of Souls*, Volume 2, p. 282.

bishops who had not received papal investiture, he would find few prelates willing to incur the anathema provided in such cases by the XXII Session of the Council of Trent. Episcopal sees, therefore, were likely to remain empty; and indeed within a space of two years twenty-seven dioceses were thus deprived of bishops.

Napoleon yielded to violent outbursts of rage. In November 1809 he contrived to assemble an Ecclesiastical Committee whose duty it was to discover a solution. Under the presidency of Cardinal Fesch it included, apart from such sycophants as Maury, men of unimpeachable character, among them M. Emery and Father Fontana, former general of the Barnabites. But the result anticipated by the Emperor was not achieved. The committee declared that it would not separate from the respect paid to His Majesty "the tribute of interest, zeal and love" due to the Sovereign Pontiff's office; it confirmed that "the Pope, deprived of his counsellors and without communication with the Churches, cannot provide for the needs of the Catholic world." All the Master obtained were some vague words asking the Sovereign Pontiff "not to hinder the functions of his apostolic ministry" for the sake of temporal matters. That was little enough, and calculated to infuriate a man who did not care for opposition.

At the same time Napoleon encountered other religious difficulties on a personal level. Founder of a new imperial dynasty, he had no son, and this fact imperiled the future of his achievement. He therefore conceived the idea of repudiating Josephine and marrying another woman who would give him an heir. After some hesitation he resolved to do so, and wasted no time in taking the necessary steps. There was no difficulty in civil law. Having warned Josephine of his intentions and called a family meeting, he obtained a divorce by mutual consent, which was decreed by the Senate on December 16, 1809. Would the annulment of the religious marriage prove harder to obtain? Napoleon expressed his certainty that it would not. "A king's marriage," he declared, "can be broken like glass." But he remembered Pius VII's determined opposition to his wishes in the affair of his brother Jérôme, nor did he like to ask a favour of his captive at Savona.

130 It was the arch-chancellor, Cambacérès, who found a solution by suggesting that the matter be laid before the ecclesiastical court of Paris.[25] Today such a proceeding would be impossible, for the *Codex Juris Canonici* (canons 1557 and 1962) expressly reserves to the Pope the right of deciding cases involving heads of state and royal personages[26]; but in 1809 it was only by tradition that the granting of divorces of reigning sovereigns was reserved to Rome. At all events, on December 22 Cambacérès summoned the members of the two Parisian ecclesiastical courts, diocesan and metropolitan, and told them of the Emperor's wishes. The four priests concerned were appalled at the prospect of so heavy a responsibility, and invoked tradition in an attempt to transfer the case to the Holy See. In order to remove their scruples Cambacérès consulted the Ecclesiastical Committee, which, after a good deal of shuffling and despite the opposition of Fesch and Emery, declared the Parisian court competent.

There was no further delay; neither Napoleon nor Josephine was interrogated. On January 6 four witnesses (Fesch, Talleyrand, Berthier and Duroc) made written declarations; three days later the diocesan ecclesiastical court pronounced the marriage null, and this judgment was confirmed by the metropolitan court on the eleventh. Those tribunals, renowned for their prudent lack of hurry, had never yet been known to dispose of such a matter in five days. Two grounds of nullity were relied upon. First, defect of form: it was claimed that by marrying Napoleon and Josephine clandestinely[27] Fesch had exceeded his powers as Grand Almoner, and that in any case he had no right to take the place of the parish priest, whose presence had been obligatory since the Council of Trent. Second, it was argued that Napoleon had given "feigned consent," and defect of consent is in fact an instance of nullity, although it is rarely put forward except in

---

25. L. Grégoire, *Le "divorce" de Napoléon et de l'impératrice Joséphine*, Paris, 1957.
26. Cases of nullity of marriage are automatically subject to appeal when the initial judgment favours annulment. The second sentence is therefore passed by the metropolitan tribunal.
27. See section 7 above.

the case of minors and defenceless girls. Canonically the whole business was sound, and M. Emery himself, who was no sycophant, declared: "I am inclined to believe that all was in order so far as concerns the ecclesiastical tribunal."

When Pius VII learnt what had been done he gave no sign of the vehement displeasure which might have been expected. He declared that "the principles of the Church had been flouted" and that "the judgment should have been approved by the Pope," but he refrained from uttering the protest which some awaited. No doubt, remembering his conversation with Josephine on the eve of the coronation, he had his own view of the matter and preferred to keep it secret. Moreover he knew that Napoleon's future wife was Marie-Louise of Austria, and he more than once voiced his hope that Austrian influence would lead Napoleon to restore good relations between himself and the Church. The real problem was not whether Napoleon's first marriage was null, but whether the Parisian tribunals were entitled to take cognizance of the question. "The affair is most important," said the Pope, "for it decides the legitimacy of his descendants."

That was indeed the crucial point. Even before obtaining his divorce Napoleon had fixed his choice on Marie-Louise, daughter of Francis II of Austria, whom he had defeated at Wagram; and Francis had agreed to hand over his child to a man whom only yesterday the Viennese press was describing as "the ogre." Negotiations therefore presented no difficulty. Mgr. Sigismund Anton von Hohenwart, Archbishop of Vienna, who had at first shown deep repugnance, bowed to the assurances of Cardinal Fesch that everything was in order, and blessed the new union by proxy. On April 2, 1810, Cardinal Fesch went to the Louvre to receive the consent of the spouses. But when Napoleon entered the Salon Carré he turned pale with fury. Twenty-seven seats had been reserved for the cardinals resident in Paris, only twelve of whom had accepted the invitation. Despite Fouche's warning that they would find themselves in trouble if they did not attend the wedding, fifteen of their eminences, led by Consalvi, had refused. "Fools!" sneered the Emperor. "I see they're trying to protest against the legitimacy of my descendants, and destroy my dynasty." Fouché had some difficulty—so at least he tells us—in dissuading him from having them shot. On April 4, however, at a great reception in the Tuileries in honour of the marriage, Napoleon created one of those public scenes at which he was so adept, by having the offenders turned out of doors. Next day the minister of cults, Bigot de Préameneu, attempted without success to obtain from them letters of apology. The brave *porporati* were immediately deprived of their property, their pensions and the marks of their dignity. Two months later they were sent into the provinces and placed under house arrest; Consalvi was taken to Rheims. Since they were forbidden henceforward to wear the purple, they became known as "the black cardinals."

On the evening of that famous reception Metternich, the Austrian emperor's representative, drank publicly to the birth of the "King of Rome," thereby anticipating nature but announcing a political truth. For on February 17 a sensational decree proclaimed that Napoleon was going to "reassemble the fragments of the western empire, reign on Tiber's banks as on those of the Seine, and make of Rome, hitherto the principal town of a small state, one of the capitals of the Grand Empire." The title King of Rome was expressly reserved for the future heir to the throne. Francis II made no objection to his son-in-law's usurpation of papal power; Josephism and Gallicanism were natural allies. As for dear Marie-Louise—Louise the Pious, as she was called in Vienna—she was far too happy at sharing the throne of St. Louis, and far too much in love with her ogre, to make the slightest protest. On March 20, 1811, the King of Rome was born. On June 9, after the baptism, Napoleon publicly restated his plans for the Eternal City, which belonged no more to the Pope but to the new-born infant and his proud father. "Now begins the most glorious epoch of my reign," he cried enthusiastically. And he really believed as much.

13. THE GRAND EMPIRE AND CATHOLIC RESISTANCE

THE years 1810 and 1811 were critical. Outwardly Napoleon seemed to have reached the summit of power. The French Empire, after incorporating Holland, Valais, the German shores of the Nordi Sea and the Papal States, in addition to Piedmont, Belgium and the left bank of the Rhine, counted no fewer than one hundred and thirty *départements*. But Napoleon's influence was felt also beyond his frontiers: in the Kingdom of Italy and the Illyrian provinces, which were directly subject to his authority; in the kingdom of Naples, Westphalia, Spain, the grand duchies of Berg and Tuscany, all of which were governed by his near relations; in the Swiss Cantons, the Confederation of the Rhine and the grand duchy of Warsaw, which he "protected"; and even in the territories of his allies—Denmark, Prussia, Russia and Austria—where the impact of French ideas led to the abolition of privileges and the introduction of the Civil Code. It was almost inevitable that a man who wielded such unimaginable power should yield to *hubris*—the temptation to excess. He could scarcely help believing himself commissioned by God to remake Europe according to his plans. Moreover he was well-nigh bound to consider the papacy as in some sort dependent on that prodigious power. He dreamed, in fact, of installing the Pope at Paris, which would thus become the spiritual as well as temporal capital, and where a basilica larger than St. Peter's would become the cathedral of the Catholic world.

There were present, none the less, mortal dangers that would gradually but inexorably lead Napoleon to disaster. Britain continued to fight, invincible; the French fleet no longer existed, having been sent to the bottom at Trafalgar; his most recent victories, brilliant as they may have been, had proved costly; relentless warfare still raged in Spain; and his allies were unreliable, especially the Czar of Russia. In almost every part of subject Europe, too, there was a threefold ferment of resistance—national, liberal and Catholic—inspired by all those who would not forgive the Emperor for having enslaved their countries, for having abolished the liberties whose message revolutionary France had brought to the world, and for having humiliated the Pope.

In France, Catholic resistance had been negligible since the signing of the Concordat, and particularly since the failure of the royalist conspiracy in 1804; but it revived as soon as the final rupture occurred between Napoleon's government and the Holy See. The Bull excommunicating the despoilers had not, of course, been publicized through official channels; the authorities had taken care of that. The bishops, too, who were striving to maintain harmony between Throne and Altar, had refrained from bringing it to the attention of their flocks; indeed they continued to pray for Napoleon, since he had not been expressly named in the Bull. After the police had dissolved the Congregation and the Society of the Heart of Jesus, a group of young noblemen, all of whom were fervent Catholics, decided to found a sort of military order known as Knights of the Faith, in order to defend the Church's cause, which they linked with that of the legitimate royal family; and until the collapse of the Empire they carried on a secret activity which the police never managed to suppress. Nevertheless some members were arrested—Alexis de Noailles, for example, d'Astros and Mother de Soyecourt; and coercive measures became more and more rigorous, but without preventing Catholics from becoming more and more hostile to the regime, notably in Italy, Germany and Spain.

As regards Italy, there was no question of unanimous resistance; the French authorities found allies among the ambitious, the venal and the timid. A number of bishops fell into line, some through faint-heartedness, others through self-interest. But few went as far as Mgr. Buschi of Ferentino, who called upon the twelve Apostles to help the new Caesar in his struggles. Some priests too showed enthusiasm for the omnipotent master; among these "collaborators" were Jansenists and their fellow-travellers, ever hostile to the Pope and his temporal power.

Such support, on the other hand, dictated by more or less selfish considerations, failed to win over public opinion, which had manifested hostility towards France ever since Napoleon's first Italian campaign, especially among the common people. For all that, the French administration in Italy was excellent, as Cardinal Consalvi later admitted. It brought order to a country that was in sorry need of discipline; it improved the roads, street lighting and public services; it kept a watch on hygiene and introduced vaccination; it also undertook extensive works (e.g., in the Maremma and the Pontine Marshes). At Rome the prefect, Count Camille de Tournon, had the Colosseum, the Forum and the Palatine cleared, the Pantheon restored and the foundations of St. Peter's strengthened. On his instructions, too, Valadier created the beautiful Pincio gardens and gave the Piazza del Popolo its noble layout. But none of those benefits sufficed to mollify the people. First there were clandestine lampoons, pasquinades, songs and jokes. But 1811 saw the beginning of armed resistance by a curious medley of Catholics under the leadership of their parish priests, highwaymen commanded by deserters from the army of occupation, and members of the *Carbonaria*,[28] a secret society more or less akin to Freemasonry. Nor was the situation improved by widespread arrests and the imprisonment of more than six hundred priests. Conscription, the hated Zeva, aroused the fury of the masses. Priests who sided with the French were treated with ignominy, driven out and occasionally assassinated. From 1812 a Spanish war in miniature, which nothing but an entire army could have quelled, raged throughout most of the Italian peninsula.

In Germany also there was considerable opposition to Napoleon. At the call of Arndt and especially of Fichte, author of an *Address to the German Nation* (1808), backed by the professors of Berlin University and encouraged by such secret associations as the *Tugendbund* (League of Virtue), a national movement came into being which enabled the King of Prussia to reanimate his country, and gave birth throughout Germany to what Napoleon himself described as "a thousand Vendées." Catholics played a part therein, even while the episcopate continued to serve Napoleon, but generally speaking their struggle was not the fruit of religious motives.

28. See Chapter III, section 5.

The most terrible example of resistance to imperial tyranny was that of Spain. In April 1808 the aged Charles IV and his son Ferdinand VII were expelled from Madrid by Napoleon in favour of his brother Joseph Bonaparte. A popular rising followed at once, inspired by the threefold sentiment of dynastic loyalty, patriotism and religious faith, this last serving as a kind of link between the other two. The insurrection began at Madrid on May 2. At first Napoleon obtained control of the situation from the military point of view; after the surrender of Bailen (July 21, 1808), his intervention in force (November 1808–January 1809) enabled him to reinstate Joseph at Madrid. Spain, however, was not defeated; the resistance of Saragossa (February 1809), which fell after twenty-three days of street fighting, showed clearly that a proud people which had long ago recovered its territory from the Arabs was very far from submission. The Spanish War was destined to last five years.

Blundering measures succeeded in making the Spanish clergy the life and soul of the resistance. One decree suppressed the Inquisition, a step with which no fault could be found; but another abolished all the monastic and mendicant orders, a third annulled the traditional right of asylum in the churches and a fourth put an end to the "privilege of clergy." Meanwhile the French authorities had Masonic lodges opened in the chief cities, and the struggle for liberty became a war of religion. The Catholic heroism of La Vendée was repeated in Spain, extended now to a whole nation.

Such was the war in Spain, which Napoleon afterwards recognized as having been for him the beginning of the end. French officials set about the deportation of suspect priests, but in vain; as they entered France, those ragged convoys, tied in groups to the tail-boards of wagons, merely roused pity among the inhabitants and infuriated the Catholic population. For every priest arrested ten came forward to fight in his place, and the Spanish clergy thus became the true incarnation of their people's soul. Far more than the regular armies, more than the British troops entrenched behind the impregnable lines of Torres Vedras in Portugal, it was they, the priests of Spain, who prepared the road to victory. Those men and their striving would deserve our whole-hearted admiration, but for the fact that some of them too often forgot their priestly character and associated themselves with atrocities which can hardly be excused by the frenzy of battle. Yet despite those blots on a page of glory, Catholic Spain taught the world a lesson of loyalty and heroism which everywhere inflamed the hopes of subjugated peoples.

14. FURTHER THAN LOUIS XIV

MEANWHILE the captive at Savona stood his ground. Cut off completely from the Church, he drew from his faith, as well as from the knowledge that he was suffering for God's cause, strength to resist the pressure put upon him and the tide of his own affliction. Of Napoleon he always spoke kindly. "My son," he used to say, "is rather obstinate, but he is still my son." On two fundamental issues, however, he remained adamant. He would never agree to surrender the Papal States; nor would he dream of conferring investiture on the bishops nominated by the excommunicate Emperor. Several approaches were made with a view to obtaining his surrender; but to them all Pius VII replied with tranquil insistence that he would never abandon his rights for the benefit of a man guilty of so much violence in his dealings with the Church.

The religious situation was manifestly deteriorating. The closing of convents in Italy had to be carried out *manu militari*, and instructions from Savona ordering resistance were all too faithfully obeyed. What was the good of sending Italian bishops and other prelates across the Alps if, as the police themselves admitted, those exiles as well as the "black cardinals" received countless tokens of respect and admiration in France? And then the problem of bishops nominated but not invested was becoming ever more tiresome. Cardinal Maury suggested recourse to the same procedure as Louis XIV had employed: appointment of "capitular administrators" pending papal investiture. But Bigot de Préameneu thought that the clergy would disapprove of such measures and that the prelates so appointed would obey "with extreme reluctance" if at all.

Napoleon resolved to try force. He ordered a certain number of the bishops whom he had nominated to go and take possession of their sees. But wherever this was done vexatious incidents occurred. At Florence, d'Osmond, formerly Bishop of Nancy, who had wisely delayed his arrival in Tuscany, found his chapter and subordinate clergy prepared to resist him. At Liège the aged vicar-general Henrard succumbed to intimidation and welcomed the new bishop, Lejéas, but the entire clergy absented themselves from the intruder's reception. At Bois-le-Duc, in Holland, there were such violent demonstrations that the culprits had to be deported. At Malines, Mgr. de Pradt was rejected by the chapter.

In Paris the crisis gave rise to a more serious episode. After the death of Cardinal de Belloy, Napoleon hesitated for eight months and then offered the see to his uncle Fesch, who was in no hurry to accept. Lyons, primatial see of the Gauls, was superior to Paris. As successor of St. Irenaeus, had he the right to leave the banks of the Saône? Perhaps so, if he were allowed to retain Lyons together with Paris. Eventually Napoleon, thoroughly exasperated, told his uncle to make up his mind, and the latter, who had delayed so long in order to see what turn affairs would take in Rome, decided not to fall out with the Pope and firmly declined. The Emperor then summoned Maury, of whose acceptance he entertained no doubt. "Now, my lord Cardinal," he said, "what would you do if I appointed you Archbishop of Paris?" Maury collapsed into a chair, trembling with emotion. Next day, October 15, 1810, the shoemaker's son from Valréas went and took up residence in the archiepiscopal palace. Neither his appearance nor his reputation was likely to captivate the Parisians. On formal instructions from the government the chapter agreed to accept this newcomer as "capitular administrator," but took every possible occasion to make him feel the falsity of his position.

The dispute turned to tragedy. Resistance to the counterfeit archbishop was organized by a vicar-capitular, the Abbé d'Astros. It was he who had edited the *Imperial Catechism*; but the Emperor's attitude towards the

Pope—not to mention his own disappointment at what he considered a trifling reward for his services—had led him to a different view of the regime. In due course there reached Paris from Savona by secret means two Briefs signed by Pius VII; one of them declared that the capitular administrators appointed by the French Government were no better than usurpers, while the other reproached Maury himself in the strongest terms. The police, having already intercepted some letters addressed to d'Astros, searched his house and discovered the papal Briefs. He was clearly the centre of a network of resistance with which some of the "black cardinals" were associated. D'Astros was apprehended and taken to Vincennes, where he remained forgotten for three years, and several of his accomplices were placed under house arrest at Fenestrelle.

That, however, did not solve the problem of episcopal investiture. Having vainly offered Consalvi and other "black cardinals" their freedom if they would confer investiture in place of the Pope, Napoleon attempted a new procedure. In January 1811 he set up an Ecclesiastical Committee; presided over by Fesch, it included, besides cardinals Maury and Caselli, five "reliable" bishops and M. Emery. He asked this committee to tell him who had the canonical power to grant dispensations and investitures refused by the Pope. The assembled cardinals and bishops were not inclined to make a public stand against the Holy See. Napoleon therefore came in person to demand the committee's advice. This was the occasion of a scene destined to become famous. After spending an hour in recriminations against Pius VII, the Emperor suddenly turned to the aged Sulpician, who, like the others, had listened to this diatribe in silence, but in whose countenance he read the clearest signs of reprobation. "M. Emery," he said, "what do you think of the Pope's authority?" "Sire," replied the octogenarian, "my view of it is contained in the catechism taught by your order in all schools. To the question, 'What is the Pope?' we reply, 'The head of the Church, the Vicar of Christ.'" Taken aback, Napoleon began harping once again on the temporal power of which he intended to deprive the Pope, leaving him only his spiritual authority. To this M. Emery replied with an apt quotation from Bossuet, of whom Napoleon professed to be a great admirer: "Sovereignty over the city of Rome has been granted to the Pope in order that the Holy See, rendered thus more free and more secure, may exercise its power throughout the world." Impressed by the calm of his interlocutor, Napoleon did not explode as the whole committee had expected. He continued to question the Sulpician on the points at issue, learning from him that there was no canonical means of resolving them without the Pope. The others were terrified and tried to excuse the presumptuous old man; but the Emperor silenced them, and thanked M. Emery for his outspokenness. When at length they congratulated M. Emery upon having escaped the thunderbolt, he merely replied: "I was just teaching the Emperor his catechism."

A final approach was then made to the Holy Father. Three bishops were sent to Savona with instructions to obtain from Pius VII investiture of the nominated bishops and a supplementary article to the Concordat authorizing the metropolitans to confer it. After seeming on the verge of capitulation, the prisoner recovered himself; once again he refused to yield, and the three mitred conspirators returned empty-handed.

There was now only one solution, the same to which Louis XIV had had recourse in his struggle with Innocent XI. This was to convoke a council of the French clergy, which would take upon itself the Pope's authority and make the required decisions. On June 17, 1811, the council met at Paris, in the choir of Notre-Dame. One hundred and forty-nine prelates had been summoned, but only ninety-six (including six cardinals) attended. In order to make up the number a group of non-invested bishops was added together with a few representatives of protected countries, among them Dalberg, "primate" of Germany. Napoleon relied upon the Gallican sympathies of the French episcopate in order to carry out his plans. He felt sure of getting his own Four Articles, like Louis XIV, and even thought he possessed his own Bossuet in the person of Mgr. Duvoisin, Bishop of Nantes, whom he called his "oracle and torch." But it was no longer 1682—nor even 1802.

Notwithstanding the increased severity of the regime, resistance to the Empire was making visible progress. Among the intellectuals Mme. de Staël published her work *On Germany* (1810), which was seized by the police; Chateaubriand, elected to the French Academy, was unable to deliver his inaugural speech, which was judged subversive; the Sorbonne was sullen. Among the rank and file, conscription, a sharp rise in the cost of living and excessive taxation were causing unrest. Royalists and republicans were active. At the international level, well-informed people considered the situation disturbing in spite of appearances: relentless warfare continued in Spain; Britain had not disarmed; and relations with the Russian ally were so bad that Napoleon talked of leading his Grand Army across the Vistula.

In such a climate the fathers of the council were naturally disinclined to submit without reservation. A small clique led by Duvoisin remained loyal; but the majority prepared to oppose the Emperor with the "strength of inertia," which the police at once noted in their reports. More courageous still, a powerful nucleus, with some clandestine backing from Cardinal Fesch, sided openly against Napoleon. On the very first day of the council Étienne de Boulogne, Bishop of Troyes and an illustrious preacher, spoke in his opening address of "the indissoluble union that must be maintained with the See of Peter." Mgr. d'Aviau of Bordeaux supported him, and all the bishops without exception renewed their oath of obedience to the Pope. Then the coadjutor of Mainz, Mgr. zu Droste-Vischering, proposed that the Emperor be asked to free the Pope before any discussion began, and a number of French bishops applauded him. On the other hand, when Duvoisin moved a protest against the excommunication of Napoleon, his motion was thrown out. The Emperor followed these debates with mounting fury, and when at length a huge majority of the council notified him that there was no means of avoiding the papal Bulls in the matter of canonical investiture, the imperial wrath exploded. The council was adjourned, and the authors of the motion, Mgr. Hirn of Tournai and Mgr. de Boulogne of Troyes, were imprisoned at Vincennes together with Mgr. de Broglie of Ghent, a resolute opponent.

The effect of these measures was disastrous. Maury and a few others persuaded the Emperor to revoke them; but the example of the three prisoners of Vincennes inclined the fathers to prudence. After some laborious sessions the majority agreed that if canonical investiture had not been granted by the Pope at the end of six months, it should be conferred by the metropolitan or by the senior bishop of the province. Thus they took the road pioneered by the Civil Constitution of the Clergy. But they were also careful to insert in the text of their decision a clause directing that the latter must receive the Pope's approval. In this way, they thought, everyone would be satisfied.

Another delegation therefore set out for Savona, led by no fewer than five "red" cardinals. Difficult negotiations began, during which Pius VII, sick, weary and perhaps not fully understanding what was at stake, seemed on the point of giving way. He was assured that if he accepted the council's resolution, the metropolitan or other bishop who conferred investitures could be regarded as his representative, thus leaving his spiritual authority intact. And he might have been duped by this argument but for the arrival at Savona of news that Napoleon, exasperated by the delay, had rejected the resolution as an insult to himself. Pius VII immediately recovered his determination and rejected any new concession.

Napoleon then completely lost his head. Would he create a schismatic Church? He had already gone further than Louis XIV; would he imitate Henry VIII of England? Had not Russia distracted his attention at that very moment he might well have done so. Meanwhile punishment rained thick and fast on all those members of the Church whom he suspected. Bishops were arrested, compelled to resign and placed under house arrest. The Sulpicians were disbanded. The junior seminaries were partially withdrawn from ecclesiastical control under pretext of their reorganization in the spirit of the imperial *Université*. The Trappists were driven from their monasteries, and the superior of the Lazarists was imprisoned at Fenestrelle. Public sermons were forbidden, and missioners in the provinces were told to cease all activity.

These vexations solved nothing. Napoleon had failed. The Church of France was cut in two: one branch, which grew visibly smaller, remained loyal to the Emperor, ready to go to any lengths, not excluding schism; the other had neither eyes nor ears for any but the Pope. What a situation ten years after the signing of the Concordat! "The Roman Priest," as Napoleon called Pius VII, the "cardboard Pontiff," as the Pope described himself, was on the way to conquering the all-powerful tyrant.

15. FONTAINEBLEAU

NAPOLEON then resolved to strike a mighty blow. On June 9, 1812, Chabrol, prefect of Montenotte, in whose territory the Pope was living, received a surprising order that was to be executed without delay. The government, said the dispatch, had learnt that British forces were preparing to land at Savona and kidnap the Pope. In order to prevent the operation Pius VII was to be transferred to France; he was to be housed at Fontainebleau, where he would be allowed to see the cardinals and bishops resident in France. Absolute secrecy must attend this journey in order to avoid popular demonstrations.

The order was carried out at midnight on the same day. The Pope was conducted through a private doorway to his carriage, which set off at once. He had been made to dress in his simplest cassock and remove his pectoral cross; even his white slippers had been blacked. Every precaution had been taken: as the carriage passed through the towns its blinds were to be drawn; at each posting station steps were to be taken to keep prying eyes at a distance without arousing too much suspicion. Thus the captive was hurried along towards France without anyone being able to recognize and cheer him on his way. However, those responsible for the arrangements had some anxious moments; for, on reaching the Mont-Cenis Pass the aged Pope, who was suffering moreover from bladder trouble, became so exhausted that he had to be nursed for several days. But he endured with heroic tranquility, and at length, on June 19, arrived at the Château de Fontainebleau. What memories must have crowded back upon the mind of the unhappy Pontiff. Eight years ago.... No festive scenes awaited him now. The authorities had given such vague instructions that no quarters had been prepared, and the Vicar of Christ was obliged to spend the first few days in a small room adjoining the porter's lodge.

Weeks and months passed without any indication of exactly why Napoleon had ordered the transfer. Life was a little less monotonous than at Savona: cardinals and bishops were allowed to visit the august prisoner, and all without exception greeted him with the utmost affection—even those upon whom he had refused to confer investiture. Every day he was given the latest news—carefully censored, of course. And what news! On June 24 Napoleon had crossed the Niemen and hurled against Russia an army such as the world had never before seen; it appeared that nothing could resist his onslaught. In September the announcement of a great victory on the Moskva and the capture of Moscow seemed to crown the triumph of the invincible eagles. Then suddenly other information began to filter through, despite the police: Moscow in flames; the French obliged to flee the city; the retreat, rendered more difficult by the arrival on the scene of "General Winter" and turning to disaster; the heroic but terrible passage of the Beresina; the Grand Army melting away in the plains of Russia like snow beneath the sun. Meanwhile, in Spain, King Joseph was on the point of expulsion from Madrid; Austria and Prussia were in a state of ferment; at Rome, St. Anne Mary Taïgi was foretelling the imminent downfall of the regime; and miraculous statues of the Blessed Virgin began to speak and prophesy deliverance of the holy captive. On the night of December 18–19 Napoleon arrived at the Tuileries after travelling across Germany with his chief equerry Caulaincourt. He knew well that his presence in Paris was indispensable.

The disaster, however, had not crushed him, and he began straightway to prepare France for the decisive struggle he had foreseen. His ambition was as great as ever. He alarmed his friends by continuing to draw up grandiose schemes: final victory achieved, he would be master of Europe and redraw the map according to his own ideas; the Pope would reside permanently in France and, together with a reorganized Curia, would help him to govern the world. In order to bring this plan to fruition, the first thing to do was to patch up the wretched quarrel which had embittered relations between the two powers. Envoys were sent to Fontainebleau to make overtures; but Pius VII, sick and filled with anguish, so thin and pale that he seemed very near to death, avoided an interview.

Napoleon realized that the hour had come for what Consalvi described as "the last assault." On January 19, 1813, under pretext of a hunting party, he arrived unexpectedly at the Château de Fontainebleau accompanied by Marie-Louise, who was to cajole the Pope into agreeing to crown her. Napoleon himself lavished tokens of respect and unbounded affection upon Pius VII, embracing him and kissing him on both cheeks. For five days the two men engaged in private talks. In order to win the Pope over to his side Napoleon played what he believed to be his two trump cards: charm and threat. The famous scene, variously reported by Alfred de Vigny and Chateaubriand, has, however, no historical foundation. Napoleon did *not* strike Pius VII in the face or even raise his arm. The Pope himself afterwards gave the lie to that story, which the two writers had found in a royalist pamphlet, *Anti-Napoléon*. Nor is it true that Pius VII uttered the two celebrated words: "*Commediante, tragediante.*" He merely observed when Napoleon lost his temper: "The affair began as a comedy, and is going to end in tragedy." Nevertheless at the end of those five days it was learnt, on January 25 and not without surprise, that Napoleon had achieved his purpose and that a new agreement had been signed.

In fact, what Napoleon hastened to describe as a new concordat was no more than a draft. Important resolutions were made in eleven articles. The question of episcopal investiture was decided in accordance with the "conciliar" decree of 1811: the Emperor had the right to appoint all bishops throughout the Empire, except those of the suburbican dioceses of Rome; and the Pope, in exchange for such of his property as had been confiscated, accepted a civil list of two million francs. Further, the principal congregations were to be re-established, while all imprisoned cardinals and bishops were to be freed and their titles restored.

How could Pius VII agree to such provisions? Was it through fatigue and weariness, or through conviction that a definite settlement of the unhappy dispute would really benefit the Church? Frédéric Masson has maintained that it was through conviction that Pius VII agreed to give way, and that he changed his mind only in consequence of external pressure. But all that is known of his character and his whole previous attitude is against this theory. The mystery of those conversations at Fontainebleau has never been solved; it is more likely that the aged warrior yielded through weakness, in a moment of exhaustion.

Napoleon, of course, immediately proclaimed his victory. At that decisive moment, when he knew that the whole of Europe was preparing for conflict, it was of capital importance that he should declare before the Catholic world that the Pope was henceforward on his side. The *Te Deum* was ordered to be sung in all cathedrals. Marie-Louise wrote to her father: "The Emperor has settled the affairs of Christendom." The cardinals who had laboured for the "new concordat" received the Grand Eagle of the Legion of Honour; those who were kicking their heels at Fenestrelle and elsewhere were set free and brought back to Paris. Scores of bishops hurried to congratulate the Sovereign Pontiff, and the people were allowed to come and kiss his feet. "The effect was astonishing," says Pasquier in his memoirs; and Napoleon delightedly announced that he had just escaped "from one of his most awkward predicaments."

But Pius VII, having appended his signature, was overwhelmed with gloom. He was seen prostrated, silent, gazing upon his visitors with a look of fevered anguish. During sleepless nights the Pope meditated upon the terms of the agreement, reproaching himself bitterly, feeling himself already damned. Among the twenty-seven cardinals who had forgathered at Fontainebleau there was a difference of opinion: some were for temporizing, but the more energetic, led by Pacca and Consalvi, urged the Pope to repudiate the treaty. The problem, however, was delicate; for papal infallibility, though not yet an article of faith, was generally admitted, and it would be a serious matter to recognize that the Pope had erred. Nevertheless this was the solution chosen by Pius VII; it hurt his pride, but quietened his conscience. On March 24 he sent the Emperor a long letter of retractation.

Napoleon at once gave vent to a storm of uncontrolled fury. He talked of imitating the Czar of Russia and setting up a patriarch in France. On March 25 a decree was published making the "new concordat" obligatory and directing all metropolitans and diocesan bishops to carry out its provisions. The authorities were instructed to quell any opposition. Twelve episcopal sees were vacant, and the new titulars were invited to go and take possession—with assistance from the police if necessary. Cardinal di Pietro was arrested; others preferred to leave Fontainebleau. Pius VII, expecting the worst, signed a Bull providing for a future conclave. But all this mattered very little. It was no longer in the lists of theology that this final dispute would be determined. In a moment of foresight Napoleon said to a friend: "For the moment let us forget Rome and investiture of bishops; that number has gone back into the urn and will not come out again until after a great battle has been won on the Elbe or the Vistula." Cardinal Fesch was even more shrewd. Learning of the retreat from Moscow he had whispered a few prophetic words: "My nephew is lost, but the Church is saved."

16. "STAT CRUX DUM VOLVITUR ORBIS"

FESCH'S prophecy was fulfilled within less than twelve months. Europe was now determined to rid herself of the man whose tyranny had weighed her down for almost fifteen years. Napoleon's allies were abandoning his camp: Prussia had recently defected; Austria was wholly unreliable. The great general decided for the last time to take the initiative, and in the spring of 1813 he launched an offensive in Germany. But the time of decisive victories was past. Success at Lutzen and Bautzen did not settle the issue. It became necessary to accept an armistice in order to rest and train his new conscripts. On Metternich's advice the allies, meeting at the Congress of Prague, seized this opportunity to wage a war of propaganda. Under colour of recognizing France's natural frontiers, they represented Napoleon as alone responsible for the continuation of hostilities and set the seal on his unpopularity. Now for the kill. "Victory," Napoleon had once said, "is always on the side of the big battalions." Abandoned by Austria, defeated at Leipzig by overwhelming numerical superiority (October 16–19), deserted soon afterwards by his own brother-in-law Murat, and betrayed by his ministers, the ageing Emperor was unable, in the French campaign of February and March 1814, to recover a spark of the genius he had shown as a young commander in Italy. Hope had now vanished. On April 6, at Fontainebleau, abandoned even by his marshals, he had no choice but to abdicate unconditionally and leave for Elba. He was obliged to travel a road of derision and opprobrium, disguised as an Austrian officer to avoid the fury of his people.

Amid that whirlwind of catastrophe, religious affairs and negotiations with the Pope inevitably took second place, though Napoleon did not altogether ignore them. Towards the end of 1813 some prelates on whom he felt he could rely suggested sending the Pope back to Rome and returning frankly to the stipulations of the original Concordat. Strange to say, he was not angered by those proposals, but carefully studied a report to the same effect. He had not, however, renounced his splendid dreams: he still meant to have his son solemnly crowned at Rome, and the authorities in the Eternal City were directed to make arrangements for the ceremony.

Pius VII was following events with close attention. Once more a virtual prisoner at Fontainebleau, he had regained his calmness and determination, and waited for Heaven to solve his problems. The renewal of war gave him hope—a hope that he was careful not to show and which was quickly suspended by the victories of Lutzen and Bautzen. On receiving news of the Congress of Prague (July 1813) he sent the Emperor Francis II of Austria a letter in which he stated his rights and demanded restoration of his sovereignty. No answer came. Britain, Russia and Prussia were of course no longer interested in the rights of the Holy See, and Austria doubtless had her own secret plans.

At about the same time Napoleon, who was then campaigning in Germany, received a letter which deeply impressed him. Feeling himself at death's door, Mgr. Duvoisin, Bishop of Nantes and his best adviser on religious affairs, had sent a pathetic note confessing his errors and begging the Emperor to end "the captivity which afflicts the whole of Christendom" and to restore His Holiness to Rome.

But it was too late for negotiation. Cardinal Pacca found no difficulty in convincing Pius VII that it would be dangerous to negotiate with a beaten man: there was risk of antagonizing tomorrow's victors. Moreover Napoleon still thought of agreement as nothing less than a treaty whereby he would impose his own will on the Pope in exchange for the latter's return to Rome. In such circumstances negotiations could achieve nothing. Napoleon therefore, from his headquarters in Champagne, where he was preparing to launch his final offensives, sent an order for the Pope's removal from Fontainebleau to Savona. Once again, therefore, Pius VII, leaving his cardinals and friends, entered a carriage for the return journey across France. But this time everything told him that deliverance was at hand. All along the route his heart was warmed by popular demonstrations, and the carriage had to be changed several times because an enthusiastic crowd had broken up the one in which he rode.

In mid-February 1814 Pius VII took up residence once again in his former lodgings at Savona. But not for long. A new character had just come upon the stage: Murat, King of Naples. Returning to Italy after the Russian debacle, he had agreed to go over to the allies, an act of treason for which he expected a great reward. At the same time, urged by the *Carbonaro* Maghella, he dreamed of unifying Italy. The first stage towards that unification had been Rome, where the Abbé Battaglia fomented trouble and Fouché intrigued on his behalf. On January 19, 1814, Neapolitan troops had entered the city in order to protect it in the name of Joachim-Napoleon, King of the Two Sicilies, and Miollis, loyal to the French Emperor, had shut himself up with three hundred men in the castle of Sant' Angelo preparatory to sustaining a forty-nine-days' siege.

When Napoleon heard of these events he was overwhelmed with rage against the "monstrous traitor." In order to embarrass him he sent instructions for the immediate release of Pius VII, who was to be conducted as far as the allied outposts. Two final acts of the drama were then played out. On the road from Savona to Cesena, his birthplace, Pius VII was joined by Murat, who came to present him with a memorial signed by some Roman aristocrats, asking him not to return—a scrap of paper which the old man threw into the fire without so much as reading it. Murat then encountered the Austrian ambassador, Lebzeltern, who informed him that the allies did not recognize his occupation of Rome and that strong Austrian forces were going to bring back the Holy Father.

On May 24, the exile re-entered the capital he had left five years earlier. The King of Spain, Charles IV, at that time a refugee in Rome, had presented him with his most sumptuous coach. A squadron of Hungarian hussars escorted it, and all the ambassadors of the allied powers had come out beyond Monte Mario to welcome the Sovereign Pontiff. At the Porta del Popolo the crowd unyoked the horses, and twenty young men who had donned the papal livery dragged the coach to St. Peter's and thence to the Quirinal. The entire city made holiday; the vanquished Emperor was everywhere lampooned; and on the façade of a house in the Corso hung an enormous painting showing Napoleon, completely naked, cringing at the Pope's feet and dragged off to hell by the devil.

Stat crux dum volvitur orbis. Never had the famous Carthusian motto seemed more true. Battered by so many storms, the Cross of Christ stood forth at last unmoved—and unmovable. The squall of the Hundred Days (March 1–June 22, 1815) may have disturbed the papacy; for Murat, disappointed by the allies, rejoined the French camp and once more invaded the Papal States, obliging Pius VII to flee first to Florence and thence to Genoa. But it was the enemy's final spasm. Before Napoleon's overthrow at Waterloo and his departure for St. Helena in H.M.S. *Bellerophon*, Murat had been defeated by the Austrians and compelled to evacuate Rome, whither Pius VII returned for the last time on June 7.

Eighteen months earlier Colonel Lagorsse of the French military police, who had been responsible for the Pope's custody at Savona, had written to his minister: "The Pope told me expressly that the Emperor would be doing him a grave injustice by supposing him to harbour notions of hatred or revenge." With those words the officer voiced an important truth; for Pius VII, who had proved himself so great in time of trial, was no less magnanimous when fortune smiled again. Soon after his return to Rome he witnessed the arrival of many of Napoleon's relatives, whom the "White Terror" had driven headlong from France. Madame Mère, repulsed by her own daughter the Grand Duchess of Tuscany, was honourably received; and Pius called on her more than once to ask, "How is our Emperor?" Cardinal Fesch too sought asylum. "Let him come," exclaimed the Pope; "We have not forgotten the way he has always tried to serve Us." Before long most of the family had gathered around Mme. Laetizia: Lucien, Louis, Jérôme, Pauline, Julie and Hortense. M. de Blacas, Louis XVIII's ambassador, protested in vain at what he called "an insult to the Most Christian King"; he never managed to secure their expulsion.

Even those who had been directly concerned in the worst aspects of the affair were allowed to go scot free; but it was towards Napoleon himself that the Vicar of Christ revealed the full extent of his mercy. In the darkest days of their struggle he had never borne him ill will. He had remained ever grateful to the Emperor; for, as he said, "the pious and courageous initiative of 1801 has made Us forget and forgive subsequent injuries. Savona and Fontainebleau were only errors of judgment, vagaries of human ambition." Accordingly, when Britain cruelly (and mistakenly) deported her beaten foe to the noxious climate of St. Helena—that foe whose exile was to make him a legendary figure, a "Prometheus on the rock"—Pius VII thought of him only as an unfortunate prisoner dying of cancer in fearful solitude. At Mme. Laetizia's request he wrote to the Prince Regent a moving letter begging him to mitigate the sufferings of so illustrious an exile. "He can no longer be a danger to any," said the Pope. "We desire that he become grounds of remorse to none." And when he learned through Cardinal Fesch that Napoleon was asking for a chaplain, he took personal steps to satisfy his wish by sending a Corsican priest.

Those gestures, so simple yet so grand, closed the story of a conflict in which two men, opposed more through principle than through self-interest, revived on the threshold of the nineteenth century the age-old quarrel between the Empire and the priesthood. Pius VII crowned his victory with the pardon he so generously accorded to one who had subjected him to such bitter suffering. The sword had indeed been vanquished by the spirit.

CHAPTER III

An Abortive Counter-Revolution (1815–1830)

1. AFTER THE DELUGE

DRAMATIC as was the conflict between Pius VII and Napoleon, it is seen today as a mere parenthesis, an episode external to the course and real significance of events. Before embarking on a career of caesaropapism in the manner of the Holy Roman Emperors, Bonaparte had assumed another and more important role: he had checked the grand assault of revolutionary forces by integrating the major ideals of the Revolution with a new political and social order. The question now was whether his disappearance from the scene would mark the resumption of that assault, and, if so, whether the allies would be capable of resistance.

Europe lay in ruins. Displaced frontiers; States abolished and others arisen from nothing; political regimes hitherto unknown to the West; subversion of the social order; in all minds ideas and principles erstwhile condemned—such were the results of a crisis that had lasted twenty-five years. The Napoleonic system had collapsed, an artificial system because it rested ultimately on the genius and determination of one man. Another would have to be erected. How?

Two problems called for solution, one concerning the nature and another the origin of that crisis which had caused so much upheaval. First, was the Revolution a movement intrinsically perverse, tainting the legitimate order of the world, a sacrilegious rebellion on the part of man against the whole divine content of an age-old tradition? Or, as its supporters maintained, did it mark the promotion of certain fundamental human values hitherto despised—Justice and Liberty? Second, was it a fortuitous incident, a rupture brought about by the conspiracy of a few evil minds, or a gigantic phenomenon whose causes must be sought in a remote past—in the neo-classical period, in the epoch of the Renaissance and Reformation, or even further back in the high Middle Ages? Conceptions of the order to be rebuilt would naturally depend on the answers to those two questions. If the Revolution were a Satanic enterprise, a revolt of man against God, there could of course be no thought of accepting any of its principles. But if it were the result of an evolution extending over almost a thousand years, it would be absurd to treat it as null and void.

We who look backwards in time can see that there is no simple answer. What renders it so difficult for us to pass judgment on that stupendous occurrence known as the French Revolution is the fact that it was an inextricable medley of good and bad, justice and injustice, truth and falsehood. Those who were about to replace the imperial officials at the head of Europe, those who were to be responsible for the remaking of that world, had just waged against the Revolution and its crowned successor one of those implacable wars in which a spirit of fairness towards the enemy appears as treason. During twenty years their propaganda had represented the Conventionals and then Napoleon as ogres and tyrants. Would their opinion alter once victory had been achieved? Quite sincerely, for the most part, they convinced themselves without difficulty that the Revolution *ought* to be undone and that in fact it *could* be.

Legitimacy, counter-revolution, restoration: it was on those three bases that an attempt would be made to rebuild the world. For fifteen years practically the whole of Europe witnessed a process that cannot be better described than by the word "reaction" in its fullest sense. On the morrow of the eagle's fall a remarkable period began, during which Europe attempted to swim against the current of history. On one side were groups of politicians, philosophers and even theologians for whom a return to the past, as complete as possible, was the only chance for society and civilization. On the other side were those who, more or less consciously, remained sons and heirs of the Revolution; they were called by the very wide and equivocal term "liberals." Among them were the adversaries of authoritarian regimes; the peoples who resented the heavy tutelage of a single master or occupying power; the Germans and Italians, who were exasperated by the sight of their countries reduced to a motley of petty States. But "liberal" included also the enemies of religion and professed anticlericals whose one resolve was to destroy the Church. Men's minds, like their choice of words, were hopelessly confused; but the historical reality was absolutely clear—between the partisans of counter-revolution and those who meant to follow up the events of 1789 there was open warfare.

2. THE SITUATION OF THE CHURCH IN 1815

SUCH was the ambiguous position in which the Church found herself emerging from a dreadful crisis in which she herself had had so much to endure. Materially her losses were immense. In many lands she had suffered the loss of more than half her property, which she would never recover, and that impoverishment was likely to hinder her apostolate.

With what could she support her seminaries, her charitable institutions and her schools? How was she to re-establish the means of parochial and conventual life? The indemnities and endowments promised by certain States appeared very small, and would be in any case precarious. Ecclesiastical administration too had been affected: many archives had been dispersed and would never be reassembled. The labour of reorganization was indispensable in every sphere.

Morally, however, there were no grounds for pessimism, though the Church had admittedly lost much of her social influence together with her privileged position. The very circumstances in which the Church had managed, once the first act of the crisis was past, to re-establish a more normal situation by means of concordats showed with what insolence the temporal power meant to limit the rights of God and extend those of Caesar. But a closer study reveals a number of more favourable elements. The possession of great wealth had never been wholesome for the Church. Impoverished, the clergy was now both purified and more numerous. The martyrs of the guillotine enabled men to forget the courtier-abbés of the *Ancien Régime*; the brave "black cardinals" eclipsed the memory of such as Bernis and Rohan. A Church more united and more worthy emerged from the crisis of the Revolution.

In one respect the papacy was seen as the chief conqueror of tyranny; it was the heroic helplessness of the man in white, no less than the allied armies, that had helped to bring down the ruler of the world. Around him were rallied not only the Catholic sovereigns, but also heretics and schismatics; for, strangely enough, the most determined supporters of Rome in the diplomatic field were Britain and Russia. The Papal States, on which powerful neighbours had so often gazed with greedy eyes, now appeared sacrosanct.

It was not only with heightened authority and prestige that the Church came forth from her ordeal. There were more and more signs of that spiritual reawakening which had been evident during the imperial age. France witnessed a large growth in the number of vocations and a remarkable flowering of the regular orders. In Germany the militant groups led by Princess Galitzin, Stolberg and Sailer were in process of rapid expansion.[1] Even in England the small Catholic flock was multiplying. Throughout the West literature showed a keen interest in matters of Catholic tradition.

But some very grave problems also required attention. It was clearly necessary to shoulder the task of remaking what had been destroyed, of setting up again what had been overthrown; and the Church was ready to fulfil that task with extraordinary zeal and courage. The work of reconstruction, however, could not go forward outside its political context, especially as the new masters of Europe included the Church among those institutions which they proposed to restore.

1. See Volume 2, Chapter VIII, section 6.

It was natural that the Church should take advantage of the goodwill on the part of secular governments; but she thereby incurred the risk of finding herself associated with authoritarian and counter-revolutionary systems which claimed to be rebuilding society on its rightful foundations, and thus of cutting herself off from those elements (not all of them hostile to Christianity) which had seen mankind's opportunity in certain ideals of the Revolution. It is easy in the light of experience to claim that the Church, transcending all regimes and all social systems, should have employed the designs of legitimist governments without allowing herself to be compromised by them. Yet in order to succeed in such a manoeuvre she would have needed to be led by men of genius far in advance of their time. As nearly always happens, immediate interests, great and small, acted as a screen to hide the future. We shall accordingly find the Church siding almost unanimously with the counter-revolution. What may surprise the historian is not so much the fact that she did so as that some of her representatives, men very close to the See of Peter—like Cardinals Consalvi and Bernetti—thought the alliance should not be pushed too far, while others realized that the fact of the Revolution could not be simply and completely reversed, that account must be taken of mental and moral evolution, and that a new attitude must be fostered in the Church. 157

3. MAISTRE AND BONALD

TWO men embodied this desire for the politico-religious restoration of the world, two writers of unequal standing. In 1796 Comte Joseph de Maistre published at Lausanne his *Considérations sur la France*. Almost simultaneously, at Heidelberg, the Vicomte Louis de Bonald completed his *Théorie du Pouvoir civil et religieux*. Neither work attracted much attention at the time, but after 1815 circumstances won them many readers.

Maistre (1753–1821) was a Savoyard from Chambery, son of the president of the senate, a former magistrate, a man of solid and stern upbringing.

In his youth, good Christian though he was, he had dabbled in the *philosophes* just sufficiently to understand later how dangerous they could be. And despite papal condemnation he had even been a Freemason for fifteen years, convinced that the lodges would provide him with allies in the work of rejuvenating Christianity. At the same time his relations with Claude de Saint-Martin, the "unknown philosopher," had planted in his mind a providential concept of human destiny, which he retained throughout the remainder of his life. The sorrows of exile, to which he had been condemned on the invasion of his little fatherland by revolutionary forces, completed his education and enlightenment. He wrote continually, first at Lausanne, then at Cagliari and finally at St. Petersburg, whither the King of Sardinia, Charles-Emmanuel IV, sent him as ambassador in 1803. Life was not exactly gay in the Russian capital, where he had worthily to represent a prince who too often forgot to send him the necessary funds. Far from his own family, Joseph de Maistre crammed his boxes with manuscripts bearing such titles as *Du Pape, De l'Église gallicane* and *Les Soirées de Saint-Pétersbourg*. After Waterloo he moved to Turin, took up a new post as minister of state and began the leisurely publication of his works. Though not bestsellers, these earned him the attention of political thinkers and of educated people in general.

Comte de Maistre's notion of the world was tragic. Heir of Bossuet, he discovered in the unrolling of historical events the unmistakable operation of a supernatural power, recognizing it as the passage of the divine will across the centuries. Carrying to extremes the harsh Christian doctrine of evil, he thought he could discover the activity of Providence in the violence and cruelty of men. Because nature has been wounded by sin, the divine law (according to Maistre) wills that blood shall flow; in this sense war and the executioner's work are both divine. "Every scourge from heaven is a chastisement," a chastisement that falls on the innocent as well as on the guilty. At the same time, however, he viewed this providential suffering as redemptive: the shedding of blood has an expiatory virtue.

Applied to the most recent events of history, Maistre's terrible doctrine passed upon the Revolution a judgment at once categorical and surprising.

At first sight the Revolution appeared to him destructive, harmful, "satanic"; yet it too entered into the designs of Providence, and could therefore prove beneficial. From the human standpoint it was inexplicable; moreover those who thought to direct it had themselves been led by it—and to what a fearful goal! The ringleader of this bloody game, therefore, was Providence, which sought, by chastising France, to make her conscious of her faults and loyal once more to her ancient Christian mission. If that were achieved, the whole world would be enlightened.

Why had France deserved the chastisement she had endured? The reasons given by Joseph de Maistre are various and of unequal cogency. Moral decadence and the frivolity of the ruling classes appeared to him as among the causes of the catastrophe. But there was also the presumption of the people in desiring a constitution and a share in government; for according to him sinful man, like a congenital invalid, is intended to be controlled by an authority derived from God alone. More justly, he blamed also the work of the *philosophes*, that "spirit of the eighteenth century," the revolt of the intellect against divine revelation, of false science against dogma; and on this point his criticism of Voltaire and Rousseau, his analysis of their errors and shortcomings, was extremely valuable.

If the "satanic" Revolution was a chastisement, its import must be understood and the mistakes to which it had given rise corrected. In order to set France once more on her foundations it was necessary to restore a power capable of bringing back true order, the power of an absolute monarch unlimited and uncontrolled, or rather, having no limits but his own conscience and subject to no control but the justice of God. Such was his notion of kingship, a notion which Louis XIV himself might have entertained. He was horrified at the idea of the people's sovereignty, even when expressed in the restrictive terms of the Charter; as an expression of God's will there could be no question of intermediaries between the sovereign and the people.

But—and here de Maistre, an ultramontanist, was violently opposed to the Gallican traditions of Capetian absolutism—the royal authority, plenary in each and every State, must nevertheless be subject to a higher authority, to the authority of God, and so to that of His vicar upon earth. In the book entitled *Du Pape* he develops the concept of a totally theocratic society. The Pope must be the unquestioned chief, the supreme arbiter and guide of all peoples and of all sovereigns. Maistre could hardly find enough splendid titles wherewith to adorn him: supreme instrument of civilization, creator of every monarchy, guardian of science and the arts, natural protector of liberty. Being infallible—and, declared Maistre (a sound prophet), that infallibility would soon become *de fide*—he lays down the principles of spiritual life and of morality: he is the manifestation of God's purpose. Moreover history itself proved that the papacy was called to rule the world: "No human institution has lasted for eighteen centuries"; amid the flux of Europe only one point was stable—Rome. Thus, under the paternal direction of the Sovereign Pontiff, Europe would regain her unity.

One may be tempted to dismiss the whole thing as medieval theory. And yet, no. Maistre was trying somehow to endow a world on the point of birth with those principles and institutions which had enabled Christendom in its finest hour to reach the summit of greatness. Nor was he under any illusion as to the intrinsic value of institutions; the counter-revolution which he desired was first and foremost an interior counter-revolution. He thought, and said, that it was necessary "to rejuvenate Christianity in some extraordinary way," failing which another religion would be born—the religion of deified man, of Antichrist. "Every law," he declared, "however excellent in itself, is useless and even pernicious if the nation is not worthy of the law." It was not by imposing upon men ready-made designs that society would be saved, but by calling them to a simultaneous renewal of soul, conscience and institutions.

In this respect Joseph de Maistre's rival, Louis de Bonald, was far less thorough. He was not much concerned with interior reform, with the spiritual rejuvenation of Christianity. If he regarded morality as the basis of all institutions, he thought of it only as applied by law, according to the methods of authority and discipline. "Man," he thought, "exists only for society, and society fashions him only for herself." Let a strong government apply the laws properly, let everything be forbidden that tended to destroy the legitimate order, let the Jesuits be given a monopoly of education and all would go well with the world.

Bonald, the ancestor of totalitarian theories, was likewise in private a worthy man whose smiling countenance reflected good intentions and an almost naïve candour. Born in 1754 at the Chateau de Nonna, near Millau, where he died long afterwards in 1840 at the age of eighty-six, he too had experienced the sadness of exile. Returning eventually to France, he was singled out by Napoleon, whom his teaching on authority could not fail to please and who appointed him counsellor of the *Université* in 1810. But Bonald remained at heart a monarchist and legitimist, and in 1815, although the Charter failed to win his approval, he placed himself at the service of Louis XVIII, who made him a minister of state, a peer of France and soon afterwards a member of the Academy.

As a writer Bonald is not the equal of Maistre. He lacks the grand prophetic intuition, the surging periods and brilliant phrases which illuminate the pages of the *Soirées*. He is a painstaking dialectician who deduces and reasons with implacable logic. His proofs, ordinarily threefold, have the air of mathematical theorems. "In cosmology God is the cause, movement the means, body the effect. In a State the government is the cause, the minister the means, the subject the effect. In a family the father is the cause, the mother the means, the child the effect." Everything in his work is built up on such patterns.

He had begun his literary career with *Théorie du Pouvoir politique et religieux*, a vigorous attack on the *philosophes*, particularly on Montesquieu's *Esprit des Lois* and Rousseau's *Contrat social*. Later, in 1818, the *Recherches philosophiques* extended the field of this rigorous but by no means irrelevant analysis. Bonald denied the so-called state of nature, the human and democratic origin of power, the social contract imagined by Jean-Jacques, the rights of man and especially the right to freedom. Even more than Maistre, he appears as one of the founders of that school which has never ceased to oppose a resolute *non possumus* to the doctrines of the Revolution. In his eyes, of course, democracy, daughter of the *philosophes* and especially of Montesquieu and Rousseau, was a monstrosity: it tainted the relationship of cause and effect between the ruling power and the individual, and he considered the Charter itself as a dangerous concession to democratic theories. In the social order he was no less horrified by divorce, to the condemnation of which he devoted a forcible work; it too breaks the trinity of cause, means and effect (i.e., father, mother and child).

Many of Bonald's arguments have not lost one jot of their value. But he did not confine himself to criticism. His *Législation primitive* (1802), his *Recherches philosophiques sur les premiers objets de connaissances morales* (1818) and later his *Démonstrations philosophiques des principes de la société* put forward a concept of the world, a complete system of reconstruction. Far less of a mystic and metaphysician in the sphere of history than Maistre, he claimed to found everything upon tradition, whose sources he traced, by methods more ingenious than reliable, to the very origins of society. His traditionalism, forerunner of that which the Church would one day condemn,[2] allowed no scope for human reason. It was in the name of tradition that he laid down a rigid social and political system, in which the very idea of liberty seemed outrageous, in which all institutions should tend to a single goal—the preservation of the past. This hard-and-fast order proceeded, so he held, from God; Christianity and the Church occupied a central place therein, for many reasons. First, they perfectly illustrated the trinary system which Bonald regarded as fundamental, God being the cause, Christ the means and human society the effect. Next one can see in the centralized and authoritarian organization of Holy Church the archetype of all regimes. Finally—and here is a profound idea—since the Revolution had been essentially a religious movement, a metaphysical revolt of mankind against divine tradition, it could be brought to an end by nothing short of religious restoration. Bonald's outlook then was no less medieval than that of Maistre.

2. See Volume 2, Chapter VI, section 5 *ad fin*.

They disagreed however, on a fundamental point. The author of *Législation primitive* does not grant Christ's vicar the pre-eminence given him by the author of *Du Pape*, for, as a good servant of the Bourbons, he was Gallican.

It is clear that the doctrine both of Maistre and of Bonald had a lofty end in view. What they were trying to achieve was a regeneration; each hoped, in substance, to establish the City of God on earth. But this class of doctrinaires generally has the misfortune to be interpreted by politicians in the narrowest possible sense they can be made to bear. These deeply intuitive thinkers, who sometimes (Maistre particularly) expressed amazingly prophetic views, could easily be made to serve the purposes of reaction.

4. A PLACE AT TABLE FOR JESUS CHRIST

ONE day in the year 1815 Metternich was invited to dinner by Czar Alexander I. Treaties had recently been concluded which were intended to redraw the map of Europe, but the Russian sovereign made no mystery of his desire to add to the diplomatic stipulations a religious pact which would make this territorial reorganization an expression of the divine will. Present also at the meal was Mme. de Krüdener, a lady who had been for several months the Czar's inseparable companion. A fourth place was laid, and when Metternich asked the name of their fellow-diner, Alexander solemnly informed him that the place was laid for Jesus Christ.

The incident, rather absurd in itself, illustrates perfectly the confusion of Christian considerations with high political interests which at that time was plain for all to see. The suggested pact was signed at Paris on September 26, 1815, by Francis I, Emperor of Austria, Frederick William III, King of Prussia, and Czar Alexander; it soon became known as the Pact of the Holy Alliance. Professing to speak "in the name of the Most Holy and Undivided Trinity," the three sovereigns declared that they wished henceforward "to base their mutual relations on the sublime truths taught us by the eternal religion of God our Saviour," and proclaimed "their firm resolve to take as their sole rule of conduct...the precepts of that holy religion, precepts of justice, charity and peace." Therefore, "in conformity with the words of Holy Scripture," the three contracting monarchs would consider themselves as brothers, and as fathers towards their subjects. They would be "three members of a single family," and would confess that "the Christian nation of which they and their peoples form part have really no other sovereign than Him to whom power properly belongs, because in Him alone are found all the treasures of love, science and infinite wisdom—God, our divine Saviour, Jesus Christ, the Word of the Most High." All princes of good will desiring "solemnly to avow these sacred principles" would be admitted into "this Holy Alliance with as much eagerness as affection."

The pact was welcomed in very different ways. While the official newspapers of Vienna, Berlin and St. Petersburg vied with one another in declaring that no such mighty and noble text had ever been signed since 847, when the sons of Louis le Débonnaire swore before God at Mersen to watch over "the safety of their common realm," and while preachers more zealous than prudent foretold the dawning of a new Christendom, the liberals muttered that this sanctimonious document marked the beginning of an era of slavery for the common folk. The Pact of the Holy Alliance deserved neither such fulsome praise nor such fierce abuse. Its good intentions had every chance before long of paving a small sector of hell, and statesmen were in no two minds about it. Castlereagh, the British foreign minister, refused to sign, remarking with a smile that he saw no need to associate himself "with a declaration of biblical principles which would take us back to the age of Cromwell's 'saints.'" Talleyrand spoke of it in biting terms as "splendid gibberish." Metternich considered it "an empty and sonorous monument, a vaguely philanthropic aspiration under cover of religion."

Much more serious was the fact that the mantle of religion was going to be used to cover not just vaguely philanthropic gibberish, but most precise and realistic combinations of interests. The man in the street was to be offered a Holy Alliance with its magnanimous Christian phraseology; but the chancelleries had elaborated with greater circumspection a re-allotment of territory and a diplomatic system that would guarantee the rights of the great victors. The final act of the Congress of Vienna, agreed on June 9 and completed on November 20 by the Treaty of Paris, had gravely weakened France. She lost all her conquests, was condemned to pay a heavy war indemnity and witnessed the destruction of her northern and eastern frontiers. Russia annexed most of Poland; Prussia devoured part of Saxony, Westphalia and the left bank of the Rhine; Austria awarded herself the Lombard-Venetian kingdom. In order to keep a more vigilant eye on restive France, there was established on her flanks a powerful kingdom of the Netherlands consisting of Holland and Belgium, a neutralized Swiss confederation and the kingdom of Piedmont-Sardinia enlarged by the inclusion of Genoa. Italy became once more "a geographical expression," while the Germanic condeferation of thirty-nine States was a mere sham. All that Napoleon had sought to accomplish was destroyed. Also on November 20, 1815, there was signed a pact of Quadruple Alliance, which translated into harsh reality the shrewd design of the agreement between the signatories of the Holy Alliance. Russia, Prussia, Austria and Britain united to protect themselves against the revolutionary hydra. Regular conferences would study the situation, and military intervention would restore order wherever the virus of 1789 seemed likely to cause trouble. The counter-revolution was transformed into diplomatic weapons under cover of lofty religious ideals.

It soon became apparent that the system was fragile. Joseph de Maistre described it as "the eternal seed of war and hatred." Those who intended to rebuild Europe had taken no account of the aspirations of her peoples; on many points indeed they had misunderstood the surest lessons of history. The Italians and Germans, those at any rate who had caught a glimpse of their national unity, were no less discontented than the French, humiliated and filled with nostalgia for their glorious past, or than the Greeks subjected to the Turkish yoke, or than the Poles at the mercy of Russia.

What view did the Church take of those high-sounding documents that were claimed to lie under the protection of the Trinity? The welcome accorded by Rome to the treaties of 1815 was reserved. The Holy Alliance did not seem particularly holy.... By omitting mention of the Pope therein, the three sovereigns had perpetuated that process of laicizing politics—a process begun by the Treaties of Westphalia, which denied the Vicar of Christ a voice in solving the great problems of the world. What was a religious agreement worth between an Orthodox, a Protestant and a Catholic? To encourage fraternization of all beliefs was surely to embark upon the most deplorable kind of syncretism. As for the territorial resolutions, the papacy regarded them with no more favour, principally because centuries of experience had shown the wisdom of mistrusting such ambitious edifices, in which a heady ideology attempts to hide the weakness of their foundations. How, moreover, could the Church have approved agreements which placed Belgian Catholics under the rule of Dutch Protestants, and subjected Polish Catholics to Orthodox Moscow? How, again, could she have pledged her support for the ominous silence maintained by the allies, despite papal representations, on the unhappy plight of Christians in Turkey, merely because the Sublime Porte was reckoned a "first-class power"? On a more strictly political plane the Holy See was naturally disturbed by the presence of Hapsburg rulers not only at Milan but also at Venice.

The policies of the Holy Alliance, then, were not approved by the Church. Still less would Rome agree to share them. In January 1816 Metternich invited the Apostolic See to join the Italian League formed to combat Jacobinism in the peninsula; but he met with refusal. All similar approaches had the same result. On every occasion the secretary of state replied that the Pope, having struggled so hard against Napoleon precisely in order to safeguard his freedom of action, which transcends all diplomatic calculations, and having refrained from joining a clique as the tyrant wished him to do, could not honestly abandon that principle. Even in 1820, at the time of the revolution at Naples, the Holy See refused military support against the rebels.

5. ROME AND CONSALVI

OF the many attempts at restoration witnessed by Europe after the Treaty of Vienna and the pact of the Holy Alliance, one deserves to be singled out and admired. I refer to the undertaking handled at Rome, until the advent of a new Pope removed him from office, by Cardinal Ercole Consalvi. Official histories are unfair to this man; they reserve the front of the stage for the great tenors of political opera—Metternich and Talleyrand. In extremely difficult circumstances, and with limited means, Pius VII's secretary of state accomplished something no less considerable, more reasonable and better adapted to contemporary needs than the achievement of the Austrian and French ministers; and he accomplished it without ever lowering the dignity of the Church to political contrivance. Nor had his contemporaries any doubt as to his merits: "He is the master of us all," said Castlereagh.

Consalvi, whom we have already met as a forty-year-old monsignor guiding the conclave with such skill in 1800, and then a year later conducting with equal shrewdness and patience the difficult negotiations leading to the Concordat, was now on the threshold of sixty, a man of vast experience and ability. During the dramatic conflict between the French Emperor and Pius VII he had given proof of wonderful dignity and firmness, accepting exile rather than surrender, a "black cardinal" under house arrest at Rheims, hidden soul of the resistance. Recalled by the Pope at the earliest possible moment, he was destined to lead the Church for almost ten years. Pius was now a very old man, exhausted by his ordeal and gradually falling victim to a slow paralysis accompanied by vertigo, which obliged him in his last years to walk with the aid of a cord attached to the walls of his room. He placed his whole trust in Consalvi, leaving the conduct of affairs almost entirely to him, though occasionally and under pressure from elsewhere intervening in a way that sometimes complicated the minister's task. Throughout those ten years the cardinal enjoyed enormous prestige; most sovereigns held it an honour to correspond directly with him on subjects not all of which were ecclesiastical or political. Without always following his advice, they treated him in some sort as the mentor of Europe.[3]

Thorwaldsen's fine bust shows the slight, delicate features, high and spacious brow, strong aquiline nose and keen eyes that sparkled with intelligence. He generally stooped a little, his tall body leaning towards his interlocutor, whom he watched with steady gaze. Artaud, a subtle diplomat, described him as "an undetermined mixture of sound logic and engaging gentleness." Beneath the guise of courtesy, reserve and a charming voice there lurked a tireless energy. Daunted by no amount of work, and giving audience even at table in order to save time, he was one of those leaders who can ask anything of their subordinates, because they can do so graciously and because they first make the same demands upon themselves. Without a trace of rancour, discreet and kindly in his judgments, but at the same time unyielding in matters of principle, he belonged in the sphere of politics to that class of men who, in Bismarck's celebrated words, manage to live "free from all sentiment and from all resentment." It may seem strange to us, but in those days it was not surprising that this great servant of the Church, a Roman cardinal, was not a priest; it appears that he remained a deacon to the end of his life. But Napoleon, a connoisseur of men, touched the rock bottom of Consalvi's character when he described him as "truly one of the most priestly men I have ever known."

Pius VII took up residence in the Eternal City once again on May 24, 1814, and Consalvi set to work on June 23. The first problem to be solved concerned restitution to the Holy See of its domains. It might have been expected that all those monarchs who spoke of nothing but legal rights would have hurried, without dispute, to restore papal territory to its lawful owner. But there was, as always, a great gulf between official language and reality. Hungry appetites were on the watch: Austria had never lost hope of laying hands on the Legations; Naples intended to keep Ancona and the Marches; France could scarcely believe she would be deprived of Avignon

3. See above, Chapter II, section 3.

and the Comtat Venaissan which she had annexed twenty-five years earlier. Consalvi, in a note to the powers, claimed on principle everything that had belonged and still belonged of right to the Apostolic See. Then, having little confidence in the nuncio Della Genga, or in the generous promises of the victors, he himself left Rome to conduct negotiations. He hurried to Paris and thence to London, where the powers were celebrating their triumph and where he played the subtlest of games with Castlereagh, Metternich and Czar Alexander. When the Congress of Vienna opened he betook himself to the Austrian capital to fight step by step against sordid interests, maintaining the dignity of a representative of the Church amid that crowd of camp followers and their bargaining, living in the utmost simplicity away from all the merry-making, engaged in diplomatic talks from which, he used to say, he emerged "sweating blood." A year and more of this ordeal brought him success. Murat, who made the mistake of abandoning the allied camp, lost (together with his life) the Marches and four hundred thousand souls, dominion over whom he had been promised. Metternich agreed to restore the Legations. Talleyrand long refused in the name of legality to hand back the duchy of Benevento which Napoleon had given him; he had to be paid two million francs, of which Rome was obliged to find three-quarters. Only Avignon, Parma and Piacenza were excepted from the general restitution; but that was a small price for a victory which Consalvi himself had believed to be "humanly impossible." When the secretary of state returned to Rome after fulfilling his task, he was presented with a picture showing him, attended by Force, Meekness and Glory, giving back to Pius VII Rome, Ravenna, Ferrara and Bologna, each represented by a kneeling woman. Modest and smiling, Consalvi declared: "Without the Holy Father's enormous personal reputation, without the respect entertained for His Holiness and his character, negotiation would have been in vain."

But another task awaited him, and other difficulties even greater. The restoration of the Pope's authority on the interior level was no less urgent than the re-establishment of his temporal sovereignty. Many mistakes had been made in the course of a single year. Pius VII had set up a kind of provisional government under the direction of Mgr. (afterwards Cardinal) Agostino Rivarola, and entrusted it with the restoration of order in Rome. The least that one can say is that it had behaved without much prudence or skill. To dismiss papal officials, prelates and even teachers who had collaborated too openly with the occupying power; to bar from the papal palace patricians convicted of having accepted posts of honour from the French; to send to the galleys those wretched individuals who had guided Radet at the time of the Pope's arrest; to deprive Maury of his bishopric of Montefiascone—all this was natural enough, and on the whole this cleansing process was in no way comparable to a White Terror. It was even understandable that the government was unable or unwilling to prevent the people of Rome from burning an effigy of Napoleon (and forcing collaborators to stand dangerously near the fire) or from sacking the houses of former imperial officials. What was truly absurd was Rivarola's decree abolishing all that the French had done, even such measures as were manifestly beneficial. It repealed Napoleon's civil and penal code in favour of the old legislation which was hopelessly confused. At the same time it re-established "baronial jurisdiction" (i.e., feudal justice), and the Holy Roman Inquisition, though the latter was advised not to use torture. The Jews were ordered to return to the ghetto, from which Miollis and Tournon had released them. Worse still, Rivarola's zeal abolished vaccination, street lighting and even measures against beggary, on the grounds that they were all horrible French innovations. Clearance of the Colosseum was abandoned, and excavations already made were filled in! Finally, a disastrous economic measure, by re-establishing the values of 1808, led to a sharp rise in prices, especially of wine and oil; nor were the people mollified by the almost daily processions with which they were regaled.

On learning of all this, Consalvi was much disturbed. He wrote at once to Rivarola and his *entourage*, saying among other things: "If fatal mistakes are made, the country we are in process of healing will not last six months." And in order to put the Pope on his guard, he showed him a copy of the letter he had written to Louis XVIII to warn him against the mistakes that were being committed by extremists in France. Even Pius VII's recently signed decree of amnesty failed to win his approval. Its terms were offensive, its scope too limited; and he described it as a half-measure unlikely to satisfy anyone.

On returning to Rome and taking charge once more of papal administration, Consalvi adopted a rather different policy. Not that he should be regarded as a liberal. Even when he said that liberal ideas lay under his skullcap, it was not true *stricto sensu*. In so far as "liberalism" and "revolutionary theory" were treated at that time as synonymous, he was undoubtedly anti-liberal. But he had a keen sense of modern needs—a rare gift in a man of his class and education. He realized that one must take account of the development of political and social theory. He saw clearly that young people, "who had never lived under papal government, took a very poor view of it," and disliked being ruled by priests; he even thought that a majority of the people were at heart against any such regime. His plan, therefore, was to start from the true facts of the situation, take over the best of the French legacy, and allow for the new current of ideas wherever they did not affect principle.

In giving effect to that plan, Cardinal Consalvi was under no illusion as to the opposition it would arouse. "I know well," he said, "that many Romans will not understand these things. Some will reject them through passion, others through lack of reflection, others through ignorance and others again through mere habit." Reaction, indeed, was not long delayed. The *gelanti*, among whom unfortunately were most of the cardinals, accused him of liberalism and denounced him to the Pope as a crypto-Jacobin. In their eyes the only solution was militant counter-revolution, a policy of repression and collaboration with the Holy Alliance. Now it was this very party of extremists that had furnished the personnel (cardinals and theologians) of the Congregation of Extraordinary Ecclesiastical Affairs, which Pius VII had created in 1814 while Consalvi was at Vienna, and whose duty it was to advise the secretary of state by examining together with him the manifold problems of reorganizing the Church. Furthermore, since the troublous times favoured the activity of secret organizations, the reactionary party had recruited many of its shock troops from among the most dubious elements. Members of the Association of the Holy Faith, the *Sanfedisti*, under pretext of counter-revolution and defence of the Holy See, indulged in the most fearful acts of reprisal and revenge.

Moreover Consalvi was no better understood, and his advice no more readily accepted. Such is the destiny of statesmen who try to follow a middle course. The liberal elements of Rome and the peninsula generally considered that he was too moderate, too timid, that he worked too closely with the *Sanfedisti* and other *gelanti*, and that he was on too good terms with Metternich and the Austrians. The *Carbonaria*, a secret society formed in Naples and southern Italy during the occupation, was in process of altering its objective. Its members used originally to meet at the huts of charcoal-burners in the forests, and then go out to harry the French. It soon became a well-organized body, divided into cells and controlled by strict discipline, with the twofold aim of unifying Italy and establishing liberal institutions. The *Carbonari* now had their centre at Ascoli, in the Marches; and as a left-wing opposition party, with accomplices even among the papal officials and the police, they were a formidable danger to the secretary of state.

It was in these singularly difficult circumstances, obliged as he was to employ such men as were available—all of them far from loyal, and some of them worse than suspect—that Cardinal Consalvi performed his task. Two factors appeared to him as the most dangerous: first, the *Carbonari*, whose liberal ideas disturbed public order and whose nationalist theories were a direct threat to the Papal States; second, the powers of the Holy Alliance, particularly Austria, which sought to control the policies of the Holy See and perhaps even once again call in question some of its sovereign rights. Against both perils he strove with equal skill and vigour. In 1801, after frequently reminding the allied governments of the danger of secret societies—which were in fact gaining ground, spreading through France and Germany—he persuaded the Pope to sign a Bull expressly condemning the *Carbonaria*. But when Metternich offered to provide a force of international police for the purpose of hunting down *Carbonari* and liberals, the cautious secretary of state declined, disliking the prospect of Austrian intervention in Umbria or the Marches. This subtle game lasted throughout his term of office. In order to make a show of giving way to the powers, he dispensed with the services of a few *Sanfedisti* and of some too zealous partisans of the Holy See; but on essentials he yielded not an inch. When Metternich advised him to carry out in the Papal States, and especially in the Legations, a firmer policy similar to that of Louis XVIII and the extremists, Consalvi replied that he was waiting for Metternich to do the same at Venice; for the Austrian, knowing the Venetians to be more than touchy, was having their city governed with the utmost caution and without altering its customs. Consalvi's refusal to intervene against the revolutionaries in Naples was part of the same picture, as was also the Holy See's unhesitating recognition of the young Latin-American States that had rebelled against Spain.

This game of thrust and parry proceeded simultaneously with a vast labour of reconstruction. At the international level the policy was one of concordats, which, thanks to the desire of governments to establish their relations with the Holy See on firm bases, was to control relations between Rome and foreign states long after Consalvi's disappearance from the scene. Thirty concordats were signed in less than forty years, and all those diplomatic instruments bore the marks of his sagacity and broad-mindedness; as at Paris in 1801, he advised acceptance of new conditions, was careful not to ask too much, and was ready to play a part in contemporary ideas. The striking results of this vast undertaking were apparent at Rome itself, where all nations wished to have their representatives, even those whose governments were schismatic or Protestant. In 1820 there were forty-two ambassadors or ministers plenipotentiary accredited to the Sovereign Pontiff, as against twenty-seven in 1789.

As regards home affairs, the great cardinal's work was equally extensive. The situation brought about by Rivarola and his colleagues was deplorable.

174 A complete return to the past led to complications which the people, used to French administration, would not accept. What meaning in the nineteenth century had the feudal organization of the Papal States, divided into the four Legations of Bologna, Urbino, Ravenna and Ferrara; the five territories of Perugia, Orvieto, the Patrimony, the Roman Campagna and Sabinia; the duchies of Spoleto, Castro, Benevento and the Marches of Ancona; and the so-called government of Città del Castello, not to mention Rome, which had separate status? How could the finances be made to work when the cost of collecting taxes amounted to one-quarter of their total sum, when a multitude of exemptions and privileges were allowed and when revenues were already mortgaged to the banks? If we add that highway robbery, of which the French police had never managed to purge Italy, was everywhere rampant, even within twenty-five miles of Rome, we shall have some idea of the problems faced by Consalvi.

A constitution enacted on July 8, 1816, by two successive decrees was manifestly, though not expressly, inspired by the French principles of unity and uniformity. It marked the end of privileged cities, provinces and fiefs. The papal territories were divided into seventeen administrative districts under governors and legates appointed by the secretary of state. The communes also were organized around a municipal council recruited by co-optation and controlled by the Apostolic See. At the same time Consalvi sought to laicize the administration by withholding from priests those offices for which he considered them ill-suited by their vocation. A similar revolution was undertaken in the field of justice, where the ecclesiastical tribunals were given clearly defined spheres of competence. All the old jurisdictions with their medieval trappings were swept away in favour of civil and criminal tribunals and courts of appeal. Torture was abolished. A civil and penal code was promulgated; it was none other than the *Code Napoléon*, to which the jurist Bartelucci was invited to give "a Roman collar." A commercial code was also published, later described by Guizot as a "monument of wisdom." Financial reform was likewise taken in hand. The land tax was based on a new survey; customs dues were made uniform;

excise on salt and tobacco was organized; and an overall tax replaced the old outmoded taxes which brought in nothing. The Congregation formed to deal with economic matters laboured to improve the *agro romano*, to create model farms and to establish textile industries. Draining of the Pontine Marshes and the irrigation of arid land were also part of Consalvi's extensive schemes. Moreover, with the powerful backing of Pius VII, he interested himself in undertakings that were destined to transform the Eternal City: the completion of the Piazza del Popolo and the Pincio gardens, the restoration of the Quirinal and Vatican, the construction of the Chiaramonti galleries, the repair of more than twenty ancient churches, excavation of the Forum, Palatine and Colosseum, and the rebuilding of the Vatican Library. Never since the age of the Renaissance had Rome witnessed such creative ferment.

It will no doubt be asked whether this vast work succeeded. The answer must be: not entirely. Although Cardinal Consalvi achieved his ends on the political level by saving the Holy See's liberty of action, his efforts at reconstruction were crowned with less good fortune. His measures provoked nothing less than sabotage; partisans of the old order (and they were many) cried, "Revolution!" For example, he never managed to secure the appointment of laymen instead of priests as heads of the administrative districts. Owing to lack of money, too, some of his most valuable schemes remained a dead letter; drainage of the Pontine Marshes was hardly begun. At Rome itself town-planning remained far from complete. Finally, Consalvi had only eight brief years in which to carry out his entire gigantic enterprise. Pius VII had placed unlimited trust in him; but the advent of that Pope's successor, a man of very different inclination, would suffice to set back the clock. Consalvi had often predicted as much, and he lived long enough to witness the event.

The Pope himself had certain limitations, and the work he accomplished, remarkable though it was in many ways, reveals a number of defects. The most serious of these was undoubtedly his failure to enlarge the framework of the Church; he lacked the world-wide vision of later popes, a vision that would give a new dimension to Christianity. Consalvi's work for the missions was negligible.[4] Nor did he lift a finger to prevent that Italianization of the Sacred College which appeared to give the Catholics of the peninsula a certain pre-eminence.[5] If Consalvi had relied more upon the Church in other lands he would probably have built his achievement on broader and more solid foundations. It cannot be doubted that he failed to understand that the question of nationhood was now so prominent in Italy that it could not be avoided simply by imprisoning a few *Carbonari*. And finally, like many others, he did not recognize the imminent confrontation of the Christian conscience with social problems.

It is, however, none the less true that few men of his time, especially within the Church, give an impression of having seen so clearly and of having acted in accordance with the historical trends. If his successors had done likewise many things would have turned out differently.

6. THE RESTORATION OF THE SOCIETY OF JESUS

IN that vast enterprise of reconstruction, which does such honour to the Holy See, two facts deserve particular attention: the restoration of the Society of Jesus and the "campaign of concordats."

More than forty years had passed since the suppression of the Jesuits by Pope Clement XIV, and the material plight of those who survived was now extremely painful. Thrown on to the roads of Europe, many had been obliged to earn a living in all sorts of petty trades or to reside in the homes of such kind souls as offered them shelter; others, the majority, were destitute. Three thousand of them had even been settled for a while in Corsica, where, despite the legendary hospitality of the inhabitants, they had not been happy.

4. See section 14.
5. In the Conclave of 1829, forty-three of the forty-nine cardinals present were Italians.

And yet, throughout their ordeal, many had preserved an ineradicable hope of better times. In 1785 Giulio-Cesare Cordara, an ex-Jesuit, wrote to a friend: "I tell you, the Society will rise again. God will move one of His good servants to restore our Institute." This conviction, general among the former sons of St. Ignatius, had gradually produced local results in the shape of more or less sporadic attempts at recovery. Survival of the Society had been favoured by a rather paradoxical and unforeseen event.[6] While Catholic states were merrily driving out the Jesuits, Russia, a schismatic power, had welcomed the Fathers in its midst. After the annexation of the Polish provinces Catherine II numbered about two hundred members of the Society among her subjects. So far from expelling these excellent teachers, she urged them to carry on with their work. Her example was followed by Alexander I, and when the Grand Army entered Russia its officers were surprised to meet French Jesuits who were educating thousands of children. The "Russian province," to which the Society had now been reduced, continued to prosper during the Revolution and the Empire; it was governed by Father Karew as vice-general, and its numbers were swelled by brethren driven from the West. Questioned on several occasions as to what he thought of this astonishing survival, Pius VI gave contradictory answers, sometimes encouraging their efforts to the extent of allowing them to open a novitiate at Polotsk, and sometimes referring to them publicly as "rebels"—which indeed they were from the canonical point of view. He was obviously embarrassed.

Meanwhile the French Revolution broke out, and one of its unforeseen results was to modify the Society's reputation in the eyes of many European rulers. Events showed clearly that the suppression of the Jesuits had been one of the most brilliant victories of the philosophical and revolutionary spirit. What more reasonable therefore, in combating that spirit, than to call upon the Fathers? Thus from 1793 onwards there was talk in Italy of restoring to the sons of St. Ignatius their legal existence.

6. *The Church of the Classical Age: The Era of Great Splintering*, Volume 2, Chapter V, section 3.

178 One man had embodied that hope of resurrection, and had worked for its fulfilment with equal prudence and intelligence—St. Joseph Pignatelli (1737–1811). Scion of a great Italian aristocratic family, but born in Spain, he was one of the leaders of that unfortunate group of Jesuits who had spent some time in Corsica. Then he moved to Bologna, and his name was thereafter associated with the whole of this most delicate affair. The first step was taken at Parma, where Duke Ferdinand of Spain reopened some Jesuit colleges and even brought a number of Fathers from Russia. Despite the initial hostility of the Spanish king and his minister Godoï, who told the young duke that he must adopt towards this question a policy different from that of his father, and despite the opposition of Pope Pius VI, the enterprise succeeded. Father Pignatelli was appointed novice-master at Colorno, not far from Parma. This Jesuit province, dependent on that of Russia, lasted until Bonaparte's invasion liquidated the duchy of Parma; but even under French rule the Fathers, disguised as secular priests, were able to continue teaching. Meanwhile, simultaneously with the undertaking at Parma, contacts were made at Naples, and conversations started by Father Pignatelli with King Ferdinand with a view to the ultimate re-establishment of the Society.

More significant, perhaps, than these essays on the part of ruling princes was the permanence, and indeed growth, of the "Jesuit spirit" in the highest sense of the phrase. St. Ignatius's ideal of discipline, faith and self-sacrifice had manifestly survived all disasters. Some had devoted themselves to the task of keeping it alive and spreading it; others, in the midst of trial and tribulation, had discovered its power. In France the heroic Father de Clorivière[7] had managed at the height of the Terror to found and propagate a small clandestine congregation known as the Society of the Heart of Jesus and modelled on that of the Jesuits. At Louvain, in 1794, some young refugees (among whom were Tournely and de Broglie, two former pupils of M.

7. See Chapter I, section 9. On his part in the revival of the Society see the article "Clorivière et les Pères de la foi" in *Archivium historicum Societatis Jesu* (1952), by Father André Rayez.

Emery) had established a small society known as Priests of the Sacred Heart. In Italy, Niccolô Paccanari, a remarkable layman who once ran an exhibition of curios but was in fact a mystic, founded the Company of the Faith of Jesus at Spoleto in 1797. The Jesuits had refused to make it part of their own Society, but it derived none the less from St. Ignatius and the spirit of his *Exercises*; Pius VI, whom Paccanari met during the Pope's transfer from Rome to France, showed himself sympathetic. The Society of the Sacred Heart and the Company of the Faith then combined to form the Fathers of the Faith.[8] These latter spread throughout France, thanks to the work of the Abbé Varin de Solmon and of young Father Barat, brother of the celebrated founder of the Ladies of the Sacred Heart. It will also be remembered that the Fathers of the Faith, protected by Cardinal Fesch and favoured to some extent by Napoleon, were able to reopen colleges in France, until the Emperor dissolved them during his conflict with the Pope.

At the time of Pius VII's accession to the throne of Peter the situation was thus favourable to the Society. Himself a Benedictine, Chiaramonti was not a particular friend of the Jesuits; but he was well aware of the error committed by the Holy See in suppressing the most devoted of its auxiliaries. Soon after his election, therefore, when the Czar asked him formally to re-establish the Society of Jesus in his dominions, Pius gladly agreed, and a Brief to that effect was signed on March 7, 1801. A first step had been taken. The new general, Father Gruber, realized this fact, and one of his assistants went to Rome to beg the Pope for a complete restoration of the Society, while Father Pignatelli received the title of Italian Provincial. Taking advantage of the tentative work already accomplished at Naples, Pignatelli managed to reinstate the Society in Ferdinand's realm, though not without much difficulty and more or less open resistance. The papal Brief *Per alias* (July 30, 1804) officially re-created the Society in the Kingdom of Naples; its colleges

8. In 1804 Paccanari's Fathers regained their independence, but their founder was doomed to misfortune. Accused before the Holy Office, he was imprisoned in the castle of Sant' Angelo, and finally perished by the hand of an assassin.

180 were reopened and immediately filled with hundreds of students; and it was possible to begin setting up houses of retreat. Personal rivalries notwithstanding, the new province gave proof of wonderful vitality, until its dissolution less than a year later by Murat, the new king of Naples.

The impulse was now too strong to be halted or slowed down, even by the quarrel between the French Empire and the Holy See. Driven from Naples and officially banned from Parma, the Jesuits continued to make steady progress. Even the French police, who mistrusted them, could do nothing to prevent their expansion. The bishops of Orvieto, Tivoli and many other dioceses sent in turn for the Fathers, who disguised themselves as secular priests in order to run schools or preach missions. Pignatelli continued until his death in 1811 to direct the advance. His personal radiance counted for much in that secret growth which was preparing the future, and it was due to him that ex-King Charles Emmanuel IV of Piedmont-Sardinia became a lay brother at St. Andrew's on the Quirinal. In France, Father de Clorivière[9] took control of the Fathers of the Faith; and these crypto-Jesuits, closely watched by the police and unable to leave their house, waged an active struggle against Napoleon, helping the young Knights of the Faith[10] to distribute the Bull which excommunicated the Pope's persecutors, and making firm friends for themselves everywhere.

Such was the state of affairs when Pius VII returned to Rome. Petitions began to reach him from bishops all over Europe, asking him to re-establish the Society, to place them once again in charge of schools, to give them back their houses and missions. The desire seemed so general that it might be regarded as the very voice of the Church. Cardinal Pacca, who had formerly shown little sympathy for the Jesuits but had since profited by experience, urged the Pope to grant all these requests; he tells us in his memoirs that he himself considered that restoration of the Society would be a notable stage in the work of counter-revolution.

---

9. He had earlier been arrested by Fouché's police, and spent four years in prison.
10. With whom they must not be confused. See Chapter II, section 13.

On August 7, 1814, less than three months after his return, Pius VII promulgated the Bull *Sollicitudo*. In order to put back "on board Peter's barque, ceaselessly tossed by the billows, those strong and experienced rowers who would conquer the might of the waves," he rescinded Clement XIV's Bull, and invited the surviving members of the Society to reassemble and resume their work.

As it happened there were few survivors—certainly not more than eight hundred; but their vitality at once became apparent. In 1820 they numbered nearly two thousand, and more than six thousand in 1850. But Russia, strange to say, rounded upon them in 1815 and exiled them to Polotsk; then in 1820 the whimsical Alexander drove the Fathers from his empire. By that time, however, all the Catholic countries, excepting Austria, had seen them recover, if not the prominence they enjoyed before 1773, at least a considerable standing in the Church.

The reconstitution of the Society was of some historical importance from many points of view, giving back to the Holy See a loyal body of men, utterly devoted to its cause and of which it would soon have need. Throughout the nineteenth century and afterwards many Jesuits exerted a discreet but profound influence upon certain papal attitudes; and a proverb became current in Rome that "the Pope's pen-holders are Jesuits." The reappearance of the sons of St. Ignatius inevitably provoked reaction, for none could fail to recognize it as a notable gesture of counter-reformation. In France the Jesuits were soon made scapegoats for all the sins of the extremists; but this was altogether unfair, since the most fervent royalists, a majority of whom were Gallicans, were just as hostile as the liberals towards the Society. It is important to remember that the restoration of the Jesuits, by rousing opposition in two otherwise mutually hostile camps—revolutionary liberals and Gallican royalists—showed clearly that the religious counter-revolution did not coincide exactly with the political.

7. THE POLICY OF CONCORDATS

To strengthen the Sovereign Pontiff's authority, and to separate as far as possible the religious from the political counter-revolution, were Consalvi's principal and largely successful aims in the policy of concordats, one of the most important of his undertakings.

It was not only Rome that appeared in 1815 to call for restoration. The Church throughout Europe, and even throughout the world, needed to be reorganized. The situation, however, varied so much from one country to another that the task was infinitely complicated. In Austria and Spain, for example, the national Churches seemed to be very much as they had been before 1789; but wherever the French had passed great upheavals had taken place and rebuilding was necessary. Again, during his four years' imprisonment, first at Savona and later at Fontainebleau, the Pope had been isolated from Christendom; it was time for him to resume a firm grasp on the helm of Peter's barque. That is what the policy of concordats was intended to accomplish. Consalvi, with the full approval and support of Pius VII, handled it with that mixture of firmness and subtlety which was the outstanding feature of his character. Striving simultaneously against the determined partisans of Gallicanism, Josephism and Febronianism, as well as against the liberalo-revolutionary menace, knowing also when to yield on a secondary point but never on a matter of principle, he showed once more that keen sense of the real and the possible for which he is so greatly admired.

The means adopted to reorganize the Church and secure the Pope's authority was the concordat, a treaty negotiated between the Apostolic See and another sovereign State. Experience demonstrated the necessity of making sure that governments signing such an agreement would not abuse their rights and obtain an unfair advantage, as in the case of the Organic Articles and Melzi's decrees. Future concordats, therefore, must be narrower than the one signed by Bonaparte; advantage must be taken of the new state of affairs to show, if possible, more precision and firmness. Over the years concordats were worked out with so many countries that we must forgo an attempt to draw up a complete list.

In Italy the situation offered few difficulties. The peninsula, once more a mere "geographical expression," was again divided into at least a dozen States of relatively small importance, not to mention several petty principalities, and all these governments needed to strengthen their authority. It was, of course, no small task to carry on negotiations in so many "capitals," but the Holy See met with no force capable of effective opposition; the Jansenist and regalist elements of yesteryear were for the time being in eclipse. It was easy to discuss without passion the restitution of ecclesiastical goods and diocesan boundaries. One by one Piedmont-Sardinia, Naples and the Two Sicilies, the principalities of Lucca and Modena, the Lombard-Venetian kingdom, the duchies of Tuscany and Parma signed agreements, and nuncios were accredited to their rulers.

The most numerous and also the most delicate concordats were negotiated in Germany. There the situation was complicated, more difficult even than before 1789, since Protestant Prussia now had many Catholic subjects on the left bank of the Rhine and in erstwhile Polish territory. The old system of prince-bishops was in ruins—no misfortune, considering that those mitred lords had never showed themselves at all submissive to the Holy See—but the French, who had destroyed it, had been unable to reorganize the German Church. The project of a German concordat, as we have seen,[11] had come to nothing; in view of Napoleon's ambition the Pope had been unwilling to entrust the reordering of Catholicism in Germany to a man who had signed the Organic Articles. But the urgency of re-establishing a *modus vivendi* is proved by the fact that only six bishops survived, of whom five were septuagenarians. All the sovereigns were clearly anxious to be rid of that curious situation.

Difficulties, however, remained. A majority of governments were unwilling that the necessary reorganization should give the Holy See too

11. Chapter II, section 6.

much influence. This was quite natural in the Protestant States; without admitting that there was an anti-Catholic conspiracy, as has been maintained, it must be emphasized that in the autumn of 1817, on the occasion of the third centenary of the Reformation, Frederick William IV launched a Royal Appeal which disclosed his plan to absorb the Catholics into a unified Protestant Church. But even in Catholic territories there were a great many obstacles. Febronianism had not died with the submission and death of its originator. It was now incarnate in the person of Dalberg. We have met him before as coadjutor of Mainz before 1789 and paying court to Napoleon in order to obtain from him in 1806 the title Prince-Primate of Frankfurt. His skill had enabled him at the Congress of Vienna not only to obtain pardon for having collaborated with the fallen Emperor, but even to retain his primacy. Assisted by Wessenberg, formerly Vicar-General of Constance, Dalberg spent the remaining two years of his life working secretly against Rome.

It seems that this ambitious man, relying on a strong nationalist current in Germany, dreamed of creating a "National German Church," whose principles would have been derived from those of ecclesiastical Gallicanism and whose head would have been a largely independent Primate, none other than himself. This National Church, too, would have formed part and parcel of a Germanic constitution for which the patriots longed. Dalberg died in 1817, and Wessenberg lacked the ability to carry out such a scheme on his own. Thus, by utilizing the particularist instinct of all the German princes, Consalvi managed to avert the danger. He was helped in this struggle by St. Clement Hofbauer, the great Redemptorist, whom he had frequently met during the Congress of Vienna and whom he had appointed as a kind of secret emissary of the Apostolic See.

Such was the complex situation in which Consalvi's negotiations led to the signature of about a dozen German concordats. The first was concluded with Bavaria in 1818. One after another all the small German Catholic States fell into line and negotiated concordats, though often revealing Josephist and Febronian tendencies; in some cases also, after signing the treaty, they attempted to encroach on the rights of the Holy See, particularly by appointing bishops without reference to the Pope.

More remarkable is the fact that Protestant Prussia joined the procession of concordats. She did so for two reasons: because it was absolutely necessary to establish good relations with her Catholic subjects in the Rhineland, and because she was unwilling that her Polish subjects should be canonically dependent on Warsaw. Berlin's example was followed by lesser states: Hanover obtained a Bull four years later, and identical concordats were signed with Baden, Württemberg, the two Hesses and Saxony, as well as with the free cities of Lübeck, Frankfurt and Bremen.

None of these agreements was perfect; at Rome it was found that they restricted the powers of the Pope more than was desirable and that they allowed too much scope to the new ideas. Consalvi, however, justly replied (1) that it was of paramount importance that all States, both Catholic and Protestant, by signing these diplomatic instruments, had recognized the Holy See as the fount of all legitimacy in the Church; (2) that the danger of national Churches (Josephist and Febronian) had been averted; (3) that the Catholics of Germany, which had recently been in such turmoil, beheld "the revival of their dioceses under the life-giving breath of the papacy."

Moreover this success in a country more than half Protestant was no isolated achievement. Throughout his period as secretary of state Consalvi carried on negotiations in the Swiss cantons, where many delicate problems called for solution; and those discussions led to the signing of a concordat in 1828. Orthodox Russia presented fewer obstacles; a concordat regulating the canonical position of Catholics in Poland was signed as early as 1818. An agreement was very nearly reached with England, where Consalvi had made several lasting friendships during his stay in 1814. George III favoured such a plan, and showed his respect for the Holy See by paying the carriage on works of art removed by the French and now restored to Rome by the allies. Castlereagh too assented to the project. It failed, however, because the Anglicans in Parliament insisted that the king should control the appointment of bishops and that all papal documents entering the country should be subject to government approval. To the first of these stipulations Rome eventually agreed, but refused the second. Nevertheless, despite this setback, the negotiations had important consequences for the future, hastening the hour of Catholic Emancipation.[12]

Only two great countries stood aloof: two countries where the Church had had least to suffer and had retained more or less the positions they had held under the old regime. I refer, of course, to Austria and Spain, in both of which regalist, nationalist and to some extent anti-Roman tendencies survived. In Austria the Emperor Francis II at first appeared to favour a concordat, and during his visit to Rome in 1817 he actually promised to sign one. But Metternich was far less enthusiastic; above all, he was a determined foe of the Jesuits. The Legislative Committee under the guidance of Döllinger and Lorenz, both of them resolute Febronians and Josephists, raised numerous obstacles on points of detail, and the negotiations failed.

In Spain the situation was more surprising and more disturbing. The Cortes, meeting at Madrid in 1812, had voted for a constitution submitted to Ferdinand VII after his return from exile. It was drawn up "in the name of Almighty God, Father, Son and Holy Ghost, author and supreme legislator of society"; and one article stated that the religion of the Spanish nation is now, and always will be, Catholic, Apostolic and Roman, which alone is true. The nation protects it by wise and just laws, and forbids the practice of any other religion. In theory, nothing better could have been desired; but in fact things were not so simple. Anti-Roman feeling had long been powerful in Spain: it had been carefully fostered by Godoï, and the liberalo-nationalist elements were ready to continue on the same lines. There could be no question of a concordat in these circumstances, and Spain had to wait until the second half of the century for successful negotiations. Rather than recognize the Holy See's right of intervention in the religious affairs of Spain, Ferdinand VII preferred to embark straightway on a policy which identified spiritual with temporal interests, and to deal

12. See section 15.

with the clergy on a basis of unrestrained reaction. He soon paid dearly for his scheme.

Apart from these two exceptions, then, Consalvi's policy of concordats was successful. Its most obvious result was to arrest the ebb of those anti-Roman tendencies which had been all too manifest during the eighteenth century. Another consequence was that, in agreeing to recognize the rights of secular governments by narrowing its own, the Holy See displayed a broadmindedness far removed from the facile policy of reaction, restoration and counter-revolution then in vogue. By refraining from a demand for the return of all ecclesiastical property Rome was preparing the way for a clergy less attached to the goods of this world. In her policy lay the seed of a purer Church, more independent of governments and more exclusively concerned with her pastoral role. But many years would pass before it was understood that this was the way of salvation.

8. THE AFFAIR OF THE FRENCH CONCORDAT

NOTWITHSTANDING this tale of success, there was an unexpected setback. It occurred in a land where such an event could least have been anticipated—France, the realm of Louis XVIII, where the union of Throne and Altar was the alpha and omega of politics, and were veneration for the Pope, especially since his captivity at Fontainebleau was virtually unanimous. A new agreement was necessary in France: it was essential to restore order in ecclesiastical affairs after the long conflict which had disrupted them. The most delicate problem was that of the "refractory" bishops, those who had long ago rejected the Civil Constitution of the Clergy and who then, at the time of the Concordat of 1801, had refused to resign.[13] Thirteen of the original thirty-six were still alive, and continued to use the titles of their sees, whether or not those sees had been abolished. Nor

13. See Chapter II, section 5.

 was all well in the ranks of the concordatory episcopate. Many bishops of the *Ancien Régime*, whom Napoleon had reappointed, regarded their ex-constitutional colleagues as usurpers. Led by Mgr. Talleyrand-Périgord, former Archbishop of Rheims, they had made it quite plain to Cardinal Consalvi, during his stay at Paris in 1814, that they considered themselves true confessors of the faith, and they went so far as to hint that Pius VII had exceeded his rights in signing the Concordat. They all demanded cancellation of the "diabolical treaty" of 1801. Now Pius VII, during his imprisonment at Savona, had refused canonical investiture of many bishops, and some dioceses were therefore without a pastor. A new concordat was thus indispensable, and there was little doubt that it would be easily concluded.

In 1814 an Ecclesiastical Commission was set up, containing a majority of "extremist" bishops and other prelates. The minister Talleyrand had an old score to settle with the Holy See for having refused to bless his marriage with Mme. Grand, and he gladly seized the opportunity to make use of the bishops in resisting Rome. On the morrow of Waterloo the commission proposed outright to repeal the Concordat of 1801 and return to that of 1516. All the old dioceses were to be re-established, and the concordatory bishops replaced by new ones appointed according to the system of the *Ancien Régime*. When M. de Pressigny, the French ambassador, submitted these proposals to Consalvi, the secretary of state received him coldly; it was he in fact, he, the negotiator of the Napoleonic Concordat, who was being disowned. Pius VII let it be known that he could not agree that he had erred in signing the treaty with Bonaparte or that he had exceeded his rights in demanding the resignation of the bishops appointed before 1789. Consalvi therefore replied by asking for the retention of the concordatory bishops, the submission of thirteen "refractories" and, in addition, an assurance that the French clergy, instead of being paid by the State, would be endowed with capital funds. Louis XVIII, in order to show his goodwill, wrote personally to the thirteen bishops asking them to resign; and this they did, though not all with equal alacrity.

Talks were resumed in Rome at the beginning of 1816; but they were handled on the French side by a new and aspiring ambassador, the Comte de Blacas, who saw in the Concordat an opportunity for self-aggrandizement. After interminable discussions he managed to persuade the Holy See (1) that it was possible, without abrogating the Concordat of 1801, to state simply that it "ceased to have effect," (2) that it was also possible to declare the retention of concordatory bishops in their sees "with a few exceptions based on grave and legitimate causes," and (3) that the clergy would again have its capital endowment under the treaty of 1516. Although M. de Blacas wrote to Paris extolling himself for having thus won a splendid victory, the fact was that Consalvi had carried the day; he had saved the fundamentals of the 1801 Concordat and had secured financial independence for the Church. As regards the Organic Articles, a typically Roman compromise was achieved whereby they were abrogated "in so far as they are contrary to the laws and doctrine of the Church." Thus all was going well. A French move to insert a clause on "the freedom of the Gallican Church" was not followed up, while the papacy's endeavour to prevent ecclesiastical peers from having to swear to a charter proclaiming equality of cults ended with a non-committal formula. Finally, on July 19, 1817, by the Bull *Ubi primum*, Pius VII ratified the new Concordat.

It was now that trouble began. The agreement had been negotiated by three men: the king, his prime minister the Duc de Richelieu and the ambassador Blacas; other ministers had not even been kept informed. It seemed unlikely that acceptance of the Concordat would meet with opposition in the political climate of the Chamber, which was zealously royalist and Catholic. But just as the Concordat's existence became known, the Chamber had to be dissolved, and its successor contained a majority of constitutionals and liberals. Portalis, keeper of the seals, whose uncle had negotiated the Concordat of 1801, observed that since the Napoleonic agreement was part of the law, it could be annulled only by statute. The Gallicans started a campaign in the Chamber, as well as in the press, supported by liberals who were only too glad of this opportunity to create a breach in the alliance of

 Throne and Altar. The government was obliged to work out a new project which formally repealed the Napoleonic agreement, invoked the right "inherent in the Crown to appoint archbishops and bishops throughout the realm," and recalled the king's right "to authorize the execution of Bulls and to transform pontifical acts into State laws in order to render them applicable." This was Gallicanism pure and simple. Lastly the project suggested that France should have seven archbishoprics and thirty-five bishoprics, and that the Church of France should be endowed, and no longer salaried.

The scheme met with unanimous opposition. Gallicans found it insufficiently anti-Roman; the provinces were indignant at the failure to restore them all their dioceses; the liberals went about complaining that the government was in effect reviving the clerical order recognized by the *Ancien Régime*. M. de Marcellus, a right-wing deputy, asked the Pope whether he could in conscience vote for the measure. He was told that he could not. Louis XVIII, as "supreme legislator," would have had the right to sign this bill without approval of the Chambers; but he dared not do so. Pending a solution, Consalvi had a *Motu proprio* signed by Pius VII in 1819, declaring the Concordat of 1801 temporarily in force. Three years later, as a result of further negotiations more skillfully conducted, the Napoleonic treaty was very slightly modified: a Bull re-established fourteen archbishoprics and sixty-six bishoprics—one for each *département*, a little fewer than in pre-revolutionary days. This "temporary" arrangement lasted until 1905.

9. THRONE AND ALTAR IN FRANCE

THE new regime consolidated by the Bourbons in France gave official sanction to the alliance of Throne and Altar. Article VI of the Charter published on June 4, 1814, declared Catholicism the state religion, not merely "the religion of the majority of Frenchmen" as under the Empire. Indeed it appeared natural that the Restoration should be at once both religious and political, since the Revolution had overthrown the Church together with the monarchy. The king, seated once again on the throne of St. Louis, of Louis XIV and of Louis XVI, was inevitably "Most Christian." A vast majority of the French Church was wholly sympathetic towards such ideals. Frightened by bloody memories of the Terror, the clergy, says Lacordaire, were "royalist to the teeth." Moreover they had "lived for centuries in the shadow of the House of Bourbon, which honoured and protected them; with the Bourbons they had mounted the scaffold or gone into exile..." It was hardly surprising therefore that French priests looked upon the white banner as a religious emblem. In particular, almost the entire episcopate entertained for the throne a degree of reverence and affection which was often expressed in fulsome terms.

Catholicism thus officially recovered the moral eminence it had enjoyed before 1789. True, it had not been given back its civil status—a loss which offended many parish priests—but in other respects it had little of which to complain. Not only were the churches reopened for worship, but Beugnot's regulations imposed the observation of Sunday, revived the custom of open-air processions, suppressed divorce and instituted military chaplaincies. In all circumstances the authorities showed the greatest respect towards the clergy; bishops took precedence of all others on state occasions, and invariably wore full canonicals. The home missions, which were then on the eve of expansion, assumed the character of a public institution. They began with a procession headed by a picket of cavalry and followed by all the civil and military officials. Salvoes of artillery accompanied the singing of hymns; and the missioners, not to be outdone in this matter of civility, took every opportunity to associate political fervour with the religious enthusiasm of the crowds. These outbursts of collective excitement sometimes led to the molestation of ex-juror priests or of ex-Jacobins who were deemed insincere in their repentance. For, as always happens when the Church is too closely linked with the civil power, the revival of respect for Catholicism, though good in itself, was associated with an endeavour to enlist conscience on the side of political intentions, an endeavour which must be viewed with the gravest suspicion. Religious authorities are always tempted to employ means furnished by the State for the triumph of their cause—or what they believe to be their cause. The clergy of the Restoration did not regard official pressure as unworthy of their spiritual mission, and the civil authorities naturally took advantage of this view.

Intellectual influences ran parallel with regimentation in the field of conscience: the schools, upon which Napoleon had foisted a militaristic discipline, retained his methods in clerical dress. Pupils went through their daily routine at the call of a bell instead of a drum, and their programme included Mass and Compline. Irreligious and even anti-clerical professors in the higher grades of their profession were dismissed. Plays were banned from the theatre if considered offensive to Christian morality or to the Church. And the *Journal de Débats*, alarmed by the enormous popularity of books by Rousseau and Voltaire, suggested that the State should declare itself heir of those two mischievous authors, with a view to destroying their works and forbidding further reprints!

An institution known as the *Congrégation*[14] appeared to symbolize and cement this alliance between Throne and Altar. It was derived from a group founded in 1801 by Father Delpuits and formed into a secret society, a sort of counter-Freemasonry, by Bertier de Sauvigny. Banned by Fouché's police, it was resurrected in 1814 as a religious body by the Abbé Legric-Duval and Father Ronsin, and at the political level by Mathieu de Montmorency. Its leaders were the former Knights of the Faith, who had earlier striven against Napoleon's tyranny and helped to publicize the papal Bulls. Known henceforward as *La Grande Congrégation*, with headquarters in the Rue du Bac at Paris, it soon attracted the élite of Catholic royalists, and the most illustrious names in France appeared on its registers. Were these devoted servants of Throne and Altar the secret agents of Catholic-legitimist reactions, as their enemies declared? Were they united by oaths worthy of Freemasons?

14. This name has been left in its French form throughout, in order to avoid possible confusion when the English word "Congregation" is used alone with reference to a religious institute or to one of the Roman ministries. (TRANSLATOR)

Had they, as the Vicomte de Carné reported, secret signs for mutual recognition? It seems that, as in the case of its seventeenth-century predecessors, the Company of the Blessed Sacrament, many legends grew up around the *Congrégation*; some went so far as to credit it with forty-eight thousand members, though the true number seems never to have exceeded three thousand. No one, however, can doubt that it wielded considerable political influence, including as it did eighteen Peers of France, several ministers, the prefect of police and many other distinguished persons. That influence, moreover, took the form of employing current circumstances to advance the Catholic cause.

Thus for fifteen years, throughout the period commonly known as the Restoration, the attitude of the Church in France was based on close collaboration between the spiritual and the temporal. But the extent of this collaboration varied. At first, immediately after the king's return, the alliance was vehemently proclaimed, and revealed itself in an often regrettable share on the part of many Catholics in counter-revolutionary reaction. Louis XVIII, however, was a man of prudence and moderation, suspicious of all extremists. Ultra-royalist bishops who had returned from exile full of arrogance and resentment appealed to him no more than did violent liberals. He meant to govern hand in hand with the moderates, typical of whom was Decazes, his "dear son Decazes," upon whom he conferred a dukedom when, after eighteen months, the assassination of the Duc de Berry necessitated his dismissal. During this short period clerico-legitimist propaganda was muted; but it grew more vociferous with the advent of M. de Villèle. An excuse was found to drive the Abbé Grégoire from the Chamber; favourites of the *Congrégation* were given office; the home missions received official encouragement; and a determined struggle began against secret societies. French intervention in Spain (1823) marked the triumph of this policy, which was enthusiastically supported by the Chamber but viewed with anxiety by the ageing Louis XVIII.

It was destined to continue during the reign of his brother Charles X, formerly Comte d'Artois. A droll and obstinate character, fondly attached to his own authority but subject to the influence of a group of extremists, Charles possessed the ardent faith of a convert, a faith very different from his brother's religious scepticism. The revival of the coronation ceremony at Rheims, with all its traditional rites, was sufficient evidence of the direction in which he would move. In this new reign confusion of the spiritual and temporal assumed the force of a byword, and many incidents revealed official pressure in the sphere of religion. A climax was reached in 1825 with the passing of the Law on Sacrilege, making theft of sacred vessels and profanation of the Sacred Host capital crimes. Meanwhile such distinguished Catholics as Chateaubriand in the Chamber of Peers and the Abbé de la Mennais in the press vainly protested against these measures, which were bringing hatred and contempt upon the religion in whose name they were supposed to be taken. The government of Charles X dared not apply them; it was more than enough that an assembly had been found to pass the law.

10. ADVANTAGES AND DANGERS OF AN ALLIANCE

NEVERTHELESS it would be false and unjust to think that this alliance of Throne and Altar did the Church nothing but harm; quite the contrary.

Following a long series of tragic events, she had to undertake a task of reconstruction on many fronts, and State protection enabled her to accomplish it.

The most striking aspect of that achievement was the reform of the clergy. In 1815 there were said to be fifteen thousand vacancies in the parochial service. Parish priests and curates numbered only thirty-seven thousand, and no more than six thousand of them were young men ordained since 1801. Moreover that clergy, though possessing real virtues, was intellectually below standard. In the seminaries which it had been possible to reopen since the Concordat, teaching was backward, preoccupied with refutation of Jansenist and Quietist errors, but ignoring contemporary problems; busy discussing the legality of loans at interest at a time when capitalism on the grand scale was emerging, but ignoring recent works of exegesis and ecclesiastical history, which later hardly entered into the curriculum at all.

Reform was consequently indispensable. Undertaken with remarkable patience and intelligence during the years of the legitimist monarchy, it was continued for a long time thereafter; not until about 1845 did its full results become apparent. Official steps were taken to encourage it. These included a substantial increase in the salaries of the clergy, larger sums earmarked for public worship, permission for the bishops to found junior seminaries, and the creation of scholarships for the benefit of seminarians. But the real architects of this work were the bishops, those Restoration bishops who are said to have been too much concerned with defence of the monarchy at the expense of their duties as pastors. The importance of their efforts is only just beginning to be appreciated. Using such influence as they enjoyed—many of them sat in the Parliament, the Council of State and the Privy Council—they laboured with a pastoral zeal reminiscent of their seventeenth-century predecessors. The task was slow and difficult. For instance, it was not until 1820 that they were able to fill the vacancies caused by death; but then the situation was reversed. Between 1820 and 1828 the surplus of ordinations was two thousand two hundred and eighty-nine, and at the latter date there were twelve hundred students in the senior and twenty thousand in the junior seminaries. The average annual number of ordinations rose to three thousand. No less impressive was the revival of religious orders and congregations. Starting, as we have seen,[15] under the Empire, the movement gained strength in the Restoration period.[16]

The third great feature of this work was the resumption of the home missions. We have noticed their shortcomings, or rather we have noticed how the regime directed their energies to the service of its own propaganda; but we must not forget that they were still pre-eminently pastoral and achieved some valuable success. Inspired with new life during the Revolution by the

15. Chapter II, section 9.

16. See Volume 2, Chapter VIII, section 9.

 Abbé Linsolas and his rivals,[17] expanded on the morrow of the Concordat, but soon afterwards halted by imperial tyranny, they no longer existed in 1815. As soon as circumstances permitted, the Abbé Rauzan of Bordeaux devoted himself to the task, of reviving them. In 1816, together with the abbés Liutard and Legris-Duval, he founded the Society of French Missioners. The methods chosen were perhaps nearer to those of St. Alphonsus de Liguori and St. Paul of the Cross than to those of M. Vincent or M. Olier, inasmuch as vulgar sensationalism was not altogether eschewed. But the labour of missioners in groups of four or five, concentrating upon single districts for a fortnight at a time, certainly bore fruit. These men preached not only in the churches but also in the open air, as well as making contact with individuals; and it was not uncommon at the end of a mission to see forty thousand people at Holy Communion. French Missioners, Picpus Fathers, Jesuits, Redemptorists and, in several dioceses, secular priests, all did fruitful work in the ancient Christian glebe.

One fact is certain: the spiritual reawakening begun in 1799 continued and spread during the whole period of the Restoration. Despite the picture afforded by the liberal press, France as a whole was drawing nearer to God. No doubt a majority of the middle classes retained the spirit of Rousseau and Voltaire, and would continue to do so as long as the Catholic faith appeared to be associated with absolute monarchy. No doubt the higher nobility had few sacramental relations with the religion they protected. But its young élite, whom we have seen emerging under the Empire, was about to do great things; it included those who were to work with Lacordaire and Ozanam in the early years of the fight for social principles. From this point of view the much-maligned *Congrégation* did some useful work. Not only did it help to rouse in the upper classes a consciousness of truths they had well-nigh forgotten, but its numerous charitable undertakings were by no means ineffective, contributing to the evolution of a new climate which gave religion fresh opportunities.

17. See Chapter I, section 12.

Unfortunately there is another side to this picture. The faith is not well adapted to situations in which religion is one element of a political system, especially if that system purposes to dominate men's minds. As invariably happens, the pressure of conformity led to falsehood. Duplicity ran from top to bottom of society, the same causes producing the same effects. Louis XVIII himself secretly preferred Horace to the Gospel, and admitted, as Lamartine afterwards said, that "his education had freed his intellect from the official superstitions of his cradle"; but he continued to take part in religious processions with all the appearances of heartfelt piety. In governmental quarters there was more than one Tartuffe for every devout Montmorency. Maréchal Souk had lately enjoyed himself pillaging Spanish churches, and yet at the ministry of war he fitted out a private chapel which he visited every day in full uniform. A certain official well known as a "Theophilanthropist" or atheist never failed to invoke divine Providence and declare that without religion there would be no human society. A barrister or physician would go to Mass hugging a large book, in order not to offend his clients; sometimes the book, though bound in black shagreen, was certainly not a missal.... Even children learned hypocrisy, rebellion and worse from official conformity; Lacordaire asserts that at one *lycée*, where daily Mass was obligatory, thirty youngsters went together to Communion in order to obtain consecrated wafers with which to seal their letters. 197

It was not only through this deplorable influence on conscience that the excessive alliance of Throne and Altar proved harmful. Frenchmen have always disliked regimes that set out to dominate the interior man. Could they accept one marked in its origins with the signs of defeat and whose blunders were innumerable? Was it right that the Church should appear to link her fortunes with those of the regime? A legend took shape at about this time, and persisted for very many years: it told of a secret society directed by the *Congrégation* and the Jesuits, whose firm purpose was to enslave the people of France and "take them back to the Middle Ages." Unfortunately appearances seemed to give this legend an air of truth. Dictatorial priests, missioners too devoted to legitimist policies, an episcopate drawn almost exclusively from the nobility and often arrogant—all these did immense harm to the Catholic cause. There is something infinitely afflicting in the spectacle of the Church at this date, so brave and so energetic in her effort to re-Christianize France, yet paying for the fall of the regime because the great movement of spiritual reconquest appeared too often, in the eyes of the masses, as a political undertaking intended to repress them.

II. NEO-GALLICANISM

THE alliance of Throne and Altar brought with it another consequence harmful to the Church, the rebirth of Gallicanism. It might have been thought that this problem was a thing of the past, since Catholicism was no longer the religion of the State. But the ancient Gallican theories too had been gathered into the granaries of the *Ancien Régime*. Many bishops remained firmly attached to the celebrated "liberties of the Gallican Church," all the more so as Rome clearly intended to exercise stricter control over national Churches. Parliamentary Gallicanism too was still alive. Some politicians saw in the latter an opportunity to disarm liberal opposition by directing its spleen against the Holy See. Above all, many regarded it as a means of subjecting Church to State and thus strengthening the forces of absolutism. Restoration France, then, witnessed the emergence of neo-Gallicanism, which, though looking back to Louis XIV, employed the authoritarian and State-socialist methods inherited from Napoleon.

The leading theorist of Gallicanism was the illustrious orator Mgr. Frayssinous, author of *Frais principes de l'Eglise gallicane*. He was as yet a moderate and declared that he wished to defend Gallican liberties "without in any way detracting from the true greatness of the Holy See." Not all Gallicans, however, exercised the same restraint, and there developed in the Church of France a spirit of suspicion, almost of hostility, towards Rome. Bossuet's Four Articles, the charter of traditional Gallicanism, were restored to honour and taught once again in seminaries and law schools. Articles began to reappear in some sections of the Catholic press, explaining that the Pope could do nothing in the universal Church without the assent of a Council, and that in any case the Gallican Church possessed immemorial and sacrosanct privileges. Mgr. Frayssinous declared ultramontanism to be a subject "wholly out of date, harmless by dint of its absurdity." The Bishop of Strasbourg, in order to excuse himself for having allowed the Jesuits to open a college in his diocese, seriously proclaimed that the Fathers were called by Providence to rebuild the monarchy on solid foundations. In 1826 fourteen French archbishops and bishops went so far as to sign a joint pronouncement qualifying the papacy's right of intervention in political affairs for spiritual reasons.

The French Church thus found itself divided between Gallicans and ultramontanists—strange consequence of so harmonious an understanding between Altar and Throne! It is against this background that one must view the problem of education, which was to be the occasion of so many conflicts. In 1815, when the entire Napoleonic heritage was regarded with detestation, the monopoly enjoyed by the *Université* was abolished by statute. Simultaneously the government proceeded to an experiment in decentralization: the *Université de France* gave place to seventeen separate *universités*, the Grand Master being substituted by a Royal Council of Public Instruction under the presidency of a bishop. This experiment, however, was quickly abandoned, and before the year was out the monopoly had been revived. On this point, as on many others, the legitimate monarchy was content to follow in the footsteps of the tyrant. In 1821 the office of Grand Master was restored, and in the following year was conferred upon Mgr. Frayssinous. Reaction against the nationalization of education was thus the work not only of liberals, but also of ultramontanists, who saw in the monopoly a means of furthering Gallican theories, and were thereby led to defend scholastic freedom. La Mennais, for example, was shocked that anyone "should credit the government with a right to enslave the reason of a whole society by taking control of instruction."

In point of fact the monopoly was not absolute. It did not extend to primary schools, since the government was not much interested in the education of the lower classes; the Brothers of the Christian Schools were allowed a free hand, as in Napoleon's day. It was mainly with secondary education that the authorities were concerned: the imperial *lycées*, where the future governmental hierarchy received its training, became colleges and were strictly subjected to the monopoly, although bishops were allowed to open their own junior seminaries, some of which they entrusted to the Jesuits. This arrangement, however, soon raised difficulties; for many families, both Catholic and liberal, preferred to send their sons to the junior seminaries and religious schools rather than to the *lycées*, where morality was believed to be lax.

This cause of dispute interlocked with another, the restoration in France of the Society of Jesus. Objective truth compels us to admit that the French Jesuits hardly deserved the pre-eminence granted them by frenzied popular opinion. In 1829 they numbered only one hundred and eight priests and two hundred and twelve coadjutors. They controlled eight colleges, in which, as they themselves admitted, the teaching staff was far from having regained the qualities it possessed in 1762 (the date of their expulsion), but in which their disciplinary methods were highly successful. Their missions were few and far between. Why were they chosen as scapegoats? They were targets of two kinds of enemies: the liberals, heirs of the *philosophes* and of the Revolution, who saw the reappearance of the sons of St. Ignatius as a defeat of their principles; and the Gallicans, in whose eyes they embodied the most detestable form of ultramontanism. A campaign was mounted against them, and its strength steadily increased. It was said that the Fathers were the true directors of the *Congrégation*, and through it of the whole regime; according to *Le Journal des Débats* they had organized a "mystical Masonry" with millions of adherents. Béranger's famous song was on all lips: "Black men, whence come ye? We come from underground...."

After the accession of Charles X the most absurd rumours were current: the king was affiliated to the Society and said Mass in secret; the Jesuit house at Montrouge was a fortress where no fewer than fifty thousand Jesuits were trained, not in the *Exercises* of St. Ignatius but in the use of firearms and artillery; an underground tunnel connected it with the Tuileries; and so on. From this period dates the custom of using the word "Jesuit" in that pejorative and almost insulting sense which is all too familiar.

The most violent attacks on the Society, however, were made not by liberals, but by Gallican Catholics. Poets such as Barthélemy and Méry revived Boileau's satire in *Jésuites de Rome à Paris*. The Comte de Montlosier, an Auvergnat, made a speciality of such venomous assaults. Mean and stubborn, ponderous in style but with occasional flashes of wit, he directed against the Fathers the heavy salvoes of his *Mémoire à consulter sur un système religieux et politique tendant à renverser la religion, la société et le trône* (1826). This work contained the most preposterous statements: that Louis XIV was an honorary member of the Society; that Saint-Sulpice, "as everyone knows," was a Jesuit foundation; that in every ward of the great cities there was a Jesuit centre for spying on the faithful. The implication was that the sons of St. Ignatius sought to impose their authority on the whole of France, especially on the monarchy, as well as to destroy the liberties of the Gallican Church and subjugate it to Rome.

Such attacks, as can be imagined, won enthusiastic liberal support. *Le Journal des Débats* referred to Montlosier as the "torch of France." A combined liberal-Gallican offensive was launched against the Society. When M. de Montlosier denounced the Jesuits to the Court of Paris, the latter decided partially in his favour by declaring its own incompetence but recalling that edicts against the Society had still the force of law in France. His petition to the Peers on the same subject was taken into account. The liberal party won many seats at the elections in 1827, and the prime minister, Martignac, thought to cajole them by sacrificing the Jesuits. He seized an opportunity to settle in favour of the State the delicate problem of secondary education, and two ordinances were signed in 1828. One of these subjected to the *Université* monopoly all scholastic establishments belonging "to an unauthorized religious congregation" (i.e. to the Society of Jesus); the other limited the number of pupils admissible to ecclesiastical schools and junior seminaries, and made the opening of new schools of this type dependent on government approval.

There was considerable indignation throughout the Church in France,[18] and those responsible for the ordinances were likened to Julian the Apostate or Saint-Just. Several bishops, even among those who were Gallican at heart, protested against measures which restricted their activity. Mgr. de Quélen delivered to the king a memorial signed by seventy-three members of the episcopate. Cardinal de Clermont-Tonnerre disdainfully refused to see the Grand Master of the *Université*, who had asked for an interview. La Mennais plunged into the fray with a book entitled *Des progrès de la Révolution et de la guerre contre l'Église*, in which he described the monopoly of education as a "tyranny unknown to the world before Bonaparte" and a "violation of the most sacred rights conceivable on earth." Thus began the struggle for freedom of education which was destined to reach its full fury some years later.

12. THE DILEMMA OF THE CHURCH AND THE "THIRD TERM"

THE danger of collusion between the Church and the counter-revolutionary system was quickly apparent. All those who, in every land, would accept neither the international order imposed by the Holy Alliance nor the legitimist regimes that flourished almost everywhere, soon perceived that this politico-religious union was the weak point in the system. They hurried to denounce it, and their propaganda represented the Church as the ally and accomplice of reaction in every shape and form. Unfortunately too many facts seemed to prove them right.

18. So much so that the authorities dared not close the Jesuit houses. The Fathers were left in possession and simply disguised themselves as secular priests.

In this connection we may cite two notable examples. In France the restoration of monarchy had failed, as was inevitable, to make all yesterday's revolutionaries and all Napoleon's loyal adherents out-and-out royalists at a single stroke. From the start there was opposition; it was reduced to silence in the first year by fear of the White Terror, but it quickly reappeared, assumed growing importance, won seats in the Chamber and eventually constituted a force most embarrassing to the government. Recruited from among the well-to-do middle classes (particularly the lawyers) who disliked seeing the nobility becoming arrogant once again, from among intellectuals reared on the teaching of the *philosophes*, and from among half-pay officers, it was certainly managed to some extent by Freemasonry. The latter had been reorganized in 1815; it still enjoyed secret and powerful protection, and it was reinforced about 1820 by the *Charbonnerie*, an energetic and audacious French branch of the *Carbonaria*. This opposition published its own newspaper, *Le Constitutionel*, which had no fewer than twenty thousand subscribers and was read by all sorts of influential people. It had also its ringleaders, its writers and its fashionable circles.

Now this opposition at once perceived that the alliance of Throne and Altar was disliked by the French people, among whom anti-clericalism has always found a measure of sympathy. Moreover the majority of "liberals" were convinced Voltaireans if not atheists. It was not safe to make a frontal attack on the political regime; on the other hand it was quickly apparent that anti-clerical satire provoked no reaction from the police. This therefore was the direction in which the liberals launched their offensive, striking at the nobility through the clergy, at the ministers through the episcopate. If they could destroy the Church, they would succeed in bringing down the whole edifice. Hence during these years, which one might have been tempted to regard as plainly well disposed, there was a flood of anti-clericalism such as France had never before experienced. Every day *Le Constitutionel* fed its readers with an irreligious article, often so dull that the paper's editors nicknamed it "the silly article." Lampoons and satirical booklets circulated in large numbers, together with cartoons repeating eighteenth-century jokes on such topics as nuns, priests' housekeepers and confession. After fifteen years of propaganda the common people were firmly convinced that the whole Church was the enemy of freedom.

In Italy a similar result was obtained by somewhat different means. As well as being "liberal"—that is, hostile to the petty despotic regimes that had been established in most parts of the country—the opposition was also nationalist: it wanted to unify the peninsula, though it did not know how or in what form that unity could be achieved. This movement also very quickly adopted an attitude of hostility towards the Church. Originally there was no such enmity; the resistance offered by the Pope and most of the clergy to the French forces of occupation had predisposed the average man in their favour, but there was a rapid change. The *Carbonaria*, for instance, the most active and most important of the sects that swarmed in Italy at that time, had at the outset no trace of irreligion. But its character altered under the influence (1) of Freemasonry, (2) of elements descended from regalist and anti-Roman Jansenism, and (3) of men imbued with the old philosophical ideas, who believed that the present Church-State forms of society should give place to organisms founded on nature. Thenceforward the *Carbonaria* worked against the Church. As in France so also in other countries it denounced the alliance of clericalism and the civil power. Rome became the target for its shafts—Rome, whose States cut Italy in two; Rome, where the old regime appeared to have been re-established more completely than ever; Rome, too, where the police were less strict and vigilant than in the Kingdom of the Two Sicilies. About 1830, just as the Italian nationalist movement (later known as the *Risorgimento*) was becoming widespread, many of its adherents saw the Church as an adversary of national aspirations.

The Church at once found herself in a dilemma. Her enemies seemed to be identical with those who sought to overthrow the established order. The truth, however, as Cardinal Consalvi realized, was not quite so simple. For in various parts of Europe and elsewhere those liberal and nationalist ideas which appeared hostile to the Catholic cause were embraced and stoutly defended by Catholics.

In Belgium, Catholics and liberals, though disagreeing on the subject of religion, united in singing the well-known refrain: "I am not a Dutchman, and I do not wish to be." Led by their bishops, they regarded with suspicion everything done by the government at The Hague, accused the "Fundamental Law" of encroaching on their rights, boycotted the state schools and objected to the suppression of teaching congregations.

In Ireland the legitimist order, modification of which was forbidden by the principles of the Holy Alliance, condemned the ancient people of St. Patrick to bear the yoke of Britain, by whom they had been deprived of their most fertile territory and, since the Test Act, barred from civil or military employment. Refusal by the British Parliament to repeal the Test Act twice provoked the wrath of Ireland, which was aggravated by a lamentable economic situation. Numerous murders were followed by savage reprisals; curfew was imposed at dusk; and police raids were common throughout the island. But Ireland never abandoned her dream of liberty.

The situation was also grave in Poland, and there it was possible to see even more clearly in what difficulty the Church found herself. The whole area annexed by Russia was long subjected to a campaign intended to wipe out national traditions, a campaign that grew in severity under Alexander I. Polish resistance steadily increased, especially among the Ruthenians with the bishops at their head. An explosion seemed imminent. What would Rome do? Alexander I was looked upon as one of the pillars of order in Europe; none had been more active in restoring the rights of the Holy See, which was therefore unwilling to quarrel with him. Notwithstanding opposition on the part of Consalvi, Mgr. Siestrzencewiecz, a catspaw of the Czar, obtained the title "Primate of the Catholic Church in Russia," though without any special powers of jurisdiction. But such an appointment meant little to the Catholics of Poland who mourned their vanished freedom.

On the other side of the world Catholics compelled the Church to make reluctant choice between the established order and the new forces of nationalism and liberty. The vast territories owned by Spain in America rose against her. One after another, almost simultaneously, the ancient colonies

 Peru, Bolivia, Colombia, Venezuela and Mexico won their independence, and Catholics were in the forefront of that struggle for freedom. What attitude should the Church adopt? By supporting the rebels she would seem to accept the new liberal and nationalist ideas. By refusal, on the other hand, she risked alienating Latin-American Christendom, which was so firm in faith and so devoted to the Catholic cause. The Church's dilemma was unmistakable, and in order to escape from it, Cardinal Consalvi opened negotiations with the young South American States in the last months of Pius VII's reign.

The way, then, was far from easy: the *gelanti* cardinals in Rome and the legitimist bishops of France were mistaken in imagining that the future of the Church could be assured by mutual support of Throne and Altar and by the maintenance throughout Europe of the system adopted in 1815 by the victorious allies at the Congress of Vienna. The revolutionary hydra reappeared as early as 1820 in Spain, where Riego compelled the king to restore the constitution of 1812; then in Portugal, where a liberal general obliged John VI to summon a Cortes; then at Naples, where the *Carbonari*, led by Father Minichini, drove King Ferdinand from power; then again in Piedmont, where Victor Emmanuel I abdicated rather than recognize the revolution. True, these early attempts proved abortive, but they were none the less ominous.

Force had been employed to restore order in each case; yet the continued application of such high-handed methods was dubious, to say the least. Britain was becoming more and more hostile to military intervention of this kind. When the Greeks revolted against the Ottoman Empire and the Turks assassinated the Orthodox patriarch as he came from celebrating Mass on Easter Sunday, Metternich declared himself opposed to any manifesto by the Christian powers against a "legitimate government." Public opinion, however, throughout the West swelled the indignation of the British Foreign Office, and after months of heroic effort the independence of Greece was an accomplished fact (1821–1822). Trouble began in France; it became more acute after the foundation of the *Charbonnerie* by Bazard, Bûchez and

Flottard. There were conspiracies at Belfort, La Rochelle and Saumur; in each case the police intervened and the conspirators were executed, crying to the last: "Vive la liberté!" But there was no certainty that the government would always be stronger than its opponents, and the prevailing unrest was accompanied by a growth of anti-clericalism.

The Church thus found herself in a serious dilemma, from which it was not clear how she could escape. She had either to remain associated with the legitimist system and the Holy Alliance (which an honest consideration of the facts showed to be weaker than appeared), or she must come to some agreement with the young liberal and nationalist forces which strove to change the established order while openly declaring their hostility to Rome and even to religion. At this juncture a handful of men in various parts of Europe conceived the idea of rescuing the Church from her predicament by means of a "third term," which can be stated as follows. Instead of opposing the new forces of liberalism, the Church should reach an understanding with them, uphold them and make them serve God's cause. Unbelievers would be defeated on their own ground, and the Church would recover her influence with the masses which she was now on the way to losing.

Such were the theories elaborated at Turin, in circles frequented by Count Cesare Balbo (1789–1853), a fervent Catholic reared on Dante, and by his young friend the Abbate Vincenzo Gioberti (1801–1852), well known for his racy eloquence. The novelist Manzoni, illustrious author of *I Promessi Sposi*, and the dramatist Silvio Pellico were in close touch with them. They called themselves neo-Guelphs—Guelphs in memory of their great forerunners who had sided with the Pope during the medieval struggle between Empire and papacy. Keenly patriotic, and determined to drive the Austrians from Lombard-Venetian territory, they wanted the Church and the Catholic religion to be the foundation of a united Italy that was striving to be born. In the federation of which they dreamed the Pope would hold the place belonging to him by right—the first place—in complete independence. Opposed in this respect to the *Carbonari* and other liberals, they differed likewise as to choice of means. To the conspiracies and insurrections whose disastrous results were all too evident they preferred the lawful process of convincing men's minds. This small group counted for little in the years before 1830; but thereafter its importance rapidly increased.

In France the nationalist problem did not arise; the new ideas found voice on the question of liberty. They proceeded from very different and sometimes unexpected sources. The fountain head of Catholic liberalism was undoubtedly Chateaubriand, at that time French ambassador at Rome and apparently a strict legitimist. In *Le Génie du Christianisme* he had written: "Christianity is opposed in spirit and determination to arbitrary power." In his preface to a new edition of the *Essai sur la Révolution* he declared: "I shall never again become an unbeliever until someone proves to me that Christianity is incompatible with liberty.... It is a religion of liberty." Far less celebrated than Chateaubriand, and today most unjustly ignored, was Baron Eckstein, a naturalized Danish Jew. Almost single-handed he edited a review, *Le Catholique*, in which he upheld the rights of the human spirit against all constraint, vehemently criticized those who "organized a convenient servility," and advised Christians not to rely upon governments for the triumph of their cause. Similar ideas were germinating in the minds of young men (e.g., the future Abbé Lacordaire) who had returned to the faith for altogether personal reasons, and who did not recognize in the contemporary Church that ideal which had caused them to live again in Christ. But the group most active in the promotion of these theories was one that published a small newspaper entitled *Le Mémorial catholique*. Most of its members were disciples of Joseph de Maistre, but they inherited from the author of *Soirées de Saint-Pétersbourg* not so much his condemnation of the modern world as the mighty impulse that was driving them towards a future of enlightenment, when Christianity would be the foundation of human society. Unlike so many complacent admirers of the past, they felt a deep sympathy for their own age, its men and its affairs. Their gaze was fixed upon tomorrow. The Catholicism for which they looked was infinitely wider than that of all the conformists who lay like a heavy weight upon the Church; that much was clear in their concentration upon the critical sciences, German exegesis, the study of oriental languages and indeed the whole current of ideas. Cautiously, almost timidly at first, they extolled the separation of religion and politics, of Church and monarchy. They believed that the cause of true liberty was not identical with that of destructive and criminal revolution. All this bears the imprint of a great man, Félicite de La Mennais, who was the life and soul of that group.

13. LA MENNAIS BEFORE "L'AVENIR"

LA MENNAIS.[19] It is not easy to write without prejudice of this man. The harvests that sprang from his toil are still lodged in our barns. One may find them bitter, poisoned with tares; but it is impossible to deny their abundance. After one hundred and fifty years "Féli" remains with us as a symbol of contradiction.

Among the many talents, great and small, that did honour to the Church of France in the early nineteenth century, his were by far the most outstanding. Among so many obtuse minds who saw no sign in the heavens, he was a visionary, "a druid resurrected in Armorica," as Lacordaire said, a kind of biblical prophet in the age of Decazes and M. Thiers. Karl Marx alone, in another age and in another sphere, can be compared to him as a prophet whose theories would later seem to be confirmed by events. Like Marx he felt convinced that he was witnessing the end of a world; like him he expected a whole series of cataclysms "so long as there remains the least perceptible scrap of the huge corpse whose decomposition began in 1789." Like Marx again he saw beyond that era of decay; but unlike the doctrinaire of *Das Kapital* he saw the future not as materialistic and atheistic, but as Christian. He discerned that Christian future with astonishing clarity: papal infallibility, abandonment of the temporal power, acceptance by

19. His real name was Félicite de La Mennais. It was not until after 1834 that he adopted the more "democratic" form Lamennais.

the Church of democracy and liberalism, separation of Church and State, together with liturgical reform, development of biblical studies, widening pastoral methods and, under another name, Catholic Action itself. All or nearly all of what the Church has achieved in our own times is to be found in La Mennais. He was undoubtedly a genius, a genius whose work would have been more effective if his innermost heart had not been tainted by a lethal pride.

Let us take a look at him at La Chênaie, that little Breton country seat which is even yet haunted by his presence. The simple white house standing in a glade not far from the high road between Dinan and Lamballe favoured recollection and play of ideas. La Mennais loved that place, which was dear to his childhood and where his troubled soul often found peace. He was surrounded by a whole group of disciples, young men whom he had revealed to themselves and to whose lives he had given orientation. Among them were Gerbet, Gousset and Doney, future bishops; Guéranger, who would one day rebuild Solesmes; Rohrbacher the historian; Emmanuel d'Alzon, who later founded the Assumptionists; the poet Maurice de Guerin, and Lacordaire. To each one he assigned a special task in the immense labour he had conceived; nor was he mistaken in his divination of their gifts. He even decided to build up at his side a religious institute, a kind of nineteenth-century Society of Jesus, destined to foster and spread abroad the revived Christianity. In this undertaking he was ably assisted by his saintly elder brother Jean-Marie, and the Congregation of St. Peter came into being at Malestroit. A whole little world was animated and borne along by this man of fire. How many would later declare that they owed their self-discovery to La Chênaie!

Appearances, however, did not reveal anything exceptional in Félicité de La Mennais. At the age of about forty he was a lean little figure, wrapped in a brown frock coat and stiff cravat; the face yellow and wrinkled, with prominent cheekbones and aquiline nose. Only the eyes were extraordinary: deep pools of grey, often shot with a cold flame. When he spoke, "head thrust forward, hands clasped or rubbing gently one against the other,"[20] his voice was at first low, monotonous, as if he followed with difficulty the thread of his own thought. Then it suddenly burst forth in fervour or anger, and his speech became an indictment or a prophecy. Such was every evening at La Chênaie, where talk continued late. And from that puny little man there went out a magnetic force which none could resist. Sometimes he annoyed his hearers, but more often he moved and convinced them.

What had he to say? What watchword did he give his young disciples? "The world is in your hands.... To save it, what is required? A message that proceeds from the foot of the Cross." Like Chateaubriand, he had unbounded confidence in the future. The noblest precepts of Christianity were on his lips: Be ye the salt of the earth. Live with the freedom of the children of God. Be transformed in order to transform the world. How far that was from the external and pseudo-Christian religion the sorry spectacle of which was inescapable!

What in fact was his goal? To realize the prayer of the *Pater*: "Thy kingdom come." Maybe there was much illusion there; perhaps he aimed too high in seeking to bring down the Kingdom of God to earth, and too low in claiming to establish by temporal means that kingdom which had been declared to be "within us." Yet how exalting and compelling was his theme, born not of intellectual reasoning but of spiritual conflict!

Félicité de La Mennais had not always possessed the faith that inspired his burning utterance; he discovered its necessity amid the conflict that raged in the depths of his own being. As a child at Saint-Malo, where he had been born (1782) into an ennobled middle-class family, he knew none but the traditionalist form of religion, a form which, in his reveries beside the surging sea, mingled strangely with mystic voices. Moreover, in the solitude of his uncle's library, he pored over the *philosophes* and was disturbed by their teaching. His attainment of adolescence coincided with the revolutionary era, during which the whole world seemed in the throes of crisis.

20. Cardinal Wiseman, *Memories of the Last Four Popes*, p. 315.

 Where find certitude? At the age of twenty Félicité had yet to make his first Communion. Through indifference? No. He was burdened with ceaseless unrest, the anguish of undying perplexity. But he groped his way forward, tearing his hands on the thorns. It required all the influence of his brother Jean-Marie, now a priest, to persuade him to receive the Host.

There was in him, nevertheless, a longing for the absolute. He could never tolerate lukewarmness. A Christian, he believed, must go to the utmost limit, must give himself to God entirely or not at all; he must become a priest. Yet when his brother suggested this to him, he hesitated and resisted. After some while he received minor orders, but would not venture upon the final step. In 1808 his first book appeared. It was a defence of, and at the same time an appeal for, the reform of Christianity; but perhaps he was not fully assured of the facts that he proclaimed. He too often repeated the great romantic lament that reached him from Combourg: "What is the use of me? To suffer.... All things disgust me." But that way lies self-destruction, as he realized during 1814 amid the sorrows of exile in London, when the Abbé Carron consoled him. Faith was the sole means of renewing his own life and of repairing all else. On March 9, 1816, he was ordained priest. Until the last moment he appeared strangely indifferent: "Let them make whatever they like of the corpse...." But while celebrating his first Mass he distinctly heard Christ murmur: "I am calling you to carry my cross—nothing but my cross, do not forget."

One of his biographers has described him as "a priest in spite of himself."[21] "Priest in defiance of himself" would be far more accurate a phrase: in defiance of one whole side of his nature, in defiance of that obscure region of the soul whose menace each man bears within himself. Bremond is right in saying that "La Mennais is seen as nothing but a priest—a priest to his very marrow even when the sacerdotal character rested with intolerable weight upon him." It was by virtue of a sort of Pascalian wager that he became a priest, in order to convince himself; and even after he had rejected

21. R. Vallery-Radot, *Lamennais, prêtre malgré lui.*

the bidding of his ecclesiastical superiors he remained faithful to the obligations of his priestly order as such, never experiencing the banal temptation of marriage. But is that almost despairing attitude sufficient to make a priest—a true priest? Félicité de La Mennais never completely vanquished his internal demons.

What he lacked was the spirit of humility and that supernatural goodness which drinks at the living fountain of Christ's charity. Some critics, including Lamartine, have seen fit to pour scorn on the "well-nigh comic" contrast between the peevish character and the great humanitarian teachings of the prophet. Sainte-Beuve, with keener insight, saw that "the less certain and self-satisfied he was, the more he impressed others." Now La Mennais was the very opposite of self-satisfied. He was arrogant, intolerant and violent in such a way as to be often unendurable. His was "the vanity of a woman and of a poet," says Bernanos; nay rather an almost satanic assurance that he alone possessed the truth, that he had been entrusted with the task of handing it on to the world. This pride deceived him, prevented him from seeing obstacles, led him to identify his passions with reason. It also inspired him to write passages from which the most scurrilous anthologies could be compiled. A priest who is also a man of letters is a sufficiently curious being; what is one to say of a priest who is also a polemist? In this combination lay the weakness of that genius, of that reformer incapable of reforming himself. Activity in his case was not the perfect flower of sanctity, as in that of St. John Bosco or the Curé d'Ars. The real trouble with La Mennais was the fact that he was not a saint.

Yet how could he escape the snare of pride? The lure of pride is not easily resisted by a successful author, towards whom rise the heady fumes of fame; it is even more unconquerable when that author happens at the same time to be a spiritual guide, when he plays as it were the part of a Father of the Church, a "dictator of the Christian conscience." By about 1806 Félicité de la Mennais had been all those things for nearly ten years. His earliest works, *Réflexions sur l'Église en France* (1808) and *De la Tradition de l'Église sur l'institution des évêques* (1814), had not proved successful, despite the prophetic views to which they gave utterance. But glory suddenly enwrapped him in 1817. The first volume of his *Essai sur l'indifférence* was welcomed with unbounded enthusiasm. Chateaubriand promised its author academic immortality. The aged Picot likened him to Pascal; young Lacordaire to Bossuet. Publication of this work seemed to offer Catholicism the charter of its second spring. The style too was good: for the most part clear and harmonious, sometimes marred by surprising faults of taste, but adorned with many sublime pages in which reasoning gave place to lyrical flight. Thenceforth the Catholic Restoration possessed no more sonorous voice.

What was the message of this blazing work? It declared that indifference is not just the bankruptcy of a soul seduced by pleasure or enslaved by error, whose misery is proclaimed by Pascal; that it can be elevated to the status of a governmental maxim or a fundamental principle of society. Herein, La Mennais held, lay all the evils from which the world, and especially his own age, was suffering. Without religion everything decays; an atheist society is doomed to collapse and annihilation. Only religion, therefore, could enable a ruined society to recover its strength.

Between 1820 and 1823 three more volumes of this work appeared, as massive and controversial as the first was brilliant and persuasive. La Mennais's purpose now was to answer the question: *Which* religion can fill this role? He was a poor theologian, and in order to prove that Christianity alone could do so, he had recourse to arguments which many viewed with grave suspicion. Though an enemy of the *philosophes*, he based the constructive side of his apologetic on a theory of the irrational and of "common sense," which savoured strongly of Rousseau.[22] True, in the course of it he emphasizes the part played by tradition and authority in the search for truth, but the foundations of his reasoning are none the less disputable. He was reported to Rome, and his book submitted to the Congregation of the

22. I shall deal with this later, when considering the papal condemnation of 1834. See section 5 of the present chapter.

Index; but the consultors ruled that he was perfectly orthodox. As a power in the Church he was untouchable; the Church was all too grateful to him for having continued the work of Chateaubriand by strengthening the intuitions of an artist with the fabric of social apologetics, and for having proved that Christianity alone could rebuild the world. She did not, perhaps, realize that the prophet of La Chênaie was leading her by unwonted paths.

In 1825 La Mennais revealed the basis of his thought in *La Religion considérée dans ses rapports avec l'ordre politique et social.* Christianity had been hitherto regarded as exclusively subjective; it was indeed true that Christ had redeemed the souls of men, but He had also promised another revelation, which had not ended with His death. Religion must therefore be enlarged. "Restricted hitherto, as regards dogma, within the limits of pure theology, and as regards morality within those of domestic life and individual relations, it had not yet penetrated the field of science or of social institutions." This teaching was far in advance of its time; not until fifty years later did it begin to be partially accepted. As expounded by La Mennais it was disturbing, because it did not lay sufficient emphasis upon the cardinal obligation which binds every Christian first to reform himself if he intends to reform the world. This idea of Christianity's penetration of society was the axis of La Mennais's thought; he had long been hoping to achieve this goal in the sphere of politics, a sphere utterly foreign to Christian morality.

It was to the search for a Christian political system that the prophet of La Chênaie ultimately devoted his life. On the morrow of Waterloo he identified legitimism with the object of his quest. A disciple of de Maistre and Bonald, he began by posing as the champion of Throne and Altar. For a time he appeared to be a member of the extremist clique, and even contributed to its journals, *Le Conservateur* and *Le Drapeau blanc*. Appearances, however, were deceptive in this case. He had believed that the king's accession to the throne of St. Louis marked the return of Christ's champion upon earth, fiery sword in hand; he had looked upon the Restoration regime as the furnace that would purify Christian France of her defilement and send her forth as hard, pure metal for service in years to come.

But he quickly turned his back on such illusions. Christ's champion had misunderstood his role; the sword of God was notched. Most unfairly, it must be said, La Mennais saw treason in the quite justifiable policy of Louis XVIII, whose purpose was to heal old wounds. There was more sense in his conviction that the war against atheism and irreligion had been waged without determination and, above all, without much skill. Worse, instead of the regime for which he hoped, in which the Spirit should govern men and institutions, he beheld an authoritarian monarchy controlling and subsidizing the Church "like a stud farm," claiming to use religion in order to domesticate its subjects, just as the Empire had done. "We expected the Restoration to terminate the chaos resulting from the action of a man who saw religion simply as a means of influencing the conscience of his people and of thereby subjecting them more easily to his despotism."[23] The opposite had happened. Disgusted with the tyranny of the State, of the party and of money, La Mennais deserted the camp of the legitimist counter-revolution and formed another of his own.

About 1825, when La Chênaie was at the zenith of its fame, the appeal to liberty became the pivot of his thought, "the liberty purchased by Christ for His people with His blood." The Church had nothing to gain and everything to lose by meekly submitting to the authority or even to the protection of the State. Let the civil power cease to pay, administer and employ the Church for secular ends; let there be no more of this pretended alliance between Throne and Altar, which had so clearly failed to rebuild France on Christian foundations. At this date La Mennais was not as yet a professed democrat, though he already spoke of the "people" as the source of true authority. But he was not seeking to substitute one regime for another; his aim was to revivify Christendom.

His grand appeal to liberty was not designed to issue in lawlessness; for in the system he contemplated there was a supreme and undisputed

23. Memorial addressed by the editors of *L'Avenir* to Gregory XVI (see section 5, above). It expresses perfectly the grievances of La Mennais against the legitimist regime.

authority—that of the Pope. Secular governments had betrayed their duty, but Christ's vicar had gained proportionately in stature: "Rome seems to me nowadays the only motherland of Christians," declared La Mennais. Logic proved the supremacy of Peter's successor: "No Church without the Pope; no Christianity without the Church; therefore no religion and no society without Christianity." Féli then, who had been an ultramontanist from youth upwards and especially since the publication of his first book, grew more and more so as he came to realize the failure, the treason of political governments. According to him the Pope is not only the Lord's Anointed, God's representative on earth; he is also the expression of the universal will of man, the trustee of the entire human race. He must consequently have the most absolute power: he must be infallible. Further, he must regain his right to intervene in the affairs of the world, so that he may give effect to the principles of the Gospel. He alone can safeguard the freedom of God's children against State interference, just as he alone can establish between nations the fraternal order of which the Holy Alliance was a mockery. In a sense this doctrine was a return to theocracy; but it also revealed a profound understanding of the future. La Mennais foresaw, in a lightning flash characteristic of his genius, the dilemma of our own age: the necessity for choosing between the authority of a deified State and that of the Spirit entrusted to the Vicar of Christ.

It was in the name of such convictions that he joined battle. Henceforward his real opponents were not the atheists, who made a frontal attack on the Church and her faith, but those Catholic extremists who set out to deprive men of liberty, those lackeys of secular government who were enslaving the Church and those Gallicans who, by isolating France from Rome through their attempt to render the temporal power completely independent of spiritual authority, were wrecking the very bases of society. He lost no opportunity of attack and denunciation. The *Université*'s monopoly of education was in his eyes a monstrosity; so too was payment of clerical salaries by the State. With the accession of Charles X, in 1825, the legitimist monarchy showed an even greater insolence in its claims; year by year the situation became increasingly tense between Paris and La Chênaie. The government was not sufficiently adroit in its proceedings against *La Religion considérée dans ses rapports avec l'ordre politique et social*—a fact which enabled Berryer and the culprit himself to find a new platform for its theories; and the thirty francs fine imposed on him for having assailed the royal authority, by criticizing the Declaration of 1682, caused much amusement and served to enhance his reputation. La Mennais's influence grew. *Le Mémorial catholique* started on its career; the younger members of the clergy admired the herald of new ideas. "He is nothing less than a Father of the Church," declared *Tablettes catholiques*, but he was a Father upon whom the official Church looked with mounting suspicion.

The Gallicans, led by Mgr. Frayssinous and his supporters, inevitably hit back; it was easy to discover "outrageous statements, extravagant paradoxes" in the works of La Mennais. Who would be persuaded that the government of so truly Catholic a ruler as Charles X was persecuting the Church and leading her to ruin? But there was also a number of ultramontanists (Jesuits for the most part) who disapproved of "this trenchant tone, this perpetual declamation." Even some non-Gallican bishops frowned upon a defender of the Church who reprimanded the hierarchy with such vigour. The crisis precipitated by the educational ordinances of 1828 fired the train. La Mennais's satirical booklet *Des progrès de la Révolution et de la guerre contre l'Église* called upon the bishops "to restore to the Church her necessary independence." It declared, moreover, that the legitimist regime was on the point of death and had no chance of survival. Mgr. de Quélen replied with a pastoral letter in which he condemned a man so rash "as to set up his personal opinions as articles of faith." La Mennais's answer was embodied in two open letters, full of invective, in which he described the official religion as "a disgusting hotchpotch of stupidity and arrogance, tomfoolery, besotted smugness, petty intrigue, petty ambitions and absolute intellectual impotence...." It is not surprising that the bishops complained to Rome.

Such was the attitude of "Catholic liberalism," which had produced Félicité de La Mennais at a moment when events offered the Restoration a challenge it could not meet. Catholic liberalism was a strange admixture of sound ideas and passions which endangered them, a curious doctrine which contemporaries failed to understand. Denounced by royalists and Gallicans, it was likewise unacceptable to the liberals, who were shocked by its ultra-montanism. Besides, La Mennais himself had long mistrusted the liberals. "If they ever come to power," he wrote, "we should have to expect all sorts of violence, injustice and persecution"; the freedom of God's children was not the freedom of the liberals. In La Mennais's eyes the future belonged to the forces of liberty—of liberty in all its forms. Christianity, therefore, could not lag behind. Delécluze had recently penned these words: "Every day I become more firmly convinced that liberty is incompatible with Christian tradition." Féli was ready to accept the challenge and prove that Christianity is fundamentally hostile to absolutism of any kind. The liberal group to which Thiers and Guizot belonged became allies, since they too condemned the regime. "Are you fearful of liberalism?" cried the prophet. "Very well then, catholicize it!" Catholic liberalism was at that moment on the slippery incline of politics, and that was a more than likely source of misunderstanding.

What of the Pope? What did he think of all those quarrelsome debates and of La Mennais's wish that he should act as the supreme champion of liberty? The Vicar of Christ, the Sovereign Pontiff, was remote—so distant that the prophet of La Chênaie had been able to fashion him into a kind of myth and "lend him the colours of his own hope." But the See of Peter was occupied by a man, the Church was administered by a whole governmental organization. How were the audacious theories of La Mennais received? In 1824 Féli went to Rome and spent some time there. Though at first unfavourably impressed by certain aspects of the Papal Court, he was quickly enchanted. Italian religion pleased him, for "always and in its every manifestation it is close to the people". Cardinals, the highest prelates and the generals of religious orders loaded him with "marks of deference and politeness." He was treated as the pride of the Church; he was given rooms in the Vatican; and it was even rumoured that the red hat would be conferred upon him at the next consistory. He had several private audiences of Leo XII, who spoke to him with touching kindness and confidence. Nevertheless, though Féli did not know it, the Pope made a very clear assessment of his character: "That man needs gentle handling.... He is a fanatic; he has talent and good faith, but he is one of those perfectionists who, if allowed, would convulse the world." Rome, in fact, welcomed La Mennais as the herald of ultra-montanism and determined foe of the Gallicans rather than as the proponent of Catholic liberalism.

When the situation in France became tense, La Mennais decided to speak out. Advised by the new nuncio Lambruschini, whose acquaintance he had made in Rome, he sent a confidential letter to the Pope, urging him to make a stand, to separate his cause from those of authoritarian governments and to defend liberty. "Would it be wise," he wrote, "to link or to appear to link the Church's cause indissolubly with those of governments hostile to the Church, especially when those governments are tottering on all sides?" Fundamentally La Mennais was right, though it was hardly fair to describe the government of Charles X as hostile to the Church; but his gesture was daring, to say the least. Protestations of respect and obedience notwithstanding, what right had an author, however famous, thus to drive the Apostolic See into a corner? Rome's time-honoured caution was unlikely to submit to such dictation.

Weeks and months went by. "Rome's silence is amazing," wrote La Mennais; "and none can tell what that amazement will become if her silence is prolonged." It was prolonged. Even when the crisis of 1828 broke, and La Mennais was in open conflict with the episcopate, the Vatican said nothing; it could not declare in favour of the bishops, whose memorial was an affirmation of Gallicanism, nor could it support the vehement polemist of the *Lettres à Mgr. de Quélen*. Denunciations poured into Rome, representing La Mennais as a revolutionary who, "torch in hand and at risk of causing a conflagration," ran about the Church like a madman. Lambruschini himself now became wary, particularly in respect of La Mennais's outpourings against the hierarchy. Silence reigned. From La Chênaie there rose an impatient wail:

"Rome, Rome, where art thou? What has become of the voice that once upheld the masses and awoke those who slept; of that message that once sped through the world in time of peril, giving all men the strength to fight and die?" It never occurred to La Mennais that Rome's attitude might be dictated by mistrust of himself, of his questionable theology, of his unspeakable violence; never for a moment did he imagine that he was damaging the cause he professed to defend. His fickle nature led him to spy treason everywhere. "I cannot persuade myself," he wrote, "that the Pope knows the real state of affairs; he is misled, unworthily misled, by the men he employs." Then his anger carried him away: "The sanctuary is empty; nothing more goes out from it." Where would such vehemence lead the great advocate of papal rights? Madrolli, an unknown but far-sighted lampoonist, described him as "the Catholic Diderot" and perceived in him, "beneath the honest appearance of a believer, the germinal shape of a dissenter."

In 1821, two days before his own death, Count Joseph de Maistre wrote to Féli: "Take care, Father; go gently. I am afraid, and that is all I can say...."

14. POPE LEO XII

THE Pope who received La Mennais with such kindness, but summed him up with such perspicacity, was not Pius VII, on whose behalf he had done battle in his early years. Napoleon's old adversary died on August 20, 1823, and the conclave, which lasted for twenty-six days, elected Cardinal Annibale della Genga. Formerly nuncio at Cologne and then at Munich, he had not achieved much success as a diplomat; but among his principal assets was the fact that he had on several occasions crossed swords with Cardinal Consalvi, who had few friends among the forty-nine members of the Sacred College.

The new Pope took the name Leo XII in memory of Leo XI, the last Pontiff of the Medici family, to which the Della Gengas had owed their fortune. Though only sixty-three years old, he was so decrepit that for a moment he was tempted to refuse the tiara. Yet beneath that outward frailty there lurked uncommon energy. His gaze, "so gentle and penetrating that it immediately won affection, at the same time commanded respect."[24] Simple and humble in himself, but keenly aware of the majesty of his position, he was by no means the blockhead that was imagined. He was described as "Pope of the Holy Alliance, Pontiff of the *Ancien Régime*," but that judgment was too hasty. It is more than probable that Leo understood the grave difficulties confronting the Church, and saw the way of escape therefrom. But he lacked so much that there was small hope of his accomplishing anything in a brief pontificate of six years; above all he lacked opportunity, that mysterious gift which Napoleon had rated so highly.

The pontificate began with an episode that showed the Pope's determination to be no one's pawn. His election appeared as a triumph for the *gelanti*. Consalvi was dismissed without any of those eulogies and supposed compensatory honours which, at Rome as elsewhere, usually accompany a fall from power. The former secretary of state withdrew to Porto d'Anzio, his birthplace, and was succeeded by the aged Cardinal della Somaglia, whose social graces barely hid a sluggish mind. The Sacred College at once increased its pressure: under pretext of concern for the Holy Father's health a Congregation of State, whose members were carefully selected, undertook the government of the Church. Within less than two months, however, a sort of revolution occurred.

In December 1823 Leo XII became so gravely ill that he was thought to be dead, but just as the various parties were preparing for yet another conclave he astonished his *entourage* by summoning Consalvi, himself a sick man. The colloquy between those two men in the shadow of death was something unique. The new Pope, wide awake to what was going on, had resolved to seek advice from an old hand in the sphere of world politics. He did not know Consalvi well, and was amazed by his intelligence. "Never," he exclaimed, "have We had, with any man, talks more important, more

24. Cardinal Wiseman, *Memories of the Last Four Popes*, p. 223.

substantial or more useful to the State." Consalvi bequeathed to the Vicar of Christ his true political testament. The fallen minister left the audience as Prefect of Propaganda; and although death prevented his achieving much in that capacity, Leo XII never forgot the advice he had received. The Congregation of State was firmly called to heel, and the Pope took Consalvi's private secretary as his own.

One of the things which the former secretary of state no doubt advised was a strong declaration of the papacy's grandeur and strength, so that all might see it on all occasions as guide of the Christian world. In 1824, as soon as he had recovered, Leo XII took some notable steps in this direction. Resuming Benedict XIV's tradition of great dogmatic encyclicals, in which the *magisterium* of the Church is exercised with full solemnity, he signed *Ubi primum* (forerunner of *Mirari vos* and *Quanta cura*), in which he denounced contemporary errors, especially those covered by the term liberalism; stigmatized "indifferentism" and the de-Christianization of society; and called upon the bishops to do their utmost for the improvement of their clergy and their flocks. At about the same time another encyclical proclaimed the celebration of a Jubilee in 1825—the first since 1775. Governments throughout Europe took a jaundiced view of the project; as Gallicans or Josephists they were unwilling thus to strengthen the authority of the Holy See among their subjects. Leo XII stood firm: missions made careful preparation for the Jubilee, and the Holy Door was opened at Christmas 1824 in a blaze of splendour. Though not an outstanding event, the Jubilee was fairly successful: four hundred thousand pilgrims went to gain the indulgence. Simultaneously Leo XII launched a world-wide appeal for the rebuilding of St. Paul Outside the Walls, which had been destroyed by fire in 1823. Then, in order to seal the return to tradition, and to show that the See of Peter intended to renew its links with past glories, he left the Quirinal and took up residence in the Vatican.

It remained to be seen what policies would flow from this change of attitude. Consalvi's firmness had always been accompanied by scrupulous care not to allow the Holy See to become involved in a particular line of policy.

 The question was whether Leo XII would prove strong enough to maintain this balance unaided. In home affairs he acted with extreme rigour, not only against the brigands who infested the Papal States, or against the embezzlers and traffickers who prowled around the Vatican, but also against the *Carbonari* and other revolutionary nationalists whose influence was continually growing in the domains of the Church. At Rome, two members of the *Carbonaria* were convicted of having assassinated a police officer, and they were executed despite protests from the liberals, who glorified the memory of these "martyrs of clerical tyranny." Leo XII, quite unmoved, sent Cardinal Rivarola to Romagna to suppress an alarming disturbance; after which an Encyclical solemnly condemned Freemasonry and all secret societies.

In his relations with foreign powers Leo XII proved less firm, less competent and on the whole unsuccessful. He was remembered as the nuncio who had achieved so little in Germany, as Pius VI's delegate in 1814, when he had failed to recover the Comtat-Venaissin and whose incompetence had aroused Consalvi's ire. Moreover the start of his pontificate was marked by a vexatious and somewhat laughable incident. Urged by the *gelante* Severoli, who was in close relations with the ultra-extremists surrounding the Comte d'Artois, he listened to all sorts of calumnies against Louis XVIII, which ended by exasperating him. He therefore wrote an indignant letter to the French king, reproaching him for not "giving sufficient protection to the Catholic clergy," for allowing "the continuance of laws injurious to religion," and for permitting "a clique of writers to hurl their missiles with impunity against religion." He concluded by asking the sovereign to "choose as collaborators men of approved piety and political talent." Louis XVIII's reply, of course, was equally sharp. It stated clearly that "reports dictated by imprudent and unenlightened zeal had deceived the Holy Father as to the true state of affairs." Leo XII, disturbed by these assurances, made further inquiries, which showed him that intrigue had once again attempted to compromise him; and he expressed his sorrow by going to pray for France at the church of San Luigi degli Francesi.

Soon afterwards another incident occurred in which he showed very little sense of reality. Under pretext of returning to ancient custom the papal government proposed to re-establish the famous "tribute of the palfrey," which the kingdom of Naples used to pay as acknowledgment of Rome's overlordship and which Consalvi had wisely replaced by a tax on clerical incomes. Francis I of Naples, good Catholic though he was, naturally declined to recognize papal suzerainty, and he was supported by Charles X of France as head of the house of Bourbon.

Not all of Leo XII's diplomacy, however, was so inept. Following Consalvi's policy, he signed concordats with Hanover, the small Rhineland States and the Swiss Confederation, and he even managed to obtain from the Sultan permission to establish a Catholic metropolitan on Turkish soil. But his obvious goodwill was not always understood, still less repaid. In France the ordinances of 1828, including those which struck at the Jesuits, revealed the power of Gallicanism in the kingdom of St. Louis. Leo XII prudently advised the bishops not to protest too strongly, and thereby avoid rousing against a Catholic government revolutionary forces that were all too manifestly prepared to quarrel with it. His advice was reasonable; not so his warning to the Catholics of Belgium. The latter were suffering persecution at the hands of the Dutch king William I, who supported the schismatic Jansenist Bishop of Deventer; but Leo counselled them "to maintain an attitude of passivity" until such time as the Holy See saw fit to intervene. This was inexcusable backing of established order, particularly in view of the fact that other pillars of the Holy Alliance were not altogether favourable to Rome or even to the Catholic Church. Leo XII had congratulated Ferdinand VII of Spain on his "victory" over the liberals; but this did not prevent friction over the choice of a nuncio, the appointment of several bishops and, of course, the rebellious colonies in South America. In Germany the States which had signed concordats interpreted them as they pleased, and numerous difficulties arose in connection with the appointment of bishops. In Russia the obstacles encountered by Consalvi, and against which he had warned Leo XII in their memorable interview, became daily more acute.

 Nicholas I was behaving more and more as an autocrat, endeavouring to Russianize the Ruthenian Church and persecuting the Basilians, with the help of the "white clergy" and of ambitious secular priests, among them Siemasko, whom the Czar on his own authority raised to the episcopate. Against all this mischievous activity poor Della Genga dared not raise the expected protest, because he, like his predecessors and immediate successors, saw czarist Russia as the paragon of established order.

Leo XII's real fault, perhaps, lay in a want of strength which rendered him unequal to the difficulties that confronted him; it would be quite unfair to regard him as a mere anti-liberal reactionary, loyal to the Holy Alliance. We must not forget that during his pontificate young French Catholics joined battle in support of the new ideas against the remnants of an earlier age, and that Leo XII, who kept a portrait of La Mennais in his room, did not condemn them. We must not forget that he encouraged the Munich School; that in England, as we shall see presently, he helped to prepare for Catholic Emancipation; that in Latin America he followed Consalvi's advice by working for the establishment of a hierarchy independent of Spain; and that he did much to encourage the growth of foreign missions.[25] Less important, still significant, are certain facts which reveal him as by no means a narrow-minded extremist or hidebound conservative. These include measures for improving the lot of the Jews in Rome, and a Bull creating institutes of higher studies. Some very curious words, reported by Chateaubriand, show him remarkably close to certain ideas which were then considered more than advanced. The French ambassador once told him: "The trouble has arisen from contempt of the clergy, who, instead of supporting the new institutions, or at least refraining from criticizing them, have let slip words of disapproval, to say no more.... Godless men have seized upon those words and used them as a weapon. It has been put about that Catholicism is incompatible with the establishment of the people's freedom, that there is war to the death between the Charter and the

25. See Volume 2, Chapter VII, section 10.

priests." The Pope replied: "I agree with you.... The Catholic religion has flourished under republican as well as under monarchical regimes; it has made enormous progress in the United States." During the summer of 1828 a bold change of policy seemed imminent with the appointment of Cardinal Bernetti as secretary of state. Tomaso Bernetti (1779–1852), a subdeacon and disciple of Consalvi, told all who cared to listen that the Holy Alliance's policy of reaction would infallibly ruin the papacy, or at any rate cause it to lose its territory. Who knows to what this new orientation might have led, had not death put an end to it, together with the pontificate, at the beginning of February 1829?

Poor Leo XII, who never lacked goodwill, died painfully aware of having failed. He was most unpopular among the common people of Rome for having had the taverns fitted with gratings, so that customers had to drink in the street. Pasquin insulted him with a bitter verse: "Holy Father, thrice you've mocked us, by agreeing to become Pope, by living so long and by dying on Carnival day." Neither the *gelanti*, who found him too soft, nor the liberals, who considered him a tyrant, approved his policies. Secular governments had not helped him in his struggle with the factions, but had thwarted him in the name of their pretended rights. On the whole his pontificate was far from brilliant, but it revealed the difficult situation with which the Church was then confronted. Only a strong, daring and far-sighted genius could have escaped from the dilemma, and it was not the fault of Annibale della Genga that he was no such man.

15. CATHOLIC EMANCIPATION IN ENGLAND

WHEN Leo XII died, in February 1829, a grand undertaking was on the point of fulfilment in England. After more than one hundred and fifty years of persecution, humiliation and suffering, the Catholics were about to recover most of their civil and religious rights. Shortly before the French Revolution the upper classes at any rate had begun to favour some relaxation of the anti-papist laws.[26] At that time the little flock appeared so insignificant—"not even a sect," said Cardinal Newman, "but a few handfuls of individuals who could be counted like the remnants of some great deluge"—that British statesmen, most of whom were unbelievers, had come to the conclusion that those few poor devils were no longer a danger to the State. William Pitt, anxious to unify the nation in preparation for the struggles which he knew lay ahead, had approached the Catholic Committee with an offer to repeal the most burdensome statutes in return for an oath of allegiance to the Crown, and the Catholic Relief Act had been passed in 1778. Catholics now had the right to practise their religion in public without fear of informers, to sign contracts, to inherit and to purchase land.

This was a first step towards complete freedom; another was the Public Worship Act of 1791. In 1787 the Catholic Committee had resumed negotiations in order to obtain true equality of rights; and they had done so with such willingness to make concessions that the vicars apostolic had felt obliged to disavow more than one of their initiatives. As soon as war with France became inevitable the government resolved to terminate all disagreement at home; it had already employed force to quell anti-papist riots. The Act of 1791 succeeded in establishing a system of tolerance: the oath of supremacy was no longer required and certain disabilities (such as that which prevented a Catholic from membership of the Bar) were removed. To freedom of worship was added freedom of education, and relations were settled as between Catholic peers and the Crown. In a word, Catholics were henceforward in the same position as Non-conformists: Parliament remained closed to them, they could not send their sons to the universities, and they were excluded from public office. More serious was the fact that only the Anglican clergy could solemnize baptisms and marriages recognized by the law.

---

26. *The Church of the Classical Age: The Era of Great Splintering*, Volume 2, Chapter VI, section 12.

The crisis of the French Revolution and Empire, however, had the most fortunate consequences for Catholics in England. By closing the schools and monasteries owned by English Catholics in France, the Convention drove a tide of priests, religious and students back to their native shores along with many French refugee priests whom England treated with splendid generosity. The dignity of their lives, their piety and the spirit of brotherhood which they manifested helped to dispel much anti-Catholic prejudice, while the French missions started in London by the Abbé Carron, Père Grou and Mgr. de la Marche did good work. The firmness of two successive popes, Pius VI and Pius VII, in face of tyranny led public opinion in Britain to take a more equitable view of Rome; after all, the Sovereign Pontiff alone, with Catholic Spain, had refused to join the Continental Blockade—an argument which Consalvi was able to exploit during his visit to London in 1814. On the morrow of Waterloo there were about one hundred and fifty thousand Catholics in England, and they were once again a force with which to reckon. The climate, too, was in their favour; Shelley married a Catholic, Byron sent his daughter to a convent school at Ravenna, and Walter Scott thrilled his readers by evoking the glories of medieval Christendom.

The decisive impulse, however, came not from England but from the neighbouring island which had always been a bastion of Catholic loyalty. On the eve of the French Revolution Ireland, whose heroic resistance had amazed the English, had lately scored several points. Britain's "Turkish despotism," as Franklin called it, had been found to relax its hold. In the Dublin Parliament a Protestant, Henry Grattan, had secured the abolition of such odious aspects of the penal laws as bonuses for those who betrayed priests, Protestant guardianship of Catholic orphans, descent of a man's entire property to any son who abjured the Faith and the rule prohibiting Catholics from owning land. The viceroy opposed most of these liberal measures, but the situation of Catholics had undergone considerable change: the hierarchy had managed to re-establish itself; Catholic places of worship had multiplied; and Trinity College, the great Anglican foundation, was now open to Catholics.

230 The French Revolution had some remarkable consequences in Ireland. Irish Catholics were so hostile to the revolutionaries, especially to those who guillotined priests, that many of them enlisted in the British Army; nor were they insensible to the wind of freedom that was blowing over the world. They did little or nothing to help the French to land in Ireland, but they took advantage of circumstances to improve their own lot. Agitation increased to the point of guerrilla warfare (1797–1798) between Defenders and Peep O'Day Boys, between Green and Orange, Catholic and Protestant. William Pitt was alarmed: the opening of a new military front in Ireland might be dangerous. His solution was to proclaim the full union of Ireland with England (1800); but Catholics thereby came to form one-quarter of the population of the United Kingdom, and to leave them in a state of humiliation was to risk an increase of the very danger the government hoped to avoid. Pitt therefore solemnly promised Catholic emancipation. Unable to obtain consent from George III, who thought such a measure contrary to his coronation oath, the prime minister had the grace and courage to resign.

The Irish were no less determined to win recognition of their rights. They gave no thought to insurrection, which in wartime would have been equivalent to treason; legal, obstinate and irreducible opposition could prove more effective. Its leader was Daniel O'Connell (1771–1854), a giant of a man with laughing eyes and a voice that thrilled crowds in Gaelic as well as in English. On the morning when news of the Act of Union reached Dublin he had addressed a meeting at the Exchange, making his audience swear to fight along with him "so long as the shame endured." He was twenty-five at that time, and for almost half a century he was to be the hero of the Irish cause, which he identified with that of the Catholic faith.

O'Connell held to one firm principle: never to violate the law of England, never to cause open conflict, but never to miss an opportunity, through meetings, petitions and protests, of letting the government in London know that Ireland existed and was not satisfied with her lot. His activity increased when he became leader of the Catholic Association founded by John Keogh. Controlled by the bishops, it included all Irishmen who were determined to struggle for their freedom; a modest subscription of one penny a month, which the parish priests undertook to collect, provided the movement with substantial funds. The association was twice dissolved by the government, and twice re-established by O'Connell under a different name. The Throne was besieged every day with petitions and complaints from Ireland. Mass meetings were held in the Emerald Isle, and the great tribune assured them that Catholics would soon be completely free. British statesmen were alarmed; the Whigs as a whole showed themselves favourable to the Irish cause, while Tories were divided on the question. In 1827 Canning, a Tory, almost managed to carry a bill of emancipation, but died before achieving his purpose. The Commons debate, however, convinced O'Connell that the time had come to strike a decisive blow.

In July 1828 a seat fell vacant in County Clare; O'Connell stood against a member of the government and was elected. Enthusiasm swept the island from end to end. "Now Ireland is free," cried the victor when he learned the result of the scrutiny. He was anticipating a little. Though ineligible on account of his faith, he went to claim his seat but refused the oath of supremacy. The House of Commons rejected him, but only by one hundred and ninety votes against one hundred and sixteen.[27] Unrest mounted in Ireland, where demonstrations assumed a more violent character than O'Connell himself had wished. Moreover the Catholics of England, led by their vicar apostolic Mgr. John Milner, joined the fray. In the atmosphere of 1829, when numerous signs foretold an imminent explosion, liberal England could scarcely cling to her old principles and risk an outbreak of civil war.

Responsibility for Catholic emancipation was taken by the Duke of Wellington as prime minister, supported by his home secretary Robert Peel. The legislative measures that debarred Catholics from their full civil rights were abolished. In March 1829 the Commons, and in April the Lords, voted

27. Disabilities were removed in the following year by the Catholic Emancipation Act, and O'Connell took his seat in February 1830.

for Catholic emancipation by large majorities. Catholics henceforward had access to all public employments, civil and military, excepting those of monarch, lord chancellor and viceroy of Ireland.

The Emancipation Act applied to the whole British Empire, and Catholics in twenty lands became once more completely free men. But this did not solve all their problems. In Ireland, on a more strictly political level, O'Connell turned his attention to independence, to breaking the union. In England, Catholics had been released from their bonds, but, as Cardinal Wiseman wrote, not from the cramp and torpor which those bonds had engendered; it would soon be the role of the Oxford Movement[28] to revive that Church and restore her to a sense of her true greatness.

News of the Emancipation Act was received with unbounded joy in Rome. It coincided almost exactly with the election of Pope Pius VIII (March 31, 1829), and the solemn *Te Deum* sung to mark the occasion seemed to prolong those others which had celebrated the glorious accession of a new Pontiff. All British establishments in the Eternal City were illuminated, and the Vatican, which had taken a close interest in the affair, rejoiced as over some great victory. A victory for the Catholics indeed it was, a victory won by their courage and determination. At the same time it was a victory for the liberal and national ideas which were at that time stirring the conscience of Europe, and which seemed opposed in so many ways to the power and traditions of the Church. Lacordaire had good reason to see the emancipation of English Catholics as "a first step towards the deliverance in future ages of all Christian peoples oppressed by the iron hand of despotism."

16. PIUS VIII AND THE EXPLOSION OF 1830

WHEN the cardinals met in conclave on February 23, 1829, thirteen days after the death of Leo XII, the ambassadors of the great powers came, in

28. See Volume 2, Chapter VIII, section 6.

accordance with the strange custom of those times, to deliver messages full of compliments and prayers. They spoke from behind a locked door, through a small orifice "not large enough to allow the passage of an egg," as Stendhal sarcastically observed. The Count of Labrador, representing the King of Spain, expressed his hope that their eminences would elect a Pontiff who would manage "to raise an insurmountable dam against the evil doctrines which, under the false name of broad-minded ideas, were undermining the thrones of Europe with a view to precipitating them and their subjects into ignominy and bloodshed." But the French ambassador, although he represented the strongly legitimist Charles X, spoke a very different language; no doubt consciousness of his own merits gave him more freedom, for he was none other than the Vicomte de Chateaubriand. "Christianity," he said, "which once renewed the face of the world, has since beheld the transformation of those societies to which it gave life. Even as I speak the human race is entering upon one of those epochs characteristic of its history." And the author of *Le Génie du Christianisme* demanded the election of "a leader who, armed with the doctrine and authority of the past, will be no less conscious of present-day than of future needs." It would have been impossible to express more truly than the two diplomats had done the choice with which the papacy was confronted. The man elected to succeed Leo XII was Cardinal Castiglioni, who took the name Pius VIII; and the question now was whether he would prove capable of making that choice one way or the other.

His outward appearance, as Cardinal Wiseman said, was not at first sight as engaging as that of his predecessors. At the age of sixty-eight, pasty-faced and flabby-cheeked, he was a confirmed valetudinarian. He also suffered from chronic herpes of the nape, which obliged him to hold his head bent forward and twisted to one side. Nevertheless he was refined and learned, an excellent canonist and sound administrator, and he had done well in the bishoprics of Montalto, Cesena and Frascati. Though normally timid, he had shown much firmness under the Empire; and Pius VII's gratitude reached the jocular yet prophetic point of addressing him as "Your Holiness."

The situation was everywhere disturbing: there was perhaps no Catholic country where grave problems did not confront the Church. In France she had to face a twofold offensive: that of the Gallicans, who had just won an obvious victory with the ordinances of 1828,[29] and that of the liberals, who were increasingly active and who, particularly since the law of sacrilege,[30] had begun to show themselves ever more hostile to the clergy. There were also La Mennais and his followers, the restless "liberal Catholics" who clamoured for an answer. In Belgium, Catholic opposition to Dutch rule foreshadowed an imminent upheaval, but could Rome give unqualified approval to an alliance of her own sons with the liberals, all of whom she regarded as revolutionaries, atheists and Freemasons? In Poland, in Greece and even in Armenia a similar question arose: must she uphold the forces of subversion? In Italy the situation was in one respect less complicated, for the *Carbonaria* was progressing on all sides and made no secret of its hostility towards the Church. In Spain there were many signs that the clerico-legitimist regime was tainted and that the revolutionary forces would renew their activity at the earliest opportunity. In Germany the Josephist current had reappeared, stronger than ever, both in the Catholic States of the western Rhineland and in Lutheran Prussia; nor did the feeble, timorous or half-loyal episcopate seem capable of resisting government interference. There were serious difficulties, too, across the Atlantic: in South America the question of appointing bishops had not yet been settled, while in North America the progress of Catholicism and the arrival of large numbers of Irish immigrants[31] had provoked Protestant reaction. Only a very great Pope could have dealt with those tormenting problems; but Pius VIII was merely a sick though saintly man, who wept much and often.

He was by no means lacking in judgment and foresight. The Encyclical which he published soon after his election, deploring the advance of

29. See section 11 above.

30. See section 9 above.

31. See Volume 2, Chapter VII, section 3.

indifference and pointing out the menace of secret societies, showed him fully aware of the perilous situation. His choice of cardinals also seemed to indicate a desire to rejuvenate the Sacred College. A rescript of November 1829, recommending to Catholics throughout the world the Fund for Propagation of the Faith,[32] proved that he had a sense of the Church's universality and of her obligation to share in the great movement of western expansion that was then taking place.

He also gave proof, on more than one occasion, of remarkable energy. For example, the discovery of a Carbonarist plot at Rome led to the arrest and trial of twenty-six conspirators. One of them, Picilli, grand master of the Venta, was condemned to death but reprieved at the last moment, while their protectors in high places left the city. Nor did Pius VIII show weakness in Germany. When the Rhineland States, under pretext of organizing the five newly established dioceses, published the Thirty-nine Articles of Frankfurt, which savoured of sixteenth-century Gallicanism and Napoleon's Organic Articles, the Pope protested twice in terms of unusual vigour. Then there was the question of mixed marriages in Prussia. The Lutheran king ventured to apply, even in his Catholic states, an ordinance obliging the children of such marriages to be brought up as Protestants; but Pius VIII, cutting short the manoeuvres of certain aspiring bishops, issued the Brief *Litteris* (March 27, 1830), which directed priests, before the celebration of any mixed marriage, to obtain from the parties an undertaking diametrically opposite to that required by Prussian law.

Unfortunately, though resolute in defending the rights of the papacy and heedful of contemporary problems, Pius VIII had neither the courage nor the strength to lay down a policy for the Church in her dilemma. On the most decisive points silence and temporization appeared to him the best, or at any rate the most convenient, solution. That is why La Mennais received no answer; why the Belgian Catholics were asked to moderate their combative zeal, so as not to risk falling under liberal tutelage; why the French

32. See Volume 2, Chapter VII, section 8.

 bishops who had protested against the ordinances of 1828 were told, as they had been told by Leo XII, that they must avoid embarrassing their king. This short-term prudence could hope for little support; and Pius VIII soon witnessed an explosion of the West.

France once again led the way. The situation there had been ominous since the famous ordinances of 1828. Attacked on the right by anti-Gallican Catholics, and on the left by liberals who demanded the expulsion from office of all ministers appointed by Villèle, Martignac's government had been dismissed in 1829 and replaced by that of Polignac, an extremist of narrow but unshakable beliefs. The brilliant success of the Algerian campaign, which the Catholics celebrated as a crusade, convinced Charles X and his minister that by relying on the army they could govern in defiance of the Charter and of public opinion. This led to resistance in the Chamber, and Polignac saw no escape from the difficulty except by way of a *coup d'état*. Invoking Article 14 of the Charter, which authorized him to "make the regulations necessary for security of the State," he persuaded the king to sign four ordinances suspending freedom of the press, dissolving the Chamber, modifying the electoral law so as to deprive the liberal *bourgeoisie* of their right to vote, and fixing the date of new elections. Revolution was inevitable, and for four days (July 26–29, 1830) Paris was in the throes of insurrection, during which the army, commanded by Marmont, proved hopelessly ineffective. Charles X fled to England without having secured the recognition of his grandson, the Duc de Bordeaux, as his successor. The middle classes, led by Thiers and Guizot, took advantage of the popular revolt to enthrone the Duc d'Orléans, son of Philippe-Égalité and cousin of Charles X.[33]

The French upheaval was no isolated event. In Belgium, in the spring of 1829, Catholics and liberals had made a formal alliance against the Dutch,

33. It has often been said that the revolution of 1830 was the work of Freemasonry. One fact is certain: "If the lodges did not directly bring about the fall of the regime...they collaborated wholeheartedly, and through the bellicose activity of their members, in the explosion of wrath which overthrew the throne of the Bourbons" (Dumesnil de Gramont).

with a view to resisting measures that would have "Hollandized" the education of their children, and tension had mounted steadily since that date. On August 25, 1830, a few ringleaders were able to hurl the mob against the occupying power, its minister and its friends. A military counter-offensive collapsed before the determined resistance of the townsfolk of Brussels. In vain King William sought aid from the great powers; they had no longer strength or inclination to help him restore order. The independence of Belgium was declared, and was quickly recognized by the rest of Europe.

In Poland also the Catholic patriots allied themselves with the liberals, even with Dombrowski's Freemasons, to fight the Russian oppressor. Throughout the summer of 1830 there was agitation and sporadic disorder, particularly in the army and in the schools. Then, in November, it was rumoured that Czar Nicholas proposed sending the Polish regiments to restore Dutch rule in Belgium and replacing them at Warsaw with Cossacks. The officers of the Military School revolted (November 29) and were followed by the troops. The white eagle was unfurled everywhere, and a war of liberation began under the leadership of Chlopiski.

The movement appeared irresistible. In Ireland, O'Connell and his Catholic Association launched a campaign for "repeal of the union," boycotted British goods and started a run on the banks. The *Carbonari* caused disturbances in all the Italian States; nor was the aged King Ferdinand VII able to halt the progress of the liberal party in Spain. The whole authoritarian and legitimist regime was crumbling—Europe of the Holy Alliance and the world of the Restoration. Metternich himself appeared no longer to have faith in his work, and opened his eyes to harsh reality.

News of all these events roused considerable anxiety in Rome. The Vatican hardly knew whether to be more disturbed at the sight of Catholics joining hands with the revolutionaries, or at that of the Church elsewhere made a target of unrestrained violence. In France especially the situation was alarming. The July Revolution seemed directed as much against the Church and religion as against the secular regime; dreadful scenes had occurred in Paris and the provinces, and religious buildings had been sacked. Such was the result of a too close alliance between Throne and Altar that had endured for fifteen years.

Pius VIII did not survive to witness all the tragic events of 1830, though shadows lay heavy across his closing years. Meanwhile, before dying on November 30, he made a decision of capital importance, which showed that Consalvi's lessons had not been wasted and that the healthy political realism of which the papacy boasted was not an empty phrase. Despite protests from the French legitimists who were leaving France, and notwithstanding the advice of Mgr. Lambruschini, his nuncio at Paris, Pius VIII immediately recognized the new regime, notified the French Government that he meant to maintain with it the same relations he had had with that of Charles X, publicly rebuked those bishops who were "abandoning their flocks in the interests of their own safety," and recommended the French clergy to take the oath to the new monarch. Furthermore he officially conferred on Louis-Philippe the title "Most Christian King." These measures were clearly of profound significance; they showed that the Church was willing to adopt an attitude of independence as regards secular regimes, an attitude which she had learned in the school of experience.

Death prevented the wise policy of Pius VIII from bearing fruit; but his decision proved how unjust were the pasquinades that greeted Castiglioni's passing. *Nacque, pianse, mori,* declared the Romans; but no, Pius VIII had done more than be born, weep and die. He had simply been too weak, physically and morally, to confront the Sphinx of History at a time of fearful challenge.

At all events his death marked the end of an epoch. The attempt made since 1815 to annul the Revolution and return to the past had evidently failed; it was now essential to take account of that new life which awaited the world and the Church. Perhaps that failure was foreseen by Joseph de Maistre when he wrote these prophetic words: "A counter-revolution must be not a revolution in the contrary direction, but the contrary of a revolution."

CHAPTER IV

Looking to the Future (1830–1846)

1. A PAPAL ELECTION IN A YEAR OF REVOLUTION

THE shock given to the fragile edifice of established order by the "July Days" at Paris continued to be felt. On the morrow of Pius VIII's death trouble had broken out in Romagna and the Marches. At Rome some conspirators found preparing to seize the castle of Sant' Angelo were arrested and imprisoned; young Charles and Louis Bonaparte, sons of the ex-King of Holland, were found to be implicated and were escorted back to the frontier under a strong guard of *Carabinieri*. It was in such an aura of dubious security that the conclave met on December 13; their eminences could not but feel anxious, and the stormy atmosphere weighed heavy upon their deliberations.

In his ritual speech to the Sacred College the French ambassador, Latour-Maubourg, declared that his master, King Louis-Philippe, expected from the new Pope "love of justice and the independence of those provinces which he would be called upon to govern." There was small likelihood of this hope being fulfilled and of a liberal Pope assuming the tiara. The *gelanti*, led by Cardinal Albani, appeared to be the strongest faction. That the conclave dragged on for fifty days was due simply to the opposition of two candidates—Pacca and Giustiniani—who were similarly inclined. But once the first had been adjudged too old, and the second vetoed by Spain,[1] it was not very difficult to agree upon a third name, one of which no one had yet thought—Mauro Cappellari. A Camaldolese monk, austere and pious but

1. As nuncio at Madrid he had sided with the Carlists. See section 7 below.

 of no great renown, Cappellari was at this time Secretary of Propaganda. He was elected at the hundredth scrutiny. In memory of St. Gregory's on the Coelian, of which he had been abbot, and of the saint who had once lived there,[2] he took the name Gregory XVI. It remained to be seen whether, in face of a situation more perilous than that of the sixth century, he would prove to be another Gregory the Great.

Soon after his election the new Pope found himself in a sea of difficulties. He was proclaimed on February 2; on February 6 his coronation took place in St. Peter's with unusual splendour, for the ceremony included the episcopal coronation of the new Pontiff. That same evening couriers reached the Eternal City with some disturbing news. Two days earlier, at Modena, the grand duke had only just managed to forestall an insurrection by ordering the arrest of its ringleader, his close friend Ciro Menotti. But he had not been able to prevent the setting up of a "political committee" whose first act had been to unfurl the tricolour, with the motto *Liberta*. Next day the movement had spread like wildfire to the Marches, the Legations and Umbria, which constituted four-fifths of the papal territory. Everywhere the troops were deserting or going over to the enemy; everywhere the yellow and white flag had been hauled down. At Bologna the prelate-governor had been forced to allow the *Carbonari* and liberals to form a provisional government. The same had happened at Ancona, and the insurgents were talking of a march on Rome. Nor was that all. An hour or so later the Pope received a message from the Czar's minister, Prince Gagarin: it complained of the part played by Catholics in the Polish revolt, reminded him that Russia had always protected the rights of the Holy See, and demanded that the Polish clergy should be ordered "not to overstep their spiritual functions."

Gregory XVI replied to Gagarin in terms that will be studied later.[3] His first and most pressing concern was to quieten Italy. He believed that

2. Pope St. Gregory I; no doubt also in memory of Gregory XV, founder of the Congregation of Propaganda.

3. See section 6 below.

clemency and a reduction of taxes would settle matters, but they did nothing of the kind. As soon as the "Martyrs of Freedom" had been released from prison they went to swell the ranks of rebellion. Would the strong hand succeed where gentleness had failed? A civic guard was raised from among well-wishers in the districts that had remained loyal, and it was placed under the command of a cardinal with instructions to restore order in Ancona. But the poor man was taken prisoner by the rebels.

The first month of the new Pope's reign was not yet over, and everything seemed to be going from bad to worse. At Bologna a "National Congress" assembled, during which patriots and liberals clamoured for an end to the *buon governo* of the priests and for the creation of a new State which would include all the papal provinces. Sinister news arrived from Paris: on February 14, following some trivial incident,[4] the mob had sacked the church of Saint-Germain-l'Auxerrois and its presbytery; after which it was the turn of the archbishop's palace. Moreover the prefect of police, instead of restraining the rioters, had taken their side by arresting the archbishop and the parish priest of Saint-Germain, neither of whom was in any way responsible. Dispatches from Brussels, though less violent, were no more satisfactory: the constitution adopted on February 17 confirmed the triumph of the revolutionaries, Catholics and liberals together, despite the fact that Cardinal Cappellari, while Prefect of Propaganda, had done his best to maintain the understanding with Holland.

2. A PERIOD OF TURMOIL

THE period which began in 1830 is one of the most confused in the whole of the nineteenth century. It is not one to which the greatest importance is usually attached, enveloped as it seems to be in the *bourgeois* dullness of

4. At a funeral service for the Duc de Berry, a legitimist had the unfortunate idea of hanging the dead man's portrait on the catafalque. The liberal press was scandalized.

 Louis-Philippe's reign. But although no decisive event occurred until the explosion of 1848, Western society was undergoing a visible change.

Political instability was rife throughout Europe—even in France, where the king's reassuring umbrella covered much unrest. There were uprisings in many countries—in Spain as well as in the Balkans, in Portugal no less than in Poland. The activity of secret societies became more insolent and more effective. The diplomatic foundations of Europe, laid as it seemed for ever in 1815, were everywhere in ruins. The several regions of Germany came to the firm conclusion that they formed a unity. Italy was incensed by the vision of herself as a mere patchwork, owned in part by a foreign power. The Turkish Empire, the sick man of Europe, began to crumble. Even tranquil Switzerland was passing through a crisis that would set the cantons at one another's throats.

Nor was political organization alone at stake; the very bases of society were in process of change. Machinery, which had made its first appearance on the eve of the French Revolution, had emerged triumphant within half a century. Thereafter it came into general use—in mines, in factories and, before long, as a means of communication. Capitalism developed along with machinery; it was indispensable to the birth of large-scale industry, but it was also a source of huge profits. The increasingly enormous concentrations of human beings which it produced revolutionized the relations between employers and wage earners. A new class arose, unknown to the *Ancien Régime*—the proletariat.

Behind those political and social events other debates were in progress, reacting upon them. The mind of man had never been so adventurous since the Renaissance. Romanticism was victorious with its claim not only to hurl down prosody and the dictionary, but also to offer a new way of life. There was also a spate of plans for the reorganization of society, for building the future upon new foundations. Bold doctrinaires asserted that the future belonged to "Socialism," without understanding the precise connotation of that term. Utopians, among them Saint-Simon and Fourier, dreamed of remaking the world according to logical and hopelessly abstract schemes.

Meanwhile in a London lodging-house a German exile named Karl Marx, besides preparing the *Communist Manifesto*, was writing *Das Kapital*, which was to be no dream, but a scientific treatise.

Napoleon had once declared that all the unrest was merely a sequel to the French Revolution, and the truth of his words was now plain for everyone to see. It was the Revolution that gave the Western world a new outlook. From it flowed three intermingled streams of change. The "principles of 1789" led first to the liberal revolution. Man's rights as a citizen had been acknowledged, and in the name of those rights he was determined to reject any and every form of tyranny that ventured to impose on him. He claimed a share in the government of his country; he demanded protection against arbitrary rule, clamouring for mastery—or at least apparent mastery—of his own future.

The same principles, being valid for nations as for individuals, gave rise to another and national revolution. Peoples claimed to determine their own destinies, to reject partition between masters not chosen by themselves. Heir of the Revolution in this respect as in so many others, Napoleon had shown the way of unity and national independence to the Germans and Italians, who did not forget it.

Finally, and even more profoundly though less obviously, the principles of 1789 led to a third lot of consequences. The words "liberty, equality, fraternity," unless they were to be hollow formulae, must bring about a new relationship between the various levels of society, a relationship all the more necessary because the emergence of large-scale industry was emphasizing class distinction. The French revolutionaries, most of whom were *bourgeois* property owners, had never suspected this result; but from 1848 onwards (if not before) the social revolution was on the way, and it was destined to surpass all others in the fury of its onslaught.

It was during the period which opened in 1830 that those three currents, issuing from 1789, began to make their activity felt, and it is that very activity which renders the period so confused. Western society would soon have to answer the riddles posed by the Sphinx of History. So also would the Church; for she too, though a spiritual congregation, is formed likewise of men with temporal interests, and she relies upon institutions that have social and political contacts. Once again, as so often before in her long life, Christianity would have to deal with a new form of civilization, to which her message must be delivered, in which the Gospel must become incarnate. What would be her attitude? How would the Church confront her new destiny?

3. A MONK ON THE THRONE OF ST. PETER

THE Pope who was about to shoulder the formidable duty of steering Peter's barque amid all those reefs and dangerous currents was Gregory XVI, whose pontificate had begun in such dramatic circumstances. Born at Belluno in Venetia on September 18, 1765, he was now in his sixties, a vigorous man whose excellent health contrasted with the frailty of Leo XII and Pius VIII. He liked to leave his carriage and walk for hours in the Roman Campagna, at a pace which hardly suited the asthmatic or gouty prelates in attendance. He was always jovial, and it was rumoured that the wine of Orvieto flowed freely at his table; but that was no doubt a calumny arising from the size and colour of his nose.[5]

With that lurid and graceless appendage, protuberant lips and jet-black eyes beneath curving brows, *Er Zor Grigorio* was far from handsome. Nevertheless he was intelligent, and could behave with dignity when occasion required. All those who knew him well agree in saying that when he celebrated Mass his countenance was literally transfigured, and that a supernatural beauty, reflecting his soul, made up for what nature had refused him. True, he lacked radiance and charm; but his enemies laid too much stress on these shortcomings, because he was a brave man and thwarted their designs.

5. Gregory XVI suffered from a disease of the nose which was aggravated by his habit of taking snuff and which culminated in cancer of the face.

Gregory had been trained to the stern discipline of the Camaldolese, who since the year 1000 had preserved almost intact the reformed Benedictine rule given them by their founder St. Romuald. A monk since his eighteenth year, he remained so on the papal throne, sleeping on a straw mattress in a room that was little more than a monastic cell, and eating frugally. But he was no ordinary monk; he had had plenty of experience. After reaching the highest dignity in his order, Cappellari had been in turn a consultor of the Congregation of Extraordinary Affairs and of the Inquisition; next it was his duty to examine the qualifications of candidates for the episcopate, and then to make visitation of the universities. Finally, he was created cardinal in 1826 and became Prefect of Propaganda, an office in which he had shown the highest efficiency. It cannot therefore be said that he was ignorant of affairs.

On the other hand, by temperament as well as by training, he was instinctively suspicious of novelty and hostile to the modern world. At the age of eighteen he had fiercely supported a thesis on papal infallibility and the rights of the Church. In 1799, while Pius VI lay dying at Valence and the Catholic world seemed in mortal danger, he had published *The Triumph of the Holy See and the Church Against the Assaults of Innovators*, a work that was quickly translated into four languages. Revolutionary ideas, accordingly, could hope for little favour in his sight. It was of course a short step from there to represent him as *laudator temporis acti* and a systematic contemner of the present. That step was taken by his enemies and by many historians, sometimes unfairly. He has been heavily censured for refusing to allow the railway into Rome; but his critics forget that the "liberal" M. Thiers took the same view of that "useless and dangerous" invention. When there was question of giving the Church world-wide stature by developing the missions, of fighting against epidemics, of cleaning up the city or of town-planning, Gregory XVI proved himself far from an inveterate reactionary.

The truth is that, at a time when the Church needed a diplomat and man of action at her head, this virtuous monk, this brave and loyal man, this great worker who studied all reports submitted to him and never hesitated to return them to the Roman Congregations if he thought their contents unsatisfactory, was a theorist preoccupied with major philosophical and theological problems, the very opposite of a statesman and leader of men. His chief concern was to clarify doctrine. For the rest, he was prepared to leave himself (much too often) in the hands of his advisers.

On the morrow of his election he appointed Tomaso Bernetti secretary of state, instead of the aged and notoriously pro-Austrian Albani. The choice was sound. Cardinal Bernetti, formerly assistant to Consalvi, was highly experienced in the management of men and affairs; he shared all the views of the great man who had trained him. His policy was one of firmness without brutality; of reliance on the secular powers so far as was necessary, but without allowing himself to be overruled by them; of vigorous opposition to the enemies of the Church, but without joining the reactionary clique. Gregory XVI, who retained him in office for six years, used to describe him as possessing "an arm of iron and a heart of gold."

Unfortunately Cardinal Bernetti was endowed with a keen but mischievous wit. One of his remarks, repeated to Metternich, gave great offence to the powerful minister, who immediately suspected the secretary of state of having made little or no effort to prevent the French from intervening against him in Italy. One day when the cardinal was confined to his room by an attack of gout he was surprised and flattered to receive a personal visit from the Holy Father. As he broke into protestations of gratitude, he heard Gregory XVI inform him, with all possible gentleness, that in view of his illness he was going to relieve him of the heavy burden of affairs of state.

Bernetti was succeeded by a very different man, Cardinal Luigi Lambruschini, formerly nuncio at Paris, who had at first encouraged La Mennais because of his ultra-montanism but had afterwards done him a disservice at Rome. The new secretary of state was a Barnabite, solemn in manner, immensely learned, but tenacious of the privileges enjoyed by his caste, supercilious by temperament, firmly attached moreover to the ideal of the Restoration, to the Society of Jesus and to Austria. Absolute master of the papal administration, from which he eliminated his rivals, as well as all-powerful with the Pope, the new secretary of state was prepared, as Crétineau-Joly said, "to leave to the severity of the law an initiative with which Bernetti had been content to threaten the Revolution." His harsh policies were not unconnected with the mounting discontent which became apparent in the papal provinces and which was destined to explode with dreadful fury after the Pope's death.

In these circumstances it was inevitable that Gregory XVI's pontificate should be one of strife. Convinced that any concession to the spirit of the age would imperil the very foundations of the Church, the Pope refused to yield an inch. He believed that Catholicism would betray her mission and compromise the efficacy of her apostolate by ceasing to be herself. It is to his credit that he spoke up loud and clear, that he tried to put an end to liberal equivocation, and that he never lost an opportunity to proclaim the authority and grandeur of his throne. Under Gregory XVI, whose own life was so simple, the papal ceremonies assumed unprecedented magnificence, and audiences became surrounded with more than royal protocol. Rome at this time enjoyed some years of splendour: many illustrious visitors resided there; new palaces were built (like the Palazzo Colonna); the venerable basilica of St. Paul was rebuilt; the Colosseum was excavated and restored; the Vatican was enriched with valuable collections.

The prestige of the papacy advanced in several respects during those sixteen years. What of its practical authority, its influence? Gregory XVI, a man of solid doctrine, lacked suppleness, tact and the ability to distinguish thesis from hypothesis. He looked upon the world situation as a fearfully tangled skein, and in all honesty he believed that the best means of dealing with it was that of Alexander in presence of the Gordian Knot. But there were men in that skein.

4. ROME AND YOUNG ITALY

THE first and terribly urgent problem that Gregory XVI had to solve was that of the revolution in Italy. When it began Francis I offered Rome the support of his bayonets for the re-establishment of order. Bernetti had refused; but the danger had spread, and since he had failed to win concerted action from the great powers, Gregory XVI unhappily resigned himself to calling upon Austria. It did not, of course, take long for the Austro-Hungarian troops to overthrow the provisional governments of Bologna and Ancona. The imprisoned cardinal was released; the papal officials resumed office; a few individuals were sentenced to terms of imprisonment; but many liberal ringleaders escaped, among them Louis-Napoleon Bonaparte, who was able to cross the frontier thanks to a forged passport supplied by the Archbishop of Spoleto, Mgr. Mastaï-Ferretti, afterwards Pope Pius IX.

Austrian intervention had proved successful, but not all its political results were beneficial. Italian patriots came to regard the Pope as a vassal of the occupying forces, and his action had established an unfortunate precedent of inviting the powers to take a hand in papal affairs. These consequences very soon made themselves felt. A few weeks after the end of the insurrection it was learned that Austria and France were proposing to summon a conference at Rome for the purpose of reorganizing the papal regime, a meeting to which Britain, Prussia and Russia were to be invited. This was the result of two different schemes. France was unwilling to leave Austria in sole occupation of the Papal States, while Metternich, aware that the Austrians were most unpopular in Italy, sought to win over the patriotic masses by proposing liberal reforms and thereby to make the Roman court alone appear responsible for a policy of reaction. The conference was held at Rome in 1831; it drew up a memorandum indicating the steps to be taken and declared that the powers would guarantee their execution. On the advice of Bernetti, Gregory XVI abstained from protesting against this insolent claim to meddle permanently in the field of his authority. The astute cardinal had guessed that agreement among the powers was precarious, and events quickly proved him right.

The ink was scarcely dry at the foot of the memorandum when the French Government, led by Casimir Périer, asked the Pope how soon the Austrian forces would evacuate papal territory, and added, in threatening tones, that if the evacuation was long delayed France might be driven to send in troops of her own. Bernetti shrewdly announced an amnesty for all rebels willing to submit; then, arguing that peace had now been restored, he asked the Austrian Government to withdraw its troops, and this was done in July. But the liberals suddenly resumed their agitation. Bologna, Forli and Ravenna announced autonomous constitutions, which were accepted more or less grudgingly by the pro-legates. Gregory XVI thereupon invoked the aid of Cardinal Albani, whose severity was notorious. Unfortunately the valour of the papal troops, who had been hurriedly recruited, was unequal to the energy of their leader, and they were defeated by a peasant army. The cardinal, without further reference to the Pope, turned for assistance to General Radetsky, commander of the Austrian troops, who restored order within a month.

By the end of January 1832 the authority of the Holy See had been re-established throughout its dominions; but a European conflict was impending. As soon as Périer's government heard of the renewed Austrian intervention it acted firmly and forcibly. A naval demonstration before Ancona led to the occupation of that city. There was indignation in Vienna and London; rumours of war sped through the chancelleries of Europe. Only the papal government remained perfectly calm. While protesting officially, Bernetti was doubtless glad that a French regiment should serve as a counterpoise to the troops of Francis I. After much sabre-rattling the occupation of Ancona was recognized as a "temporary measure"; it lasted until 1838, when the situation was again peaceful and two papal regiments, recruited from among the Swiss, went to garrison the Adriatic port.

From that crisis, however, Gregory XVI learned one lesson: reforms were necessary in his States. He had been unwilling to make them under pressure from the powers, but he undertook them as soon as he could do so freely, though not of course in the political sphere. The French Government would have liked Rome to become a sort of parliamentary monarchy modelled on that of Louis-Philippe; but of that there could certainly be no question. Gregory XVI intended his government to retain its absolute and ecclesiastical character, which precluded anything that might resemble a liberal regime. The Sovereign Pontiff's authority was even strengthened by the creation of a papal army of mercenary soldiers and by the reorganization of the functions of the secretariat of state. Reforms were confined to administration, to the courts and to the exchequer; even so they fell short of those recommended by the powers in their memorandum.

But the result of these measures was not that which the Pope had expected. This was due to the fact that their happy effect was offset by the counter-propaganda of such public calamities as floods, earthquakes and an epidemic of cholera, which brought ruin to the treasury, distress and increase of taxes, all of which seemed to bedevil this unfortunate pontificate. It was partly due likewise, and even more so, to the way in which those reforms were carried out, rendering them unpopular. Instead of enabling the people to feel themselves associated with the work, reform was imposed authoritatively from above; some even talked of "enlightened despotism" and "tyranny"—words hardly applicable to a government that was after all paternal. Moreover the Pope's adversaries found plenty to criticize: Gregory XVI, they said, had not unified the Papal States; he had restricted the powers of communal councils; he had ruined the Romans by his outlay on armaments, as burdensome as it was useless; and he had farmed out to Rothschild the excise on tobacco. These recriminations, justified or not, were spread abroad by liberals and patriots. Even among loyal Catholics other reproaches were directed at the austere Camaldolese Pontiff: he was not working for the internal reform of the Church and her clergy, or for the recruitment and training of priests, let alone of the Curia and Papal Court. Rosmini, a protégé of the Pope, was about to give expression to such criticism in his *Five Wounds of the Church*. Raffaello Lambruschini too, nephew of the cardinal, thought that religious and political reform should go hand in hand. All this created an unstable and confused situation. While Gregory's efforts deserved better treatment than they received, it must be admitted that they failed to achieve their purpose. So far from allaying discontent, the Pope's reforms helped to exasperate his adversaries. Once the Austrian and French troops had withdrawn, in 1838, revolution became more or less constant in all the papal territories—and elsewhere too.

Failure of their attempts in 1821 and 1830 had not disheartened the Italian liberals and patriots. Longing for independence and unity became more imperious year by year. Lampoons were current throughout the peninsula, denouncing all forms of tyranny. Silvio Pellico stirred countless hearts with his book *My Prisons* (1832), a narrative of his detention in Austrian jails. Leopardi's harrowing verses, Manzoni's *Sacred Hymns* and *I Promessi Sposi* seemed to promise Italy's recovery of world-wide renown in the field of literature. Vincenzo Gioberti was soon to publish his famous *Moral and Civil Primacy of the Italians* (1843), and Balbo his *Italian Hopes* (1844). The forces of national and liberal revolution were not such as could be for ever held in check by a few regiments from Austria.

The several groups that laboured in this cause were very different from one another. They agreed in a passionate desire for a united and free Italy, as well as in resisting foreigners who occupied Italian provinces and paternalist or absolutist governments which deprived their peoples of liberty while conferring some small measure of material welfare; but they differed fundamentally as regards other aims and also as regards means.

The most violent of those groups was that known as Young Italy, founded in 1831 by Giuseppe Mazzini during his exile at Marseilles. Realizing the futility of the methods employed by the *Carbonari*, he had conceived a new association stripped of the complicated hierarchy and cabalistic rites inherited from Masonry, which had fettered the *Carbonaria*. His ideas, set forth in a number of remarkably well-written booklets, were quite simple: the new Italy must be "republican and Unitarian"; republican in order to put an end to the tyranny of princes, Unitarian because all federalist systems ran the risk of perpetuating those divisions which were the curse of the peninsula. As to the methods he proposed, they too were very simple. First, the people must be educated; they must hear repeatedly the words "regenerators of liberty, rights of man, progress, equality, brotherhood" as against the vocabulary of tyrants—"despotism, privilege, slavery." As soon as the people were imbued with these principles the new age would begin, and that new age would be one of revolution. Mazzini was not daunted by the possibility of violence, bloodshed or even the assassination of kings and princes who opposed Young Italy. There must be no foreign intervention for the achievement of those noble ends: "*Id Italia fara da se*"—Italy would do it herself. What of the Church and the Pope in this scheme? Mazzini declared himself a Christian; but his Christianity, detached from dogma and linked only with "the admirable man Jesus," was very far from Catholicism, very close to the vague and humanitarian beliefs of La Mennais after the latter's fall. As for the Pope, in his character of temporal sovereign he would have to submit and lay aside his absolutist methods; as master of Rome, the only possible capital of united Italy, he would have to resign himself to the loss of his temporal power.

There is no doubt that Freemasonry was at work behind this revolutionary enterprise. Although Young Italy had no use for the rites of Masonry, its spirit remained, as did the law of absolute secrecy under pain of death provided by Article 30 of its regulations. Mazzini himself may perhaps have been a Mason; the principal ringleaders of his movement certainly were, among them Garibaldi and Francesco Crispi. Masonry was, beyond any doubt, the source of Young Italy's anti-Roman orientation. But it found support and even complicity in other very different circles—those of the old Italian Jansenism, mingled with regalism and Febronianism, whose influence it had preserved and whose inmost aspirations were towards autonomy of religious thought. Jansenist influence, moreover, helped to endow even the most anti-Christian leaders of the *Risorgimento* with an undeniable moral dignity. Mazzini himself had been brought up in a Jansenist atmosphere, and it need hardly be said that these descendants of Scipione Ricci were no friends of Rome or upholders of papal power.

Meanwhile other movements arose in opposition to Young Italy: the revolutionaries were opposed by the reformists, who were equally patriotic but disapproved of the recourse to violence advocated by Mazzini and were not republicans. On the morrow of 1830, and during the next ten years, the most important were the neo-Guelphs, who had come into being unobtrusively under the Restoration.[6] Their leaders were Cesare Balbo and Vincenzo Gioberti. Like Mazzini they exalted the greatness of Italy, and summoned their country to new heights. But the anti-Roman radicalism and methods of Young Italy had shocked them. Both were sound Catholics, and they saw Catholicism as the bond linking all their compatriots, as their common ideal and as the mainspring of all activity. The papacy, which Gioberti described as "ancient protectress of the nation, generous refuge of tolerance," must hold the primacy in a united Italy. The methods they urged were negotiation, the way of law, diplomacy. To these they would have recourse even for the liberation of Lombardy and Venetia; Austria would be offered compensation in the Balkans—Moldavia and Wallachia, for example. Distinct from the neo-Guelphs, who operated mainly from Turin, Raffaele Lambruschini in his Tuscan hermitage dreamed of a constitutional monarchy, in which the Pope would retain executive power of direction, but would be assisted by counsellors elected by the major districts of Italy.

There was of course some degree of illusion in this neo-Guelphism which sought to make the Pope sovereign of Italy, and even more so in the dream of attaining its ends by peaceful means. Besides, discord soon reared its head within the very heart of the movement. While Gioberti was writing that an Italian confederation should have "two roots, Turin and Rome, the former representing Italy's strength and the latter her holiness," Balbo quickly realized that one single root was needed and that only the house of Savoy was capable, by its power and geographical position, of expelling

6. See Chapter III, section 12.

 the Austrians and unifying Italy. The neo-Guelph ideal gradually yielded to this more realistic political concept. But for fifteen years, covering most of Gregory XVI's pontificate, the grandiose theories of Gioberti penetrated large sections of the clergy, including the senior ranks of the hierarchy; and their influence would become apparent in the conclave of 1848.

The Pope thus found himself face to face with an extraordinary ferment of ideas, doctrines and projects. Censorship notwithstanding, the press debated them; books written by leaders of the *Risorgimento* were widely and avidly read; an unusual number of supposedly scientific conferences met, and devoted themselves mainly to political discussion. What attitude should the Pope adopt towards this agitation? He certainly failed to understand it clearly; he mistrusted all who sought to change the established order, neo-Guelphs no less than revolutionaries. It must be acknowledged that some things written by Gioberti were calculated to rouse his suspicion, such as: "Authority and freedom are harmonized dialectically by Christianity." He did not realize the opportunity afforded the Holy See by the excessive enthusiasm of Gioberti and his friends. Urged by Cardinal Lambruschini he shut himself within an attitude of rejection that was dogmatically sound but politically unwise. Perceiving in all this agitation nothing but the work of secret societies, he busied himself exclusively with countering their activity. For this purpose he summoned a French writer, Crétineau-Joly, well known as the author of a military history of La Vendée as well as of a history of the Society of Jesus, and instructed him to "trim his quill and write...a history of secret societies and their consequences." Year by year, under the stern direction of the cardinal secretary, the administration of the Papal States became more severe. Without taking literally the vehement denunciations of Massimo d'Azeglio's *Recent Events in Romagna* (1845), we are entitled to believe that all was not false in the picture he drew of a regime in which the police could "imprison a man, place him under house arrest, deprive him of his civil rights, lose him his employment, open his letters and force their way into his house, as well as close shops and impose fines, at their own good pleasure." Even though in practice such events were not of daily occurrence, the very fact that they happened at all sufficed to bring grave discredit on the papal authority.

Moreover this policy of coercion—which was practised not only by the government of Rome, but also at Naples, Milan, Venice and elsewhere—ended in failure. Although prisons everywhere filled, rioters and murderers sprang up on all sides, while the Pope's faithful adherents could no longer do anything but fear for their lives. It was like a smouldering fire that bursts into flame one day here and another there. In 1833 a riot had broken out at Genoa, then the Savoyard States had been disturbed by rebellious subalterns and other ranks who had created a veritable reign of terror in certain cantons. In 1845 the whole of Romagna was seething; so too in the following year was Calabria. The most serious incident was the capture of Rimini, on December 20, 1843, by conspirators from San Marino. Their success was ephemeral, for six days later order was restored by the papal Swiss; but during those days the rebel leader Farini was able to make a pathetic appeal to Europe and at the same time to propose a scheme of reform which cunningly recapitulated point by point those suggested in the memorandum of the powers. Cardinal Lambruschini replied by refusing any kind of reform and sending out itinerant courts to deal with offenders. The situation remained explosive. Almost everywhere policemen, papal militiamen and even magistrates heading committees of inquiry were found murdered. At Imola a brigand chief tried to kidnap Cardinal Mastaï-Ferretti and two other members of the Sacred College whom His Eminence was entertaining. When his attempt misfired he flung himself on the city, and was only just repulsed. Eighteen months later, in 1845, the Legations were once more aflame, and it required all Cardinal Lambruschini's energy both to restore order and to forestall Austrian intervention. The prisons were filled with political suspects while others fled the country.[7]

Thus the rigorous methods employed by Gregory XVI, however justified they may have seemed to him by the need to defend the truths of

7. See section 11.

religion and the sacred rights of the Apostolic See, ended in failure at the political level. Would they prove more successful at another level, that of ideas, where their application was an even more delicate business? A celebrated affair, which disturbed the beginnings of Gregory's pontificate, rendered this question one of practical and immediate significance.

5. THE TRAGEDY OF LA MENNAIS

THE revolution of 1830 inspired Félicité de La Mennais with mixed feelings.[8] He was not in Paris during the July insurrection, being detained at La Chênaie by his disciples, his displeasure and his financial difficulties. On receiving the news he did not hide his satisfaction—the bitter satisfaction of a prophet who sees his gloomiest prognostications fulfilled. The legitimist regime was collapsing as he had foretold, and like Lamartine in 1848 he might have said: "I see my revolution come to pass."

But he quickly altered his tune. The political climate introduced by the new rulers was unlikely to please him. No matter how grave he considered the clergy's error in making themselves vassals of the Bourbons, he could not as a priest do aught but grieve over the detestable anti-clerical incidents which took place and which the government allowed through weakness or complicity. Gallicanism, his *bête noire*, was as strong as before—and less justified, since the State declared itself neutral. The whole Voltairean *bourgeoisie*, too, gathered beneath the "sentimental umbrella" of Louis-Philippe—the whole horde of self-styled Christians who crowded theatres to applaud *Papesse Jeanne* or *Voltaire chez les Capucins*—filled him with disgust.

Within less than three months after the July Revolution La Mennais had turned his back on all its principles. Having worked for the overthrow of men who wanted God without liberty, he was not now going to support others who preached liberty without God. "Catholics," he cried, "break

8. See Chapter III, section 13.

for ever with the men whose incorrigible blindness imperils this holy religion!" Rejected by the State, the Church should "withdraw from political society and concentrate upon herself, with a view to recovering, along with her essential independence and the fulfilment of her destiny, her pristine and divine strength." A decrepit form of Catholicism had just collapsed together with the regime, and the new monarchy was hostile to religion; but there remained a great hope, one that stirred a young, ardent and combative generation which was ready to answer the call of the Druid of La Chênaie and promote new ideas. In order to guide and give voice to that generation he had to found a journal—*L'Avenir*, whose motto was "God and Liberty."

The idea originated with Harel du Tancrel, an obscure publicist, who communicated it to the Abbé Gerbet, one of La Mennais's disciples. Gerbet began by seeking the necessary financial backing; when he had obtained it he revealed the plan to La Mennais, who, delighted to take up the journalist's pen once more, went to reside at the Collège de Juilly in order to prepare for the bold enterprise. An office was rented at 20 Rue Jacob, and on October 16, 1830, the first number appeared.

L'Avenir caused an immediate sensation. It bore no resemblance to such earlier Christian journals as the Gallican *Ami de la Religion* or the discreet *Mémorial catholique*. "Never had the Catholic faith been expressed in prouder and more vibrant language." Every number of this paper was like a manifesto, an order of the day issued before battle. Talent streamed through its columns; and La Mennais, a master of his native tongue, took care to maintain a high standard, keeping a firm check on those of his friends who, like Guéranger, thought well but wrote badly. The greatest literary figures were among his collaborators, including even some of those whose adherence to Catholicism was doubtful. There were Lamartine, who contributed his *Réponse à Némésis*. Victor Hugo, whose *Hymne aux morts de juillet* was first published in *L'Avenir*, and the unbelieving Vigny himself. *Avant-garde* literature supported the undertaking in the persons of Balzac, Michelet, Sainte-Beuve and Alexandre Dumas.

The youthful team which ran the paper[9] consisted mainly of La Mennais's own disciples: the abbés Gerbet, de Salinis, Rohrbacher and, among the laymen, de Coux, d'Eckstein, Daguerre, d'Ault-Duménil, Bartels and Harel du Tancrel, the last of whom was chief editor. Two outstanding personalities, however, soon emerged from the group and became the master's intimates, his most trusted advisers.

One was a young man of twenty years recently back from Ireland, his mind inflamed by what he had seen in "that island where the sacred cause which had just uttered a call for help in France had been for centuries incarnate in the lives of the clergy and their people." Son of a French ambassador by an Englishwoman, and descended from a noble Burgundian family, his handsome countenance with its curly beard, his grey eyes and his lively gestures bespoke that sovereign ease, blended with watchful irony and delicacy, which blood alone can give. Without affectation, moreover, and wholly devoid of charlatanism, he endowed his every act with a degree of generosity and sincerity which he would never retract. "All that I am, all that is in my power to do, I lay at your feet," he had written to La Mennais. His name was Vicomte Charles de Montalembert (1810–1870).

The other, his elder by eight years, was Henri Lacordaire (1802–1861), a young barrister from Dijon, a plebeian by birth, training and faith, who had been converted at Paris in the fullest Pascalian sense and had gradually discovered in Catholicism his notion of the world and the motives of his life. Thin and sallow, with deep-set eyes and an air of recollection, he concealed beneath an outward reserve a temperament of fire; a "charming and terrible" being, as Montalembert described him, a born polemist with the soul of a mystic, he was endowed also with brilliant and inexhaustible gifts as an orator.

The team thus gathered around the illustrious priest-author was from many points of view worthy of admiration. It had breeding, it had style, it had courage enough and to spare, it had generosity to intoxicate the hearts

9. Their average age was thirty-two.

of men. But it had also some obvious defects. Style is not everything, *pace* Bremond; in politics it is often responsible for a deal of nonsense. Thirty years later, when relating his memories of those days, Montalembert acknowledged that *L'Avenir* combined "intemperate and rash theories" with some correct ideas, and that the whole was sustained "with that unrelenting logic which ruins the causes it does not dishonour." Oratorical passion is a poor disguise for serious lack of foundations. None of the little group was a theologian; one only, de Coux, was an economist; while Rohrbacher alone passed as an historian. The most difficult problems seemed easy to solve, because their complexity went unrecognized. A good deal of romanticism flowed through the office in the Rue Jacob, and romanticism has never been accepted as a school of sound policies. To these defects we may add the shortcomings of all coteries, literary or otherwise: a deep-rooted contempt of others, an assurance of being always right and a conviction that no one else has attained ultimate truth. Column after column spoke as "We, the Church"; but what did their writers know of the real Church with her Pope, bishops and parishes, her sufferings and her terribly concrete interests?

The theories upheld by *L'Avenir* were fundamentally those propounded by La Mennais, who believed them to be justified by circumstances. The West, he declared, was on the flood-tide of transformation; its political and social bases were in the throes of change; evolution was irresistible, and it was up to the Church herself to choose whether the process should work with or against her. Her choice, proclaimed *L'Avenir*, was dictated by her very vocation. "The Cross betokens the victory of light over darkness.... The world's emancipation dates from the birth of Christianity. Catholicism delivers man from the yoke of man. The day is approaching when it will mold the nations themselves into one great society." The Church would then be seen "between Heaven and Earth, as a consoling sign".

How was this prophecy to be given substance? How was the motto "God and Liberty" to be translated into reality? According to La Mennais, by a threefold work of liberation. The Church must free herself from "the onerous protection of secular governments," for their protection had made her "the instrument of their policies and the plaything of their whims," as well as compromising her in the eyes of her loyal members. There must be no more of those concordats which entrusted the appointment of bishops to atheist governments. No more salaries must be paid to priests: "The scraps of bread thrown to the clergy are the title-deeds of her subjection.... It was not with a cheque drawn on Caesar's bank that Jesus sent His Apostles out into the world." There was only one solution, only one hope: the separation of Church and State. Then Catholicism, free to follow her own path, would be able to undertake her true mission.

That mission, he continued, was to ensure the liberation and advancement of peoples. They must be free not only at the national level, by ridding themselves of foreign oppression, but also in the political and the economic spheres, by refusing the ascendancy of the middle classes and putting an end to exploitation by employers. For the free people is the true source of sovereignty: democracy underlies the new legitimacy. "Where the people is, there is Christ. Their struggle is Christ's struggle."[10]

But together with this work of liberation the Church must undertake another, which would hallow the accomplishment of all her efforts: she must free herself of all that drags her downward, of all that entangles her in the sordid interests of politics and finance. The sublime dream of a return to Christian origins, to the age of apostles and martyrs, to the days of the catacombs, haunted the offices of *L'Avenir* as it had long haunted many a monastic cell and has more recently haunted many an editorial chair. By regenerating herself Christianity would liberate the world—a splendid vision, which La Mennais and his fellows bore within themselves as an indefectible hope. That hope was perhaps utopian, and it may be that those theories were too far in advance of the age; but no one can ponder them without emotion across the gulf of a hundred years.

In order to foster their teaching, La Mennais and his friends did not confine themselves to the publication of a daily paper. *L'Avenir* became the

10. Michel Mourre.

core, the bond of union and the means of expression of an entire movement. It never had more than twelve hundred subscribers, but from the start its influence was out of all proportion to that modest circulation. Its campaigns were sensational, for example when it attacked by name a number of bishops chosen by the government and whom it considered unworthy, or again when it fulminated against a high official's interference in a matter of religious burial. Small groups of readers and friends of *L'Avenir* sprang up in the provinces and even abroad. In December 1830 an organization called the General Agency was formed to concert the activities of liberal Catholics, to defend the rights of the Church and to confound her enemies. The Agency and the affiliations which it established in the provinces were supposed to confine themselves to the field of religion and to avoid political activity; but where did politics begin or end when, for instance, there was question of demanding freedom of education and the end of the monopoly? At length the editors of *L'Avenir*, reaching beyond the boundaries of France, conceived an even more comprehensive plan: they proposed to unite in a single movement all those who, in every land, thought as they did—the Poles locked in conflict with the Czar, as well as O'Connell's Irishmen and the Italian patriots of the *Risorgimento*. The ultimate goal of those intrepid doctrinaires was a liberal and Christian International Workers' Association. Such was the Act of Union, which La Mennais called "the Great Charter of the Age."

Those measures were not, of course, to everyone's liking. The position adopted by *L'Avenir* was so unfamiliar as to be at first misunderstood; in left-wing circles there were sarcastic references to "this song compounded of psalms and the 'Marseillaise.'" Heinrich Heine, a virulent atheist, denounced those "humbugs in disguise" who pretended to wear the red bonnet whereas in fact there was nothing to see on their heads but the purple skull-cap of a prelate. Théophile Gautier guffawed over the "hypocrisy" of those who "coupled Robespierre with Jesus Christ." On the other side wrath was more fiery and resistance more determined. The government of Louis-Philippe reacted by prosecuting the impudent journalists who had dared to criticize the choice of bishops. The oft-repeated assurance of *L'Avenir* that "a republic is inevitable," that it was in fact just around the corner, infuriated all those for whom the word "republic" was synonymous with disorder and anarchy. "Revolting absurdities!" exclaimed Montalivet, the minister of public worship. Among the clergy opinion was no more favourable; while a few young curates devoted themselves heart and soul to the movement, many parish priests felt no calling to the heroic life of poverty urged upon them by the ascetics of Rue Jacob. The bishops were equally disturbed; separation of Church and State appeared to them as nothing less than heresy, in line with theories that sought to laicize society. One of their number, Mgr. d'Astros, Archbishop of Toulouse,[11] came to the conclusion not only that La Mennais was vulnerable at the political level, but also that his theological and philosophical teaching contained grave errors. Episcopal denunciations were sent to Rome, where they were reinforced by others from secular authorities who regarded the Act of Union as a charter of revolutionary subversion, and members of the small Mennaisian groups as formidable anarchists—a new sort of *Carbonari*.

Episcopal warnings, followed by condemnations, began to fall thick and fast. *L'Avenir* was banned from the diocese of Chartres; Cardinal de Rohan and Mgr. d'Astros launched vehement pastorals against its foolhardy editors; and the nuncio publicly declared himself "appalled by such insolence." News of the Act of Union upset certain readers who did not approve the violent methods of some liberals, and many cancelled their subscriptions. Moreover, since the editors of *L'Avenir* professed the loftiest disdain for the rules that must govern the sound administration of any journal, funds quickly ran low. At the end of thirteen months, in October 1831, the situation was so critical that the shareholders decided to suspend publication—not, they said, for sordid financial reasons, but in "the interests of the theories defended by *L'Avenir*, which are far more precious in their eyes."

---

11. For his earlier history see Chapter II, section 8.

Who was it that then conceived the idea of turning to Rome, of appealing to the highest authority in Christendom? Almost certainly Lacordaire; he confessed as much later by acknowledging the move to have been a tactical error. "We must go to Rome," he told La Mennais, "in order to justify our designs and submit our thoughts to the Holy See." Without taking time to reflect or to seek advice, the master rallied to the opinion of his young disciple. More than ever, now that political legitimacy was passing to the people, he felt himself an ultramontane, entirely devoted to him who in some way embodied this supreme legitimacy. "Soon," he cried in one of those oracular outbursts for which he had such a flair, "soon a powerful and calm utterance, spoken by an old man in the Queen-City at the foot of the Cross, will give the signal for the final regeneration awaited by the world." He conceived no union of peoples other than in submission to the common father, "who stretches forth his hand only to protect, and opens his mouth only to bless." He had even welcomed with enthusiasm the election to Peter's throne of an austere monk. And so in the final number of *L'Avenir* he announced that Lacordaire, Montalembert and himself were about to leave for Rome as "pilgrims of God and liberty, just as in ancient times Israel went to call upon the Lord at Siloë."

Never for a moment—despite some more cautious remarks let fall by Montalembert—did he think that he might find in Rome the very opposite of approval. Never for a moment did he tell himself that he would cruelly embarrass the Pope by asking him to choose between him, La Mennais, his school and his ideas on the one hand, and the episcopate and princes on the other. He did not then know that Gregory XVI, on receipt of numerous complaints, had already ordered an inquiry into the Mennaisian theories. The Holy Father had appointed three examiners, chosen quite impartially: Father Ventura, general of the Theatines and a friend of La Mennais; Father Banaldi, founder at Modena of a newspaper that was by no means reactionary; and Cardinal Lambruschini, who had known the author of the *Essai sur l'indifférence* in Paris. All three, while paying tribute to the "real merits," the virtues, and even the "extraordinary genius" of La Mennais, had concluded that there were certain errors in his teaching. None of the three, however, was in favour of a public condemnation, for which the Christian Druid's enemies were hoping.

He had indeed no lack of enemies. At Rome there were the ambassadors of governments which *L'Avenir* had denounced as oppressors: Saint-Aulaire of France, and the representative of Austria, who was carefully briefed by Metternich. Cardinal Lambruschini himself had lately warned the Holy See against the extravagance of certain theories and certain observations touching the episcopate. A clique of émigrés too was working against the innovator; at its head was the youthful, wealthy, elegant and ostentatious Cardinal de Rohan-Chabot, whom the Roman wits had nicknamed *il bambino* but who spoke on behalf of the French bishops. The Jesuits were unanimously hostile; La Mennais had dealt with them very harshly on several occasions, and the democratic views of *L'Avenir* inspired them with horror. The Sulpicians were no more friendly.

It must also be acknowledged that no worse moment could have been chosen for a talk with the Holy Father on the liberty of peoples. He was in process of learning, in Romagna and elsewhere, to what excesses popular freedom led. *L'Avenir* had contained numerous articles re-echoing the "cry of deliverance" from the Belgians, Poles and Irish, a cry which "Italy, pensive and suffering, stifled deep in her breast like some secret hope." The Pope could hardly have been expected to applaud this constant reference to "Italy pensive and suffering" at a time when couriers were bringing him news of successful insurrections.

Of all that, however, the "pilgrims of God and liberty" had not the least suspicion. Their journey from Paris to Rome was triumphal. At Lyons (where their arrival coincided with the silk-weavers' riots), at Marseille, at Aix-en-Provence and at Genoa they received a warm welcome. Their reception in Rome was less cordial, and La Mennais, recalling the flattery that had attended his last visit, was disappointed. This time no delegations of admirers came to welcome him; he was offered no rooms in the Vatican. Father Ventura received the Frenchmen at his monastery, but did not hide his anxiety. Only Cardinal Wendt invited them to supper. And when they asked for an audience they were told that the Sovereign Pontiff would first like to read a memorial of their teaching and their aims.

The early days in Rome, therefore, were spent in drawing up this memorial. It recapitulated the main points of that which La Mennais had formerly addressed to Leo XII, as well as those contained in an article outlining the policy of *L'Avenir*, and it ended with reference to the journal's activity during the past year. The result was an indictment of the policy adopted hitherto by the Church in alliance with secular powers, a plea for the separation of Church and State, a justification of the work undertaken by *L'Avenir*, the Agency and the Union, and finally an act of submission to the Pope, whose decision the pilgrims declared that they awaited with the docility and confidence of children.

Weeks passed, saddening the three friends. While Lacordaire and Montalembert discovered the splendours of Rome and the poignant melancholy of the surrounding countryside, La Mennais champed at his bit, not hesitating to send highly indiscreet letters to acquaintances in France, or even to explode in public against Rome ("this great tomb"), the Curia, the cardinals and the Pope himself. Somebody present at one of these outbursts whispered that "his political heterodoxy might well plunge him into religious heresy."

An answer to the memorial came at last. Cardinal Lambruschini had proposed two solutions: either the Pope himself could send for La Mennais and tell him that he censured his revolutionary theories, or he could pass the memorial to the Holy Office. Gregory XVI was more gentle. He asked Cardinal Pacca to tell the pilgrims that "while recognizing their good intentions he was sorry to see that they had revived certain controversies which were dangerous, to say the least; that their teachings would be examined, but that this might take a long time; and that he enjoined them meanwhile to return to France, where he would let them know his decision in due course." This was plain speaking. Lacordaire at once recognized as much and told his companions that to linger in Rome would be "to fall short of their promise of absolute submission and to disobey the Pope." But La Mennais, stunned by the rebuff, stubbornly determined to remain, in order "to furnish the necessary explanations and answer objections."

Worse, he took it into his head to press for an audience with the Pope, and went so far as to ask the French ambassador Saint-Aulaire, his declared enemy, to obtain one for him. The request was granted, but the audience proved, as it was bound to prove, disappointing. On arrival the "pilgrims of God and Liberty" found that the meeting was to be attended by Cardinal de Rohan, who had censured them. The Sovereign Pontiff was all kindness and affability. He talked to them for a quarter of an hour about this and that: about the Abbé Jean-Marie and his pious undertakings; about Montalembert's mother, who was famous for her devotion; about the art of Michelangelo and the bells of St. Peter's; and also about snuff, of which the Pope offered Féli a pinch. But not a word was said about *L'Avenir* or the memorial, and the audience terminated with a distribution of medals and blessing of rosaries.

Many historians, and even more numerous biographers of La Mennais, have blamed Gregory XVI for his attitude. Some have imagined that the sequence of events would have been altogether different if the Pope had opened his arms to the great champion of the Catholic cause; if he had talked to him like a deserving son who needed only the correction of his errors; in a word, if he had remembered the far-sighted observation of Leo XII: "He is a man who must be handled gently." That all might then have been different is quite possible, but not certain. La Mennais was never one to be restrained by counsels of moderation when his own pet views were at stake; neither his brother nor Lacordaire nor, later, Montalembert was able to prevent him from travelling to the end of the road upon which he had set out. Would a few words from the Pope have sufficed? Moreover it should be emphasized that Gregory XVI was very different from Leo XII; good-natured though he may have been, he lacked the glow, the manner, the gift of words that go straight to the heart. In order to quiet the restless soul of La Mennais and bind up its wounds, someone other than a strict theologian was required.

Gregory XVI's reserve had been no doubt increased by news from France that a group of bishops had just submitted La Mennais's theories to a committee of expert theologians, most of them Priests of Saint-Sulpice, and that that committee had formally condemned them. The teaching of La Mennais thus examined included not only his views on liberty, which formed the bases of *L'Avenir*, but also his philosophical and theological tenets which could be read in the final volumes of the *Essai sur l'Indifference*, particularly his theory of common sense. On this last point La Mennais was still more vulnerable; for by claiming to establish the foundation of belief in God on the unanimous testimony of mankind, was he not setting aside the part played by reason in demonstrating faith, and treating revelation as worthless? Such argument carried weight with Gregory XVI, a thoroughgoing Thomist.

Meanwhile La Mennais stayed on in Rome without knowing exactly why. Lacordaire had quitted the Eternal City after begging him in vain not to be stubborn; even Montalembert, who would have liked to remain at his master's side, was on the point of leaving in order to visit Naples and Pompeii. Withdrawing to a Theatine hermitage at Frascati, where Father Ventura had given orders for his reception, the stricken prophet, filled with bitterness, thought of writing a work to be entitled *Les Maux de l'Eglise*. His letters showed him harsh, ill-humoured, full of wrath against all those, whether cardinals or Jesuits, whom he accused of responsibility for his defeat. All the news he received from the Curia strengthened him in the conviction that his cause was lost, and that the Pope was irrevocably committed to a course of action that would lead to disaster. La Mennais had nothing more to hope for in Rome, or from Rome; at the beginning of July, therefore, he departed in company with Montalembert.

The two unhappy pilgrims returned to France by way of Munich, in order to warm their hearts again at that friendly fireside of vigorous and enthusiastic Catholicism, whose flame was kept alight by Schelling, Görres, young Döllinger and a pleiad of artists. There they were received with open arms. There too Lacordaire joined them, bringing the bad news from

 France: their defeat was known, and it was being exploited by clerical and Gallican circles. It was during a banquet in his honour that La Mennais was handed a package from Rome, brought by an envoy of the nunciature; it contained a copy of the Encyclical *Mirari vos* (August 15, 1832), which Gregory XVI had lately signed. With it was a letter from Cardinal Pacca.

Rising from the table, La Mennais took Lacordaire by the arm. "I've just received a papal Encyclical directed against us," he said; "we have nothing more to do but submit." True, he was not named in the document; Gregory, of course, had hoped thus to humour him, and the Encyclical was framed in general terms like those which the Popes were accustomed to publish at the start of their pontificates. But there could be no mistake about it: the main theses of *L'Avenir* were condemned, those on liberty and the separation of Church and State as well as those on the regeneration of Catholicism. Indeed the union with "liberal revolutionaries" was explicitly denounced as a grave error.

That evening, with his two disciples, La Mennais made a close study of the text. "Condemnation of liberty! Abandonment of Polish nationality!"[12] he murmured sorrowfully. Silence. Then: "God has spoken.... *Fiat voluntas tua.* His Vicar on earth has forbidden me to serve either cause with my pen. There remains prayer...." In presence of the two young men, dumb with surprise and admiration, he proceeded to write a letter of submission. The three editors of *L'Avenir* bowed before the Pope's decision, declared that they were "withdrawing from the lists," begged all their friends to follow their example and renounced further publication of the journal. That was the attitude of a true Catholic, of an obedient son of Holy Church, the only attitude possible for a resolute ultramontane, a fanatical partisan of the Pope's omnipotence.

Later, recalling those pathetic hours, Lacordaire wrote: "If he had been humble and submissive, or even merely shrewd and far-sighted, he would

12. During La Mennais's last days in Italy a papal Brief addressed to the Polish bishop had condemned the patriotic revolt (see section 6) and ordered submission to "the benevolent Emperor of Russia".

have found himself once again, in 1841, head of the liberal Catholic school,
leader of a fresh crusade, greater, stronger and more respected.... No one has ever perished more gratuitously." La Mennais in fact did not preserve the noble attitude he had at first adopted; he did not abide by that initial gesture of submission. Why? Because his adversaries celebrated their triumph too noisily and turned the dagger in his quivering wound? That has often been said, and it is to some extent true: as we know only too well, there is something relentless about clerical hatred. But dates prove that even before those cruel shafts were loosed against him many symptoms showed him to be on the way to rebellion. The explanation of his recalcitrance must be sought in the depths of his being, deep down in that divided soul where a struggle between darkness and light was waged without ceasing. Was the cause of La Mennais's rebellion, then, that rugged pride which was the principal characteristic of his nature, that inescapable conviction of being always and alone right? Not entirely. True, he was embittered at finding himself rejected after having been so enthusiastically acclaimed, but that was not the only grievance that led him astray. He believed firmly that his doctrine represented true Christianity. If the Pope condemned him, he was failing in his eternal mission; but by the same token the promise made by Christ to Peter, and by him transmitted to Christ's vicar, was shown to be null and void. And if Christ was mistaken, the light was dying, the world was in a state of collapse. The whole tragedy of the impetuous dialectician was contained in that all too simple theorem.

Returning to La Chênaie with a small group of disciples, among whom were Gerbet, Lacordaire and Maurice de Guérin, La Mennais plunged into bitter rumination on his grievances. His financial situation was bad and was causing him extreme anxiety, for he had been ruined by an unfortunate venture in the field of publishing. Now he would have to write, and write a great deal, in order to live. He repeatedly went back to the document which had smitten him and derived from it some strange exegesis: *L'Avenir* had not been truly the object of censure; the Encyclical was "an act of government," but it had not condemned his teaching in the strict sense of the word." As always, of course, he too often allowed himself to be carried away by anger both in his letters and in conversation with his disciples: Rome was the most infamous sewer that had ever soiled human eyes," and so forth. All this was so painful that Lacordaire could no longer endure the atmosphere that now prevailed at La Chênaie; one evening he fled without even saying goodbye to his master, but leaving him a cruel and mournful letter of farewell.

Then the enemy awoke. The Gallicans of *L'Ami da la Religion* poured sarcasm on the papalist condemned by the Pope, insinuating that his famous submission was a decoy. His beloved brother, the Abbé Jean-Marie, was harassed, persecuted and threatened with dismissal from his charitable institutions. News came from Rome that Father Ventura, Féli's best friend, had had to resign from his generalship of the Theatines. The kindly moderation shown by the Pope in refraining from any personal reference to La Mennais was not imitated by all the bishops. Some required of candidates for ordination "an oath rejecting the theories of M. de La Mennais"; and one of them went so far as publicly to describe the unselfish apostle of *L'Avenir* as a venal place-seeker. Such meanness ended by exasperating Féli and anchoring him more firmly in his ideas.

Nearly two years passed thus, amid mounting tension. Informed of what La Mennais was writing and saying, Gregory XVI decided to send Mgr. d'Astros a Brief expressing his sorrow at the change of attitude manifested by the solitary of La Chênaie, a sorrow proportionate to the satisfaction afforded by his original submission. This was another fatherly invitation; the Pope was asking La Mennais not to content himself with the shadowy retreat into which he had withdrawn, but to issue a retractation. Unfortunately Mgr. d'Astros published the Brief in *L'Ami de la Religion*, to the delight of Féli's enemies. The stricken prophet replied by writing a letter submissive in tone but containing many obscure phrases which left those who saw it to read between the lines. In fact he now based his attitude on a casuistical distinction: "Provided that in the religious sphere a Christian manages to do nothing but listen and obey, he remains...quite free in respect of his opinions, words and deeds in the purely temporal order." This distinction, questionable enough with regard to a layman, was quite unacceptable in the case of a priest. Obviously the Pope could not allow it, and the Bishop of Rennes suspended La Mennais. Rupture was inevitable.

A remarkable episode now occurred which throws strong light on the tragic, contradictory and headstrong character of La Mennais. Quitting La Chênaie, after bidding his disciples farewell in the course of a dramatic Mass during which he fainted with emotion, he went to Paris, partly to earn a living. The archbishop was instructed by Rome to see him and try to bring him to repentance. His Grace was none other than Mgr. de Quélen, whom the polemist had berated some years earlier. Contrary to all expectation, the two Bretons understood one another. There were polite discussions, and a new message came from Rome begging La Mennais to consider his position, "as a Catholic and a priest, at the foot of the crucifix." Everything appeared to be moving in the right direction, and La Mennais sent Cardinal Pacca a letter of total submission, undertaking to follow the teaching of the Encyclical without the slightest deviation. Joy unbounded! The suspension was lifted, and the nuncio talked of inviting him to dinner. But at rock bottom the prophet had not renounced his ideas; he told Montalembert so, and the Vicomte was mightily disturbed. Why then had he signed the act of submission? Was it because he feared "the violent storm" which his refusal would have provoked; or because he was so utterly weary of all these disputes and all this bitterness; or because he wanted "peace at any price"? Perhaps a spring grew slack within him. But immediately afterwards he stiffened once again. Wild cries poured from his lips: "I signed! I signed! I would have signed a declaration that the moon had fallen in China...that the Pope is God, the great God of heaven and earth, and that he alone must be adored." The author of so many splendid tributes to the infallible Pontiff had descended to such blasphemies. Mgr. de Quélen, who had been filled with so much happiness at the return of that soul to its obedience, almost collapsed with amazement one day in January 1834, when La Mennais informed him that he renounced his priesthood and would no longer celebrate Mass.

 Thereafter a chain of events led with fearful logic to total rupture. In that "entirely new life" upon which he declared that he embarked with absolute serenity, Féli imagined, like Renan later, that "while abandoning the Church he was remaining faithful to Jesus"[13]; but schism, heresy and apostasy lay ahead. On April 20, a few weeks after he had notified Mgr. de Quélen of his decision, he published a strange book entitled *Paroles d'un croyant*,[14] which is beyond doubt his literary masterpiece. It deals with two great themes: first, the inexhaustible wretchedness of man, an exile upon earth, guest in a "lodging-house"; second, Christian hope, which must liberate mankind from all servitude and lead him to the only true light. The book describes the opposition of two camps into which the world is divided. On one side are the people, living embodiment of the City of God; on the other the city of Satan, its executioners and oppressors, kings and priests. The success of this work was prodigious: one hundred thousand copies were sold in two months. But stern critics were not wanting, not only in the governmental press, where "the gospel of insurrection" was dragged in the mud, but above all in religious circles. Lamennais was sure that Rome would do no more than utter "a few complaints," but he was gravely mistaken. Gregory XVI considered this publication an act of treachery; Cardinal Lambruschini expressed the view that its author's previous reserve and hesitation could no longer hide the truth. Mgr. de Quélen alone counselled silence in order not to give the book fresh advertisement. There was no need, as Lamennais thought, for Metternich to intervene in person; the Pope was determined to strike at the revolutionary priest. In due course the Encyclical *Singulari vos* appeared, condemning the book and comparing its author with such earlier heretics as the Waldenses, Wyclif and John Huss. The blow fell direct and hurled the rebel to the ground. In vain he continued to protest: "I have certainly not broken with the Church, I have not

13. *Souvenirs d'enfance et de jeunesse.*

14. It was from this date that, in order to democratize his name, he signed himself Lamennais instead of Félicité de La Mennais.

imitated Luther." After this formal condemnation the career of Lamennais as a Catholic was ended; his best friends abandoned him, even Montalembert. He was alone.

The events and publications that marked the remaining twenty years of his life had less and less to do with the history of the Church. In *Troisièmes mélanges* and *Affaires de Rome* he continued to denounce what he called the errors of the Church, the meanness of Rome, "papal Christianity"; and he drifted further and further from the faith towards a kind of humanitarian socialism which true socialists despised. *Le Livre du Peuple* (1837), *Le Pays et le gouvernement* (1840) and *Du Passé et de l'Avenir du Peuple* (1841) recapitulated his earlier theories on the messianic role of an idealized Demos, adding little except an indictment of the ruling *bourgeoisie*. Even the actions brought against him by the government of Louis-Philippe did not restore him to the fame which, since the *Paroles d'un croyant*, had gradually deserted him. Henceforward he was just the gaunt little man described by Tocqueville, with parchment face topping a striped cravat, dressed in a green frock coat and yellow waistcoat, moving with short and hurried steps, never turning his head or looking at anyone, still bearing the stamp of a priest "as if he had just emerged from a sacristy, but with the pride of one who walks on the heads of kings and defies God."

Nevertheless bitter disappointments awaited him. In 1848, when his dream was realized and the Republic was inaugurated, he soon detected the imposture. As a member of the National Assembly he witnessed the collapse of that Second Republic, which had failed to establish a truly popular regime and had been so firmly and so quickly taken in hand by the oppressors. In 1851 his health began to fail. He never again left his room, where he busied himself in peevish discussion with his nephew over the sales of such works as a translation of the *Divine Comedy*, friendless except for Béranger—a strange pair.[15]

15. Chateaubriand, who had never despaired of bringing him back to the Church, died in 1848.

274 Lamennais never returned to the Church. When he became seriously ill, at the beginning of 1854, his niece begged him in vain to accept the help of a priest. "No," he said, and turned his face to the wall. On his instructions his executor forbade the erection of a cross over his grave. The day after his death his brother, the Abbé Jean-Marie, said Mass in the little chapel where the master used to give communion to his disciples. Then he went out on to the terrace: "Féli, Féli, where are you?" he cried aloud in anguish, and fell unconscious to the ground.

The tragedy of Lamennais, his apostasy and fall, was a terrible loss to the Church. One begins to think of what he might have been, of what he might have done, had he been more humble of heart, had he really possessed the mind of the Church, had there been men to sympathize with him and "handle him gently." Perhaps a nineteenth-century St. Dominic. Nevertheless it would be unfair to underestimate his role. Surely his one-time disciples owed to him much of their subsequent achievement. It was he who pioneered the road to an organization of Catholics above party interests; it was he more than any other who laboured for the defeat of Gallicanism, for the spread of those ideas which triumphed at the Vatican Council sixteen years after his death; it was he, again, who brought about between the people and Christianity an atmosphere of confidence radically opposed to the hatred revealed in 1830. It may have been for these reasons that no Pope excommunicated him by name.

On the Sunday following Féli's death Father Gratry, preaching in the Oratory, spoke these noble words which close the mournful tale: "Must we despair of this poor soul's salvation? No. That this great example might serve as a lesson, God has allowed this ending to be stripped of hope. But this soul had helped to revive religious feeling in our country. May we not think there was a turning hidden from our eyes and that it obtained mercy?"

No Christian can think without emotion of Félicité de La Mennais, a brilliant apostle who was not a saint.

6. A GRIEVOUS EPISODE: GREGORY XVI AND THE TRAGEDY OF POLAND

THE attitude adopted by Gregory XVI towards Lamennais was the natural outcome of his character and training. He was a doctrinaire, and that is a facet of his personality and conduct which must not be underestimated. Nothing is more unfair than to attribute his rigidity to mere political considerations, to represent the successor of St. Peter as terrorized by the powers of oppression or as consulting none but his own interests. The truth is altogether different. Amid extraordinary intellectual confusion the Camaldolese Pope, taking his stand on the unshakable principles of Christianity, tried to arrive at truth, to determine how Catholics should behave, and to denounce the lethal errors that menaced the world.

Gregory's doctrinaire attitude, firmly based on principle and regardless of the human consequences of their application, was subjected throughout his pontificate to the test of events. Nor did it stand that test at all well; those sixteen years, confused and in many respects decisive, were far from being adorned with victories for the Church. Indeed the terrible dilemma in which the papacy seemed to be caught by liberal and national revolution ended in a manner singularly painful and unsatisfactory for the Catholic cause. This was so above all in the tragic episode of the Polish rebellion.

That rebellion, which broke out at Warsaw in November 1830, shortly before the death of Pius VIII,[16] lasted for less than a year. Heroic, but insufficiently organized and led by men more courageous than capable, the Poles fought numerous battles worthy of the *chansons de geste*, without thereby profiting a cause doomed from the outset by inequality of strength. The affair was settled at the beginning of September 1831. Instead of remaining, as it had been since 1815, a constitutional kingdom within the Russian orbit, Poland became a province of the czarist empire. The Organic Statute replaced the Charter of 1815, and the knout reigned over an unhappy land.

16. See Chapter III, section 16.

 Europe as a whole did not react to this drama. Nevertheless every man in Europe with any "liberal" leanings at all, everyone who was striving to rebuild the world, quivered with loving anguish for conquered Poland. The tragedy of a martyred people moved thousands of hearts.

What of the Pope? For him the problem was more than delicate. A huge majority of the Polish fighters were Catholics; their ranks included very many priests, and several bishops encouraged the insurrection. Badani, sent by the rebels to show Gregory the justice of their cause, emphasized one aspect of the struggle, which, as events proved, could not be ignored: the resistance of Catholicism to the oppression of Orthodoxy. At the same time, however, the Czar's representative, Prince Gagarin, assured the Pope that the leaders of the rebellion belonged to the same secret societies which were threatening law and order in Italy and elsewhere; that his master, guarantor of peace, had no intention of destroying the Catholic Church in Poland; and he asked for a "fatherly exhortation" inviting the clergy "not to overstep their spiritual duties."

The Czar's protestations were submitted to Gregory XVI on the day of his coronation, at a moment when disturbances in Italy gave him little cause for sympathy with liberalism; and they carried more weight than heart-rending appeals from the Polish Catholics. Gregory began by writing a letter to the bishops of Poland, advising them "to preach obedience and submission as advocated by St. Paul"; it was entrusted to Gagarin, but was apparently deemed inadequate by the government at St. Petersburg and never reached its destination. Gagarin intervened once more, supported this time by Metternich, who dropped a hint to the Holy Father that a measure of condescension on his part would enable the Czar to arrange an advantageous settlement of all Catholic problems in Poland. It must also be remarked that the lyrical outbursts and vehement recriminations of the liberals—those of *L'Avenir* and those of the *Risorgimento*—did not help to sway the mind of Gregory XVI in favour of the rebel cause. On June 9, 1832, the Brief *Superiori anno* stigmatized "those authors of lying and trickery who, under cover of religion, defy the legitimate power of princes, break all the ties of submission imposed by duty and plunge their country into misfortune and mourning." It directed Polish Catholics to be on their guard against baneful doctrines, and advised them to obey their "mighty emperor who would show them every kindness."

It is not hard to imagine the effect of this document, first in Poland where it arrived and was solemnly published by the Russians just as the occupying forces were beginning an orgy of repression. In France, even outside liberal Catholic circles, it caused widespread grief, and in England the Protestant press emphasized its disgraceful character. It was not then known that the Brief had been accompanied by another addressed to the Czar, in which His Holiness energetically denounced "the wicked chicanery" of the Russian government in Poland, cited examples of near-persecution, and suggested sending to St. Petersburg a papal *chargé d'affaires* to make a careful study of the whole situation. But Russian diplomacy, of course, had hurriedly interred this second document in that abyss of silence which it has always had at its disposal. Furthermore, in 1835, when Cardinal Bernetti eventually asked for a reply, Gagarin brought one which declared that all the deplorable events in Poland were the fault of Catholics and particularly of the ungrateful clergy whom His Majesty's Government was doing its best to reorganize with paternal solicitude.

That solicitude revealed itself in striking fashion. While the Poles found themselves deprived of all political rights, there took place a hateful process of Russianization and subjugation in the religious field; yet Russian propaganda spread abroad a rumour that these measures had been taken in agreement with the Holy See, conformably with the famous Brief *Superiori anno*.

After ten years Gregory XVI at long last learned the truth. In July 1842 he delivered a consistorial allocution which took the form of a moving protest, denouncing "the fraudulency responsible for a rumour that the Holy See has betrayed the Catholic cause," setting out clearly all the Russian encroachments on the rights of Catholics in Poland, and begging the Czar for a change of heart. This courageous but sorrowful speech made a great impression throughout Europe; it was praised in France, even by the liberal paper *La Réforme.*

After maintaining silence for several months the Russian Government decided to reopen negotiations, doubtless through fear of a fresh explosion of wrath in Poland. For two years and more its diplomats did their best to delay a settlement, assuring Gregory time and again that by adopting such an attitude he was siding with revolutionaries. But Czar Nicholas had begun to feel that he was losing the sympathy of Europe, even of his Austrian allies. In December 1845 he went to Rome and asked to be received by the Pope. What happened between those two men during the long audience? Cardinal Wiseman, without quoting his sources, tells us that the all-powerful autocrat strutted proudly into the Pope's room, but came out pale, "with dishevelled hair and downcast eyes, as if he had experienced during that hour all the sufferings of a prolonged fever." Twenty years later this narrative was confirmed in its main outlines by Pius IX, but again without reference to his source of information. Cardinal Acton, however, who served as interpreter, has left a far less dramatic account of the audience. According to him the dialogue was perfectly calm and the interview ended with a kiss of peace, though the Pope reminded the Czar in no uncertain terms that he was abusing his rights as a temporal sovereign by endeavouring to change the religion of his subjects. At all events that audience was the starting-point of negotiations which ended, under Pius IX, in the Concordat of 1847.[17]

"The papacy has shown itself worthy of its splendid past," wrote *La Réforme*; "justice, law and liberty have found a spokesman in the Roman sanctuary; the modern conscience can feel satisfied." True; and that firm reaction must be placed to the credit of Gregory XVI. But had it entirely erased the memory of *Superiori anno*?

17. See Volume 2, Chapter V, section 10.

7. GREGORY XVI AND THE "VICISSITUDES OF STATES"

THE problem raised in Poland, which Gregory XVI had thought he could solve in a way suggested by his personal and strongly conservative inclinations, was raised in several other countries and in a manner likewise delicate. The Poles, whose insurrection had failed, might be told that by vainly attempting to overthrow the established order they were compromising the Church to no good purpose. But how about the liberal movements which had succeeded? What attitude should he adopt towards governments that had come to power by way of triumphant rebellion? Ought he to ignore them, refuse diplomatic relations with them, at the risk of driving them into the camp of irreligion, which several of them were unwilling to join?

The question had been answered some years earlier by Leo XII, who, confronted with a declaration of independence by the Spanish colonies in America, had established relations with the young republics without reference to Madrid. Following his example Pius VIII had not hesitated to recognize the "revolutionary" government of Louis-Philippe. But the same problem arose in so many cases that Gregory XVI thought it necessary to lay down a general rule. He did this in August 1831 by the Constitution *Sollicitudo Ecclesiarum*, which decided that in cases of "vicissitudes of States" and changes of regime "the Roman pontiffs would enter into diplomatic relations with those who were *de facto* in power." He certainly did not consider this as a concession to the Revolution. The document made clear that in acting thus towards revolutionary governments the Holy See intended "neither to confirm them in authority nor to grant them any source of new rights". It was not adhesion to the theory of *fait accompli* which Pius IX condemned in the *Syllabus*; Gregory XVI was far from admitting that "an act of injustice crowned with success does not offend the sanctity of law." He merely defined a practical attitude by recognizing *de facto*, but not *de jure*, political system resulting from the Revolution.

This distinction, due in large measure to Cardinal Bernetti, was shrewd. It enabled the Pope to condemn revolutionary movements from the legal standpoint and yet to accept their results, to practise within the boundaries of his own States a policy of counter-revolution and yet remain on good terms with the governments of France and Belgium, which had resulted from political upheaval. Gregory XVI, however, adopted it with some hesitation. Pressure of events rather than conviction led him to apply this policy; and he endeavoured to restrict its consequences, ready to abandon it in favour of counter revolution pure and simple as soon as circumstances permitted. When Lambruschini replaced Bernetti at the secretariat of state the Pope urged him strongly along this path.

In Belgium revolution had triumphed, thanks to an alliance of the liberal revolutionaries and the Catholics, of which Cardinal Cappellari had formally disapproved. It was natural that, on becoming Pope, Gregory should be in no hurry to form links with the government of King Leopold. He recognized it, in accordance with the principle laid down by *Sollicitudo*, but remained cautious. The Belgian Constitution proclaimed freedom of worship, recognition of the religious orders, appointment of bishops by the Holy See and other rights of the Church—proof that the Catholics, while triumphing with the liberals, had at the same time won a victory for their own religion. But the new regime stood for separation of Church and State as well as for equality of all religions in the eyes of the law, a fact that did not please Rome. The formula "A free Church in a free State," repeatedly used by the Catholics, smacked of Lamennais. Thus when Leopold I asked the Pope to establish diplomatic relations with him, Gregory XVI at first turned a deaf ear. The Belgian Catholics, remembering that they had won their freedom in spite of the Holy See, feared that their interests might be harmed by the presence in Brussels of a papal representative. Ten years of negotiations were necessary before the Pope agreed to send King Leopold a nuncio in 1841.

Nor did things run smoothly thereafter. The first nuncio, Mgr. Fornari, made so clumsy an attempt to control the Belgian episcopate and the Catholic party that he had to be recalled. His successor, Mgr. Pecci (afterwards Leo XIII), adopted a conciliatory attitude; but the secretary of state rebuked him for lack of energy in defence of papal rights and recalled him in 1845, leaving at first only a *chargé d'affaires*, then, when the king protested, replacing him by a notorious anti-liberal. This matter of the nunciature showed all too clearly how ambiguous was the Holy See's attitude towards Belgium.

It was, however, undeniable that the Catholic cause had gained much by the establishment of the new regime. Those fifteen years were for Belgium a period of expansion at all levels—intellectual, political and spiritual. Taking advantage of the presence of Catholics in those "mixed governments," which lasted until 1847, the Belgian Church founded primary schools (nearly half of those in the entire country), secondary colleges, and a university which was opened first at Malines in 1834 and transferred to Louvain in 1835. In the political field the Catholics formed so strong and well organized a party that after 1847, when they broke off their alliance with the liberals who returned to anti-clericalism, they were able to offer them strenuous resistance. But all this was accomplished with little or no co-operation from the Holy See.

The situation was far less satisfactory in the Iberian Peninsula. Both states that lie within its boundaries were in the throes of dynastic crises which led to opposition between the liberals and anti-revolutionaries—a great temptation for the Holy See to take sides. In Portugal the crisis had begun long before 1830, but it became more acute shortly before the accession of Gregory XVI. When the country was occupied by Napoleon's troops in 1803 the royal family fled to Brazil, a circumstance of which the colony took advantage to declare itself independent and proclaim the Infante John emperor. In 1816 the latter, as John VI, returned to Lisbon, leaving in Brazil his son Don Pedro, who had himself crowned emperor in 1822. Meanwhile the country was troubled by revolutionary disturbances: there were violent clashes between the liberals, who were imbued with Carbonarist ideas and instigated by Freemasonry, and the conservatives, whom most of the clergy supported. The death of John VI in 1826 complicated the situation still further. Was his elder son Don Pedro his legitimate heir? No, replied some, for by agreeing to become Emperor of Brazil he had violated the famous oath, taken in 1139 on the battlefield of Ourique by all the Lusitanian nobility, never to allow a foreigner to reign. Moreover Don Pedro, fearing that his departure from Brazil might cost him the imperial crown, had decided to remain in America and had sent his seven-year-old daughter Maria da Gloria to reign at Lisbon under the regency of his own brother Don Miguel. At the same time, in order to mollify the opposition, Don Pedro had promulgated a fairly liberal charter.

Don Miguel, after hesitating for some while and wondering whether it might not be more advantageous to marry his niece as soon as she was old enough, eventually resolved, at the instigation of his imperious mother Donha Joachina and of the more violent absolutists, to seize power. For six years he imposed upon Portugal a reactionary regime compared with which that of the French extremists in 1815 seemed like heaven on earth. Not only was the Catholic religion given back all its rights, and the Society of Jesus readmitted, but courts modelled on the Inquisition were set up. Nearly forty thousand persons suspected of liberalism were exiles, and others were imprisoned or sentenced to be flogged. In 1831, however, Don Pedro, having lost the crown of Brazil, returned to Portugal and claimed the throne. Civil war broke out. Supported by all the liberals, and with the help of secret societies, Pedro conducted some bold and successful operations against his brother. Notwithstanding the aid of French legitimist volunteers, Don Miguel was beaten before Porto, before Lisbon and then in the neighbourhood of Evora. He capitulated (1834), and agreed to renounce the throne in return for a comfortable pension.

The Church found herself involved in this struggle; for although the Patriarch of Lisbon and two or three bishops had shown sympathy for the constitutional regime, a large majority of the clergy had seen its own victory in that of Don Miguel. Gregory XVI himself had recognized Don Miguel's government in accordance, as he said, with the Constitution *Sollicitudo*, but without concealing his personal sympathies; and when Don Miguel was obliged to flee the country he received a warm welcome in Rome.

The result of this policy was disastrous. As soon as the liberals came to power they once again confiscated the property which the clergy had recently recovered; the Jesuits were expelled after suffering insults reminiscent of the great eighteenth-century persecution[18]; priests were stoned in the villages; convents, schools and even hospices were closed; and episcopal appointments made by Don Miguel were annulled. In vain did the Pope, whose nuncio had been escorted back to the frontier, protest against these measures. Don Pedro's death in 1834 settled nothing; it was not until six years later that Queen Maria da Gloria, a fervent Catholic, managed to improve the situation and send a representative to Rome in order to negotiate a concordat. The Pope expressed his thanks by presenting her with the Golden Rose. But the anti-clerical crisis had made a deep impression on political circles in Portugal; Freemasonry had taken firm root among the intellectuals, and growing British Protestant influence was on the way to enfeebling the Lusitanian Church. A situation had been created that was to last until Salazar's accession to power in our own day.

Events in Spain were no more encouraging. Curiously similar to those of the small neighbouring kingdom, they too resulted in a clash between a niece and her uncle, between a liberally minded queen and an absolutist pretender. The queen was Maria Cristina, niece and fourth wife of the unhappy Ferdinand VII, to whom, shortly before his death in 1833, she bore an heiress (1830). The pretender this time was Don Carlos, brother of the late king. To whom should the throne pass? According to the so-called Salic Law of Bourbon tradition, to Don Carlos; according to the older Spanish custom, to Isabella. Behind this dynastic question lay a formidable political problem. Around Don Carlos were gathered all those who had lately approved the violent reaction of King Ferdinand: the more traditionalist members of the clergy, the conservative peasants of Biscay and Navarre, and the powers of the Holy Alliance. Maria Cristina, regent during Isabella's minority,

18. *The Church of the Classical Age: The Era of Great Splintering*, Volume 2, Chapter V, section 3.

 enjoyed the goodwill not only of the royalists and Catholic moderates, but also of the liberals, the survivors of the Trocadero, and even the revolutionaries and Freemasons. Britain and France favoured the queens; so did the foreign liberals, notably those of the *Risorgimento.*

Gregory XVI was embarrassed. When the regent's minister, Zea Bermudez, asked him to recognize her government, he sidestepped the question under pretext of uncertainty that Maria Cristina really held the reins of power. The result was tension between Madrid and Rome; the nuncio left and was not replaced. Appointment of bishops also was delayed, the Holy See refusing to write the traditional clause "on presentation by the Queen of Spain." It was quite clear that the Pope's sympathies lay with Don Carlos, and his attitude helped to drive the "Cristinist" government towards anti-clericalism, to which it already showed leanings. Following in the footsteps of France, the Cortes passed a bill placing a certain proportion of religious property at the disposal of the State, and examined a "civil constitution of the clergy." Gregory XVI protested against these measures, but in vain.

The situation quickly deteriorated: hostility between Carlists and Cristinists developed into civil war. In the north of Spain particularly a vast rebellion flared up, reminiscent of the war of La Vendée. Fighting for and with Don Carlos, the Navarrese peasantry believed that they were defending the ancient faith, the local *fueros* and the grandeur of the monarchy. But this bitter conflict gave rise to an even worse atrocity—an outburst of anti-religious fury. An epidemic of cholera broke out in Madrid; the population accused the monks of having poisoned the wells, and eighty of them were butchered. At the Puerta del Sol there were shouts of "Death to Christ! Long live Satan!" Monasteries were burned and churches sacked. The government followed suit by again expelling the Jesuits, suppressing nearly eight hundred religious houses and announcing a plan for the separation of Church and State. The new nuncio, who had only just reached Madrid, could do nothing but leave for home. Once more Gregory XVI protested strongly in a consistorial allocution.

Meanwhile the civil war drew to a close; after six years of fratricidal strife people were growing tired. The Congress of Vergara put an end to hostilities, but Carlism was not dead. With the return of peace the regent Maria Cristina sought to allay passions and restore quiet in the religious field. But she was opposed by General Espartero and driven into exile, leaving little Isabella II on the throne. This was the signal for a new anti-religious crisis, new measures of persecution, the final closing of the nunciature and yet another allocution by Gregory XVI condemning these acts of violence and calling upon the whole Catholic world to pray for Spain.

It was not until Espartero's fall and flight in 1845 that the religious situation improved. The new leader, General Narvaez, determined to calm the spirits of his fellow countrymen. A concordat was negotiated, and would doubtless have been signed if Gregory XVI had been willing formally to recognize Queen Isabella as rightful sovereign. Not until six years later, under Pius IX, did the negotiations bear fruit.

Thus in Spain as well as in Portugal the Church found herself involved in the great struggle between the "liberals," heirs of the French Revolution, and those who were determined to resist them. She found herself likewise involved in the affairs of a country where trouble might have been least expected—the peace-loving Swiss cantons. There antagonism emerged over the view entertained by the Swiss of their own famous union. The "federalists" stood for the independence of the cantons by virtue of ancient traditions hallowed by the treaties of Vienna in 1815. The "radicals" wanted a more centralized State. To this cause of dissension was added another—one that existed at this date in all unsettled countries. Switzerland had become the refuge of many liberals, *Carbonari*, Freemasons and other revolutionaries, among whom Mazzini was regarded as a prophet. In shameful violation of the elementary precept that refugees must not meddle in the affairs of their hosts, all these *fuorusciti* did their best to help the radical party, urging it along the road of anti-clericalism; seeing which the Catholics sided with the federalists.

In 1832 the liberal radicals tried to obtain a revision of the federal pact, but were outmanoeuvreed by their Catholic opponents. Two years later they made a bid for revenge. The predominantly Catholic cantons had persuaded the Holy See to create six exclusively Swiss bishoprics and to install a nuncio at Lucerne. Their adversaries replied with the Conference of Baden, which voted in favour of a bill of fourteen articles whose effect was nothing more or less than a civil constitution of the clergy. Gregory XVI condemned this document, whereupon the radicals expelled the nuncio and offered a chair of theology to the German professor Strauss, who was famed for his attacks on the divinity of Jesus Christ.[19] At the call of their energetic leaders, Joseph Leu and Meyer, the Catholics set themselves to fight against the decisions of Baden, which ignored their rights; they even obtained the intervention of the great powers, who asked the Swiss Government to exercise moderation. On August 1, 1842, Gregory XVI declared null and void all measures taken in violation of the rights of the Church, and he invited the Catholics to withstand such "criminal attempts."

The situation was now explosive. The Catholics formed themselves into defensive groups. Lucerne, where the majority was once again Catholic, rightly recalled the nuncio, though the city's conduct in opening its theological institute and seminary to the Jesuits was somewhat provocative. The radicals hit back by expelling Leu from the Grand Council and even imprisoning him for a time, and soon thereafter by employing force. In the canton of Vaud, in 1845, a *coup d'état* overthrew the conservative and federalist government; armed bands set out for an attack on Lucerne; and the unfortunate Leu was murdered in his bed. In face of this peril the seven cantons with federalist and Catholic leanings united to form a defensive confederacy, the *Sonderbund*, on December 11, 1845. The board was now set for the hideous game of civil war which was destined to begin a few months later.

19. See Volume 2, Chapter VI, section 2.

8. O'CONNELL'S IRELAND

THROUGHOUT that series of events the Church and the papacy found themselves committed by circumstances to a well-defined course of action. In Spain and Portugal, as well as in Switzerland, Gregory XVI could not have hesitated in the matter of his choice, since the holders of liberal ideas showed themselves everywhere more or less hostile to Catholicism. Even in Belgium his rather indeterminate attitude seemed justified by events when opposition between liberals and Catholics proved fatal. But he was confronted with a more delicate problem in countries where the Catholics themselves were defending their rights in the name of liberty and where the national movement went hand in hand with a great Catholic upsurge; in Ireland, for example, and in Germany.

The Catholic Emancipation Act, obtained in 1829 thanks largely to their activity, had not fully satisfied the Irish. They complained, not without reason, of having to pay enormous sums for the upkeep of Protestant churches while their own clergy lived on the alms provided by a far from rich population. Moreover the landlords charged them exorbitant rents, and evicted them from their holdings if a bad harvest made it impossible for them to pay their dues; nor could the poor farmers voice their grievances, for they were inadequately represented in the Commons. Religious, economic and political problems were therefore interlinked; could they be separately solved? Would not religious freedom be always illusory and precarious so long as full political freedom remained to be won? Catholic Ireland would never be truly herself until the repeal of the Act of Union, which associated her destiny with that of England.

Such was the opinion of O'Connell, the great leader to whom all earlier successes had been due. In the evening of the day upon which the Catholic Emancipation Act was passed he had exclaimed: "Those who believe that all is finished are mistaken. It is now time to begin the struggle for the nation's rights." Aged fifty-four, full of vigour and at the height of his reputation, he continued his work with the same energy and the same methods as before, refusing to break the law but making use of all the resources they allowed for the triumph of his ideas.

He started at the parliamentary level, and his eloquence caused a sensation in the House of Commons. Firmly supporting the Whigs, who were much less attached than the Tories to the Established Church, he obtained undeniable results: the appointment in Ireland of unbiased magistrates, partial abolition of tithes paid to the Anglican clergy, and rejection of the Coercion Bill which would have dangerously strengthened the powers of British officials. But he was still far from securing repeal of the Act of Union, which remained the ultimate goal of his programme; very far, especially in 1841, when the Tories returned to power.

The great warrior then resumed his campaign of agitation. Steps were taken to boycott English goods and to undermine the credit of the banks. Meetings were held at which O'Connell addressed huge audiences. The British Government was alarmed, though violence was absolutely forbidden at those assemblies. Thus when an unusually large gathering was due to take place at Clontarf, troops and artillery were sent to disperse it; but on receipt of this news O'Connell called off the meeting at the last moment. The ministry was foolish enough to order his arrest for conspiracy, a measure which the House of Lords rescinded as an abuse of power. If O'Connell's effort failed to achieve its end, it nevertheless scored several points. When the Commons voted in favour of Income Tax (1842) they decided that the Act should not apply to Ireland; and in 1844, when three new colleges were founded in Ireland, no attempt was made to prevent the admission of Catholics.

How was O'Connell's work viewed within the Church? Though supported almost unanimously by the Irish clergy, it was largely misunderstood elsewhere.

The Catholics of England showed themselves more than reserved—almost hostile. This may have been due to the fact that they were at the same time Englishmen and regarded the course of events in Ireland as harmful to the interests of their own country. But there were other reasons. O'Connell barred no one, not even Protestants, from joining the Society for Repeal of the Union; and his disciple Charles Gavan Duffy had appointed an Anglican and two Nonconformists, as well as three Catholics, to the editorial staff of the *Nation*. This alliance appeared suspicious to diehard Catholics, and not in England alone. Wiseman, a future cardinal, identified the nationalist liberalism of O'Connell and his friends with philosophical and theological liberalism and denounced both as inimical to dogma.

Rome adopted an attitude of extreme caution. Unlike La Mennais, O'Connell took care not to involve the Holy See or to claim the Pope as moral leader of the struggle for freedom. Gregory XVI therefore was not obliged to commit himself, and gladly maintained silence on the Irish movement. It is possible and even probable that he was, as has been said, "shocked by its exuberance." At all events his diplomatic activity was in no way calculated to assist the efforts of the Catholics.

The Pope's wariness helped to darken O'Connell's closing years. Moreover his country was prey to a terrible ordeal—the potato blight which resulted in such famine that the population fell from eight to five million, and more than half a million Irishmen emigrated, most of them to the United States. He was disturbed also by the growth of a new movement known as Young Ireland. It was strongly influenced by the example of liberal movements in Italy and elsewhere, and made no secret of its intention to defeat the English by means of physical force.

On the death of Gregory XVI and the election of his successor, Pius IX, O'Connell set out for Rome with a heavy heart, in order to tell the Holy Father of his troubles and assure him of his absolute loyalty. But death overtook him at Genoa (1847). The Italian liberals at the head of the *Risorgimento* claimed him as having been one of themselves, and thus appeared to justify the suspicions of Gregory XVI and Cardinal Lambruschini. In an eloquent panegyric Father Ventura spoke of "this new Maccabaeus, this new Moses," as a model for the leaders of Young Italy, and he concluded by advising the Romans to strive for the liberation of Italy as O'Connell had done for that of his own country. It was, however, precisely in order to avoid such confusion of ideas that Rome had remained silent.

9. "THE EVENT OF COLOGNE"

THE problem in German-speaking lands was one that had existed since the Reformation, the problem of relations between Church and State. German princes made a habit of meddling in ecclesiastical affairs, of acting as local popes within their own dominions. Even in Catholic Austria, Joseph II had worked along those lines.[20] But in the first half of the nineteenth century the problem was complicated by two factors: (1) the ambition of the Prussian monarchs, who sought to unify the whole of Germany under their own tutelage; (2) increasing tension between the Rhineland and eastern Germany, between Cologne and Berlin.

The wish to subject the Church to the State was frequently accompanied by a plan of Protestantization, more or less clearly revealed. Churches born of the Reformation willingly accepted royal tutelage; but the Catholic Church was much less ready to do so, and thereby tempted governments to subjugate her by force. That is what had happened in the Rhineland States which had sought to impose on the Church the Thirty-nine Articles of Frankfurt.[21] In Württemberg, for example, the government went so far as to appoint parish priests, to cancel holidays of obligation, to forbid the exposition of relics and even to alter the routine of confession. Baden notified the Archbishop of Freiburg that he might publish no pastoral letter without leave of the government, and that the State would thenceforward appoint sixty of the eighty parish priests in his diocese. In Hesse, Catholic clerics were requested to attend the Protestant and violently anti-Roman University of Giessen instead of the seminary at Mainz.

In Prussia this campaign was waged still more systematically and energetically. In order to bring about the unification of Germany under their sceptre the Hohenzollerns had first to achieve some measure of unity in the

20. *The Church of the Classical Age: The Era of Great Splintering*, Volume 2, Chapter V, sections 5, 7, 10.

21. See Chapter III, section 10.

anomalous States of which their dominions consisted. The Rhineland territories in particular needed bringing into line with the Prussian regime. In the absence of geographical continuity or common tradition it was necessary to impose on the various peoples the abstract principle of an all-powerful State, a principle embodied since the time of Frederick the Great in a caste of dedicated and even fanatical administrators, most of whom were Protestants. They naturally took the view that religion should play a part in this process of unification, and consequently that differences between the Churches should be eliminated, or at any rate reduced to a minimum.

In order to achieve this goal Frederick William II relied on the teaching and influence of Father George Hermes (1775–1811), a professor at Bonn, who was then at the height of his reputation. Hermesianism, a mixture of Kantian criticism and illuminism, reduced faith to mere feeling, emptied belief of its intellectual content, misinterpreted the role of grace, ignored that of freedom and appeared to offer a means of reconciliation with Protestantism. Though attacked by many Catholic authorities, especially by the Jesuits Perrone and Kleutgen and by Mgr. zu Droste-Vischering, coadjutor of Münster, and even condemned by the Brief *Dum acerbissimus* in 1835, the dangerous doctrine continued to spread, backed by the Prussian administration and aided by the strange connivance of certain bishops.

The conflict came to a head on the question of mixed marriages.[22] The Brief *Litteris* of 1830 had directed priests to require from spouses wishing for a Catholic marriage an oath to bring up their children in the Roman faith; in case of refusal they were to confine themselves to passive attendance, without giving a blessing. The Prussian Government forbade publication of the Brief, and sent Bunsen as ambassador-extraordinary to Rome with instructions to ask Gregory XVI for new concessions—which he failed to obtain. Then the government, without further reference to the Holy See, enlisted the services of a few pusillanimous or aspiring bishops, chief among whom was Mgr. von Spiegel, Archbishop of Cologne. In 1834, at Coblenz,

22. See Chapter III, section 16.

 these prelates made an agreement whereby, under pretext of interpreting the papal Brief, its principal clauses were annulled. Parish priests were no longer obliged to demand the oath, and had to refuse the blessing only if they knew that contrary arrangements had been made. Rome was informed; but Cardinal Lambruschini, who had just taken office as secretary of state, was unwilling to quarrel with a sovereign who was looked upon as one of the keystones of order in Europe, and he therefore accepted the explanations offered him by Bunsen.

Resistance came from the German Catholics themselves, particularly from a number of bishops who were disgusted by the servile attitude of their colleagues. The movement was headed by Mgr. zu Droste-Vischering. He had been elected Archbishop of Cologne in 1835, when the government, in asking the Chapter to cast their votes for him, thought that it was installing its own servant in the see. An old man, he was said to prefer cloistered retirement to political activity. But Prussian psychology, not for the last time, was at fault. The new archbishop proved himself another Ambrose, another Athanasius, another Gregory VII. His first measures left no doubt as to his resolution. He refused to recognize the validity of the agreement of Coblenz and directed his priests to enforce the terms of *Litteris*; then, without seeking a governmental *placet*, he published the papal Brief condemning Hermes. In vain an envoy of Berlin asked him to modify his rigour, and to refrain especially from public denunciation of the professor. "The Brief is there," he replied with a smile; and the envoy withdrew discomfited.

After eighteen months of fruitless negotiation the Prussians had recourse to violence, a procedure which they ordinarily regarded as the *ultima ratio*. Their police broke into the aged archbishop's palace, and he was sent under strong guard to the fortress of Minden in the heart of Westphalia. This was the "Event of Cologne" (November 20, 1837). It caused a sensation, but not the kind expected by the king, whose intuition once again proved faulty.

Europe was scandalized, and not only in Catholic circles. Even Lamennais, who had just cut himself off from the Church, joined the vehement protests of Görres, Dollinger, Montalembert and others. Rome reacted firmly. Less than three weeks after the event Gregory XVI assembled the Sacred College and delivered a vigorous protest against the insult done to the Church and the Holy See in the person of the archbishop, whom he praised in the warmest terms. He also sent the text of his allocution to all diplomats accredited to the Holy See. The Prussian Government hurriedly forbade the admission of this document to the territories under its control, but it was nevertheless circulated clandestinely, even in Prussia.

Berlin felt considerable embarrassment. Mgr. von Dunin, Archbishop of Gniesen-Posen, was imprisoned for having ordered his clergy to apply the papal provisions concerning mixed marriages; and the more extremist members of the government talked of nothing less than a military expedition to the Rhineland in order to bring the Catholics to heel. But it was very difficult to subdue one-third of the population of the Prussian State.

The accession of Frederick William IV made negotiation possible; as heir apparent he had already dared openly to criticize the "blunders of charlatans." Mgr. zu Droste-Vischering became a martyr on the altar of liberty. The twelve bishops of North America, meeting in council at Baltimore, sent the valiant warrior a message of their admiration; Montalembert praised his example from the tribune of the French Chamber; and there was news of grave disturbances in Westphalia and in the part of Poland annexed by Prussia. The new king hastened to free the two archbishops.

The great prelate who had fought so well for his cause stood triumphant; but the fruit of his victory, alas, was bitter. No one knows exactly what arguments were brought to bear by the Prussian negotiator upon the secretariat of state. Cardinal Lambruschini and Gregory XVI himself may have thought it inopportune further to humiliate the Prussian Government by allowing the archbishop too much glory. They may also have feared that the revolutionaries might make use of him. When Mgr. zu Droste-Vischering returned to Cologne he learned that he had been given a coadjutor to administer the diocese in his stead. He was deeply offended; for, as Goyau says, "he was one of those to whom the spontaneity of martyrdom is easier than simple obedience." It is none the less certain that the "Event of Cologne" is a date of capital importance in the history of German Catholicism. There was no more trying to subject the Church to the State, or attempting to blend Catholicism with other religions. In 1841 Prussia authorized the clergy to communicate freely with Rome, and outstanding difficulties were settled by bilateral agreements with the episcopate.

10. THE BATTLE FOR FREEDOM OF EDUCATION IN FRANCE

IN France the struggle of Catholics against State control took a less violent turn than in Germany. True, the beginnings of the July regime had been marked by deplorable incidents of anti-clericalism; and some legislative and administrative measures had confirmed that irreligious tendency. But this was in no way the result of a concerted plan; Louis-Philippe was too much of a sceptic to adopt a policy of persecution. The only consequence of a brief anti-clerical crisis was to give back to the Church the liberty she had surrendered to the late regime.

French Catholics were divided into three groups. Some remained faithful to Charles X. Others, indeed the large majority, held aloof from politics. As for the advance guard of liberal Catholics, as yet small in numbers, it grew continually, until at last it formed the skeleton of a regular Catholic party.

The misunderstanding between Catholics and the July regime was short lived; popular agitation soon saw to that, though the more friendly attitude of the government was dictated exclusively by self-interest. There was danger that Catholicism might join hands again with the regime; but an opportune quarrel arose to parry the threat, a quarrel turning upon the question of freedom of education, which the July monarchy had inherited from its predecessor[23] and which had not been resolved by the inclusion of

23. See Chapter III, section 11 *ad fin.*

educational freedom as a principle of the Charter. *L'Avenir*, almost from the start, had endeavoured to obtain implementation of that principle. A huge petition bearing fifteen thousand signatures was tabled in both Chambers, demanding a law that would formally allow free schools. Casimir Périer replied by closing the "choir schools," in which many parish priests gave free instruction to poor children. The editors of *L'Avenir* decided to hit back.

On May 9, 1831, without permission, La Mennais, Lacordaire and de Coux opened a primary school in which they themselves went to teach. The government had it closed, and the three were prosecuted. A minimum fine of one hundred gold francs showed that their defence had carried weight. And indeed two years later, in 1833, Guizot secured a law granting full freedom to primary education.

The real battle, however, was destined to be joined in another field. Primary education was not of fundamental interest to the middle classes who were for the time being in control of France. What mattered to them was the more advanced education their sons would receive. The State *lycées* still had a bad reputation as hot-beds of irreligion and even, it was rumoured, of debauchery. But the laws of 1828[24] had struck a heavy blow at religious establishments, and the number of their pupils had declined alarmingly. Was it preferable therefore to retain the monopoly of the *Université*, or to allow another educational system to develop concurrently? Certain liberals of yesteryear, as soon as they came to power, showed themselves strongly attached to the monopoly. Guizot, more honest and a sincere Protestant, remained a partisan of freedom. In 1836 he tried unsuccessfully to extend to secondary education the freedom he had won for primary. During the next four years the question was raised periodically from the tribune, Montalembert taking every opportunity to return to the subject; but little or no progress was made. At length Villemain, minister of public instruction, pretended to resolve the problem; but his project hedged the grant of freedom with such strict conditions regarding the qualifications of teachers and State

24. See Chapter III, section 11.

 control that it seemed a mere provocation. Thrice Montalembert remounted the tribune, and the bishops, anxious though they were to remain on good terms with the government, protested.

A campaign was launched from the episcopal side by the bishops of Chartres and Langres, Mgr. Clausel de Montais and Mgr. Parisis, and on behalf of the laity by Montalembert and his friends, supported by *L'Univers*, a new Catholic journal. There soon entered the lists one of the greatest polemists ever employed by the Church, Louis Veuillot (1813–1883). Son of an Orleans cooper and educated in a "mutual school"[25] at Bercy, he had remained a man of the people and the very antithesis of an intellectual; but thanks to an exceptional intelligence he had rapidly climbed the social ladder. Starting as errand boy and then clerk with Me Fortune Delavigne, a solicitor, young Louis became a journalist in the provinces and later in Paris. Then, in February 1840, he joined *L'Univers.* His convictions had been wholeheartedly and passionately Catholic ever since he had received a sudden enlightenment in Rome two years earlier. To this matter of educational freedom he devoted a vigorous intellectual talent, prolific of striking and wounding phrases, though not always careful as to choice of arguments, and even less careful as to fairness and moderation. The place left empty by La Mennais had been filled.

Wrangling over the question of the schools lasted for three years. In *L'Univers,* whose subscribers increased from day to day, Veuillot seized every pretext for demanding scholastic freedom and for berating those who opposed it. Mgr. Parisis published an *Examen de la question,* which was approved by fifty-six bishops. Ministers who had formerly been liberals felt ill at ease in face of this campaign waged in the name of that very freedom they had once so earnestly demanded, and Victor Cousin strove in vain to find some basis of agreement. More violent, the *Journal des Débats* and the *Courrier français* stigmatized the "intolerance of the ultramontanes," while the fanatics of the *Revue Independente* mounted a full scale

25. One in which the more advanced pupils taught the younger.

counter-offensive. The Jesuits once again provided a welcome subject of diversion: everything that happened was their fault. 297

Government opinion was divided. Villemain, more and more embittered by the attacks of his enemies, defended the *Université*, until he fell victim to hallucinations and had to be locked up for a while. Guizot and the minister of public worship, Martin Du Nord, were anxious to settle the affair. As for Louis-Philippe, he would have preferred not to be involved, but he was anxious that Catholic education should not be given too much importance. However, since agitation continued and increased, further consideration became necessary. In 1844 Villemain introduced a second bill. Once again the qualifications he required from teachers were such that recruitment would have been impossible; and for fear of the Jesuits he proposed that no religious congregation should be allowed to teach. The Abbé Combalot criticized the bill in such terms that he was given fifteen days' imprisonment and ordered to pay a fine of four thousand francs. Veuillot suffered likewise for having supported him. In the Chamber of Peers, Montalembert rallied a minority of fifty-one votes against the bill.

There was still no progress, until Montalembert realized that a change of tactics was desirable. All these attacks in open order were leading nowhere. It would surely be better to form the Catholics into a party which would hold aloof from all others and intervene in the political field with a view to forcing the government's hand. A Committee for Religious Defence was set up, taking as its motto "God and My Right." Its mouthpiece was *L'Univers*, although Veuillot, who had become chief editor, refused to commit himself wholly to the party. Some bishops objected, thinking that the laity were taking too much upon themselves; but others, notably Mgr. Parisis, approved the new formation. One of its most distinguished members was the Abbé Félix Dupanloup, at that time superior of the junior seminary of Saint-Nicolas-du-Chardonnet. His name had become known to all Europe in 1838, when he managed to reconcile Talleyrand *in articulo mortis*.

The enemies of the Catholic party awoke to the danger indicated by the trend of public opinion. They resolved to strike a mighty blow, and a target was quickly found—the Jesuits. The government was asked to approach the Holy See with a request for the suppression of the Society in France. Count Pellegrino Rossi, a naturalized Frenchman, was sent as envoy-extraordinary to Rome. He expressed no hostility towards the Fathers, but suggested to Cardinal Lambruschini that men of such great merit would be wise enough to sacrifice themselves for the common good. The two men reached an agreement, which was accepted by the general, Father Rothaan. It was given out that the "Congregation of Jesuits" would cease to exist in France, the members dispersing of their own accord; but the Fathers, having become plain abbés, would not leave the country, and their colleges would remain under their control.

The Catholics of France took a poor view of this manoeuvre, but they were due for yet another disappointment. At the elections of 1846 their appearance on the scene proved decisive; in the new Chamber there were one hundred and forty-four deputies who had included freedom of education as a plank in their programme. It seemed then that the goal could be attained without difficulty. However, the new minister, M. de Salvandy, a practising Catholic but strongly prejudiced in favour of the *Université*, put forward a fresh and unsatisfactory plan: again exorbitant qualifications were required, again religious congregations were barred from teaching, again control of free education by the *Université* was laid down as a principle. In face of vehement protests Guizot declared that the matter must be reconsidered; he took a grave view of this widening gulf between Catholics and the regime, and was well aware that it was not the only source of discontent. The revolution of February 1848 did not allow time for any plans he may have had to mature.

The Catholics did not appear to have succeeded in their long struggle; but their efforts had been far from useless, as was evident a very few years later when Falloux's law crowned them with victory. That struggle, too, had other results. It had shown that Catholics, by uniting, could exert strong political pressure. Above all, while it led to no systematic hostility on the part of the French Church towards the July monarchy, it separated once for all the cause of religion from that of the political regime.

Throughout that great contest the Holy See had played little or no part, and the papal nuncio, Mgr. Garibaldi, had considered it his duty to remain silent. At no time during the educational dispute, in which so many grave principles were at stake, did Rome take the initiative. Would the world march into the future without her? 299

11. "DA FRATE, NON DA SOVRANO"

WHETHER or not Gregory XVI suspected that his policy had been so disappointing, his last years were filled with sorrow. In his will one reads between the lines a burden of discouragement. Nevertheless, to judge him objectively, he had many reasons to feel consoled. During his reign a great ecclesiastical task was accomplished or at least begun. The hierarchy had been reorganized; the old religious orders had been reformed and many new congregations founded; the foreign missions had expanded to such an extent that there was hope of regaining in those distant lands what Catholicism had lost in Europe.[26]

But the aged Pope's heart was saddened by the ceaseless activity of those revolutionary forces against which he had fought with such determination, and by the knowledge that Catholics were prone to be led astray. What he saw around him was disturbing. Order seemed threatened everywhere. In France the July monarchy was opposed to all reform; but there were many signs of ominous discontent among the lower classes, and some thought an explosion imminent. In Germany the liberal and national ferment was daily more obvious, and Prussia's avowed intention to use it for her own purposes was not reassuring. In Switzerland civil war between Catholics and liberals was on the point of breaking out. In the Austrian Empire the iron hand of Metternich no longer sufficed to muzzle the revolutionaries—Hungarians, Croats and Czechs—who were clamouring for liberty. In the Italian States

26. See Volume 2, Chapter VII.

 Ferdinand VII of Naples was unable to check the activity of secret societies, and assassinations were numerous; would he agree to make the concessions desired by the Grand Duke of Tuscany and Charles Albert, the "see-saw" King of Piedmont-Sardinia?

In the Papal States agitation was incessant.[27] The disturbances at Rimini in 1843 were followed in 1845 by others affecting all the Legations. Everywhere, even in Rome, the lower classes were restive and political crimes were committed. To deal with this situation Cardinal Lambruschini had recourse to strong measures: special tribunals sat permanently; thousands of people were prosecuted for their opinions; at least four hundred were in prison, and more than six hundred had fled. All this was highly dangerous; the advance of liberalism could not be halted, and there was risk of its turning against Rome. The Pope had become unpopular—his ways had never been ingratiating—and the Roman populace no longer acclaimed him when he appeared in public.

Sickness was a good excuse for his remaining as far as possible indoors. It gained upon him slowly but surely: at the beginning of May 1846 a facial cancer was aggravated by an extremely painful attack of erysipelas. He was fully aware of his condition, and his end was worthy of the pious and austere life he had led even upon the throne. To a friend who found him gloomy and reminded him of the great achievements of his pontificate he replied: "Never mind about that. I want to die as a monk, not as a sovereign—*da frate, non da sovrano*." The Camaldolese Pope deserves respect for those words, and they would command unqualified admiration if the principle they express, so noble in face of death, had not too often been that of his life and of his government.

As soon as he died, on June 1, 1846, tongues were loosened. The entire press was severely critical; very few newspapers thought fit, like the Catholic *Quotidienne*, to praise the man's courage and firmness in defence of principles, or to observe that account should be taken of circumstances in order

27. See section 4 above.

to judge him fairly. History itself would too often re-echo that injustice and treat Gregory XVI with undue severity.

At Rome reaction was immediate and lively. Pasquino loaded his memory with cruel epithets, and the satirist Belli gave full vent to his spleen. There was talk of dealing sternly with Cardinal Lambruschini; and the aged Capuchin Cardinal Micara, who had been set aside, was carried in triumph. The situation indeed appeared so explosive that Metternich had military precautions taken in Lombardy, and he informed the Sacred College through Cardinal Gaysruck, Archbishop of Milan, that his troops were ready to intervene to restore order in Rome and enable their eminences to deliberate in peace. There was no need for that; but while the Conclave of 1846 was able to take place untroubled by revolutionaries, it produced a most surprising result.

SELECT BIBLIOGRAPHY

THE following are among the principal works cited by the author.

GENERAL

I. *Secular History*

F. Ponteil, *L'Histoire generale contemporaine, du milieu du XVIIIe siècle à la Seconde Guerre mondiale.*

E. Préclin and V. L. Tapié, *Le XVIIIe siècle* (1952).

L. Villat, *La Révolution et l'Empire* (1947).

J. Droz and others, *L'Époque contemporaine, I: Restaurations et Révolution* (1953).

R. Mousnier and E. Labrousse, *Le XIXe siècle* (1953).

R. Schnerb, *Le XIXe siècle* (1957).

J. Droz, *L'Histoire diplomatique* (1952)

P. Renouvin, *L'Histoire diplomatique* (1954–1955).

J. Pirenne, *Les Grands Courants de l'Histoire universelle* (1951–1953).

G. Le Gentil, *La Découverte du Monde* (1952).

S. Hardy, *La Politique coloniale et le partage de la terre au XIXe siècle* (1937).

P. Rousseau, *Histoire des techniques* (1956); *Histoire de la Science* (1945).

C. Gide and C. Rist, *Histoire des Doctrines économiques* (1949).

II. *Religious History*

J. Leflon, *La Crise révolutionnaire* (1949).

R. Aubert, *Le Pontificat de Pie IX.*

E. Jarry, *L'Église contemporaine* (1935).

J. MacCaffery, *History of the Catholic Church in the Nineteenth Century* (1939).

T. W. Marc-Bonnet, *La Papauté contemporaine* (1946); *Histoire des Ordres religieux* (1949).

SPECIAL

Chapter I. *An Epoch of History*

A. Latreille, *L'Église catholique et la Révolution* (1950).

C. Ledré, *L'Église de France sous la Révolution* (1949).

P. De La Gorce, *Histoire religieuse de la Révolution française*, 5 vols. (1909–1925).

A. Mathiez, *La Révolution et l'Église* (1910).

A. Aulard, *Le Christianisme et la Révolution* (1924).

J. Leflon, *Monsieur Emery* (1944); *Bernier* (1938).

Chapter II. *The Sword and the Spirit*

V. Bindel, *Histoire religieuse de Napoléon* (1940).

B. Melchior-Brunet, *Napoléon et le Pape* (1958).

S. Delacroix, *La Réorganisation de l'Église de France* (1952).

Chapter III. *An Abortive Counter-Reformation*
& Chapter IV. *Looking to the Future*

G. Weill, *Histoire du catholicisme libéral* (1939).

P. de la Gorce, *Louis XVIII* (1926); *Charles X* (1928).

G. de Bertier de Sauvigny, *Le Comte Ferdinand de Bertier et l'énigme de la Congrégation* (1948).

G. Goyau, *Pensée religieuse* (1912).
L. Dimier, *Maîtres de la Contre-Révolution* (1907).
M. Mourre, *Lamennais* (1955).
M. Escholier, *Lacordaire* (1958).
A. Billy, *Écrivains de combat* (1931).
B. Ward, *The Era of Catholic Emancipation* (1915).

Designed by Fiona Cecile Clarke, the Cluny Media *logo depicts a monk at work in the scriptorium, with a cat sitting at his feet.*

The monk represents our mission to emulate the invaluable contributions of the monks of Cluny in preserving the libraries of the West, our strivings to know and love the truth.

The cat at the monk's feet is Pangur Bán, from the eponymous Irish poem of the 9th century. The anonymous poet compares his scholarly pursuit of truth with the cat's happy hunting of mice. The depiction of Pangur Bán is an homage to the work of the monks of Irish monasteries and a sign of the joy we at Cluny take in our trade.

"Messe ocus Pangur Bán,
cechtar nathar fria saindan:
bíth a menmasam fri seilgg,
mu memna céin im saincheirdd."

www.ingramcontent.com/pod-product-compliance
Lightning Source LLC
Chambersburg PA
CBHW020339100426
42812CB00029B/3181/J

* 9 7 8 1 6 8 5 9 5 3 0 1 0 *